Palgrave Studies in Green Criminology

Series Editors
Angus Nurse
Department of Criminology and Sociology
Middlesex University
London, UK

Rob White
School of Social Sciences
University of Tasmania
Hobart, TAS, Australia

Melissa Jarrell
Department of Social Sciences
Texas A&M University - Corpus Christi
Corpus Christi, TX, USA

"Timeworn and dogmatic speciesist views of nonhuman animals, including those woven into worldwide legal statutes, maintain that animals other than humans cannot be murdered. With rigorous scholarly clarity, Piers Beirne shows how it's high time to place nonhumans squarely into the gallery of beings who can, in fact, be murdered. This move is long overdue and *Murdering Animals* could well be a game-changer."
—Marc Bekoff, *University of Colorado, Boulder, USA*

"Professor Beirne and colleagues have produced a splendidly researched, well written and timely book that challenges us to consider the many ways humans kill other animals ("theriocide"). *Murdering Animals* is a wonderful combination of history, animal imagery in art and literature, emphasis on language, and the potential of legal personhood for animals—all to persuasively argue that the killing of animals should be named murder. It is destined to be required reading in the field of Animal Studies."
—Linda Kalof, *Michigan State University, USA*

Criminologists have increasingly become involved and interested in environmental issues to the extent that the term Green Criminology is now recognised as a distinct subgenre of criminology. Within this unique area of scholarly activity, researchers consider not just harms to the environment, but also the links between green crimes and other forms of crime, including organised crime's movement into the illegal trade in wildlife or the links between domestic animal abuse and spousal abuse and more serious forms of offending such as serial killing. This series will provide a forum for new works and new ideas in green criminology for both academics and practitioners working in the field, with two primary aims: to provide contemporary theoretical and practice-based analysis of green criminology and environmental issues relating to the development of and enforcement of environmental laws, environmental criminality, policy relating to environmental harms and harms committed against non-human animals and situating environmental harms within the context of wider social harms; and to explore and debate new contemporary issues in green criminology including ecological, environmental and species justice concerns and the better integration of a green criminological approach within mainstream criminal justice. The series will reflect the range and depth of high-quality research and scholarship in this burgeoning area, combining contributions from established scholars wishing to explore new topics and recent entrants who are breaking new ground.

More information about this series at
http://www.palgrave.com/gp/series/14622

"*Murdering Animals* lays the long overdue foundation for a criminology of theriocide by weaving together a powerful and new understanding of crime, rights and violence. A landmark achievement that makes it impossible to ignore the use and abuse of animals in a field that has preferred for too long to look away. Piers Beirne sets out a daring and rigorous analysis that is genuinely interdisciplinary, wonderfully written and provides fresh understandings of social processes and cultural categories in both the past and the present. It will appeal to students across the humanities and social sciences. Indeed, it will be indispensable to anyone seeking to understand the moral complexities surrounding the killing of animals."
—Eamonn Carrabine, *University of Essex, UK*

Piers Beirne

Murdering Animals

Writings on Theriocide, Homicide and Nonspeciesist Criminology

with
Ian O'Donnell and Janine Janssen

Piers Beirne
Department of Criminology
University of Southern Maine
Portland, ME, USA

Palgrave Studies in Green Criminology
ISBN 978-1-137-57467-1   ISBN 978-1-137-57468-8   (eBook)
https://doi.org/10.1057/978-1-137-57468-8

Library of Congress Control Number: 2017964597

© The Editor(s) (if applicable) and The Author(s) 2018
The author(s) has/have asserted their right(s) to be identified as the author(s) of this work in accordance with the Copyright, Designs and Patents Act 1988.
This work is subject to copyright. All rights are solely and exclusively licensed by the Publisher, whether the whole or part of the material is concerned, specifically the rights of translation, reprinting, reuse of illustrations, recitation, broadcasting, reproduction on microfilms or in any other physical way, and transmission or information storage and retrieval, electronic adaptation, computer software, or by similar or dissimilar methodology now known or hereafter developed.
The use of general descriptive names, registered names, trademarks, service marks, etc. in this publication does not imply, even in the absence of a specific statement, that such names are exempt from the relevant protective laws and regulations and therefore free for general use.
The publisher, the authors and the editors are safe to assume that the advice and information in this book are believed to be true and accurate at the date of publication. Neither the publisher nor the authors or the editors give a warranty, express or implied, with respect to the material contained herein or for any errors or omissions that may have been made. The publisher remains neutral with regard to jurisdictional claims in published maps and institutional affiliations.

Cover credit: ANDREW WALTERS / Alamy Stock Photo

Printed on acid-free paper

This Palgrave Macmillan imprint is published by Springer Nature
The registered company is Macmillan Publishers Ltd.
The registered company address is: The Campus, 4 Crinan Street, London, N1 9XW, United Kingdom

Foreword

What are rights? In their most distilled form, rights are expectations of treatment or behaviour that are presumptively guaranteed by some authority tasked with creating the conditions for the enjoyment of those rights, and punishing violations of them.

Since the rise of the political state, governments have served as the politically authorized guarantors of rights. Before that, clans or tribes served this function. Regardless of how temporally near or distant one might choose to locate the origin of rights—as close as the eighteenth-century 'Rights of Man [sic]' revolutions, or as far as the dim past of pre-state societies—it remains a truism that wherever rights-like expectations are present, there will be conflicts over the scope and fulfilment of rights.

Rights conflicts typically take two forms. The first is contestation over who has a *right to rights*. That is, how extensive is the moral boundary that encompasses those who are assumed to have a rightful claim to the full suite of social benefits constructed as rights in a given society? Does it encompass all those in a society? Most people, but not all? A small elite, but few others? Or some other distinction between those who are believed to enjoy full rights, those who are accorded some, and those who are given none?

The second form of rights conflict coalesces around claims that, while they may exist under law, certain rights lack *substance* for particular segments of society. This disjuncture between the juridical and substantive rights may occur because the conditions for the enjoyment of particular rights do not exist (e.g. freedom of the press in a country where most people are illiterate), or because the guarantor has failed in its obligation to protect statutorily established rights (e.g. Jim Crow era transgressions in the US South of the legally established rights of African American citizens).

The question of whether a state fulfils its obligations to provide substantive enjoyment of rights for all who have the right to those rights is a key source of political conflict in contemporary societies, as well as a frequent focus of critical intellectual inquiry. However, conflicts over who should have these right in the first place raise even more fundamental questions. They question core conceptions of social relations, with all the implications for societal organization, culture and state practice that are raised whenever we ask who should have the right to rights.

From the rise of civilizations about 10,000 years ago, human history has been punctuated by struggles over who has the right to rights. Every expansion of the moral community thought to have a right to rights was associated with fundamental societal transformations. Consider the historic consequences of establishing that human beings had a right to not be enslaved. Or the ways that a growing recognition that women, racial and ethnic minorities, gay, bi and transgendered people, and the differently abled have the same rights as other citizens is altering social practice and consciousness in many societies, particularly (but not exclusively) in the Global North. These extensions of rights and the struggle to make them substantive rather than merely juridical involve much more than legal arguments. They demand significant rethinking of taken-for-granted assumptions about the nature of the world and how people live in that world.

Until the latter part of the twentieth century, debates about rights were focused almost exclusively on humans. While animal protection sentiments and animal protection groups such as the Society for the Prevention of Cruelty to Animals emerged in Britain and the United States in the first half of the nineteenth century, most debates over rights remained largely focused on what rights *human* beings of different sexes, colours, shapes, origins, social position and so on should be able to enjoy, and whether the state was fulfilling its obligation to enable the enjoyment of those rights.

The hegemonic linkage of the term 'rights' with 'human' to create what became the international organizing principle of *universal human rights* remained relatively unchallenged until the rise of what could be termed a new animal rights movement in the 1970s. This new movement combined rights philosophers, direct-action animal liberationists such as People for the Ethical Treatment of Animals (PETA), and insights from an emergent deep ecology movement. This ideational mélange created a growing awareness in some quarters that not only are all living beings on our planet linked systemically but also that this systemic linkage imposes an obligation on the planet's human inhabitants to protect *all* life. Some see doing so as a moral obligation. For others it is an anthropocentric practical necessity. In either case, however, acceptance of a 'responsibility to protect' (to borrow a term from international human rights debates) foregrounds the inadequacy of a concept of rights that stops at the borders of *Homo sapiens.*

Into this mix comes *Murdering Animals*, from Piers Beirne, Professor of Sociology and Legal Studies at the University of Southern Maine. Over the past two decades Professor Beirne has blended insights from criminology, the sociology of law, art history and literary criticism into a lens for examining the use and abuse of animals. In *Murdering Animals*, Beirne utilizes his earlier work on anthropocentrism in human–animal relationships, including the use and abuse of animals as food, objects of sport or sexual release, rendering animals the objects of judicial punishments, and the link between violence against animals and violence against humans to frame a consideration of when abuse of animals may be deemed morally blameworthy violations of animals' species being. Beirne is not the first to ask whether animals have (or should have) a right to rights. However, in this book he focuses the question of animal rights in two important directions.

First, *Murdering Animals* interrogates whether animals have a right to legal *personhood* and, second, if they do, under what possible criteria might the intentional killing of animals, or the creation of the conditions that will force them to die (animal necropolitics?) be considered the moral equivalent of the murder of human beings. While these questions bookend *Murdering Animals*, the overall narrative reaches beyond philosophical and criminological theorizing about the rights of animals. It does this by interrogating the social construction of animals across a broad cultural canvas, particularly as reflected in art and literature.

The methodological vehicle for understanding the social construction of the animal kingdom and its rights is analyses of works of art depicting animals, killing, and oftentimes the killing of animals. Here we encounter something more than philosophical arguments regarding whether animals have a right to be free from human exploitation for individual and species benefit, or from the casual and careless destruction of their environments by human action. That something more is what we can learn from studying the second-level exploitation of animals. Not the exploitation of their flesh, but the use and exploitation of their images. What role has the depiction of animal images played in validating their exploitation to satisfy human needs or whims? Conversely, how has, and how long has, animal imagery been used to question taken-for-granted assumptions about the right of humans to exploit animals. The answer to that last question I found to be a bit of a surprise.

For those interested in creating nonspeciesist modes of inquiry in philosophy, sociology or criminology, and/or in creating societies that practise some kind of species equality, *Murdering Animals* suggests we need to look beyond modernist modes of reasoning. We need to understand more fully how images of animals imitate the life of animals and, of equal importance, the degree to which the life of animals has come to imitate our constructed images of animals. What role is played by animal imagery in producing and reproducing the human practice of rendering animals as either property to be exploited and allowed to die when they are no longer productive, or as nuisances to human life to be eliminated when they stand in the way of comfort or progress?

Murdering Animals offers no easy or facile answers to the fundamental problematic of whether animals have, or should have, a right to rights. This is as it should be. While, as Beirne documents, there are contemporary movements in the direction of expanding rights beyond the human–animal boundary, we remain at the very early stages of considering just what such a change would mean as a moral, practical and legal matter.

By asking us to consider whether there are conditions under which killing animals is equivalent to murder, *Murdering Animals* asks us to *see* animals, and to think about their role as part of our moral community in challenging ways. It is a challenge that should be taken seriously by anyone in green criminology or the animal rights community.

Raymond J. Michalowski
Flagstaff, Arizona

Acknowledgments

For their kindnesses and patience during the lengthy gestation of *Murdering Animals* I wish to express my gratitude to scholars and friends almost too numerous to name. First, to my co-authors Janine Janssen (Chap. 3) and Ian O'Donnell (Chap. 6): working with you two has been a great privilege and a continuing delight. Many thanks as well to Ray Michalowski, a pioneer in the field of zemiology, who has generously consented to write the Foreword.

Maurice Herson, Willem De Haan, Tony Jefferson, Ragnhild Sollund, Ray Michalowski, Avi Brisman, Paul Friedland and Ian O'Donnell each helped enormously with their guidance on drafts of one or more chapters or on successive versions of the same chapter. Also kindly offering advice of one sort or another and at one time or another were Eamonn Carrabine, Lucinda Cole, Amy Fitzgerald, Nic Groombridge, Douglas Hay, Caitlin Kelty-Huber, Bernd Krysmanski, Ronald Paulson, Nicole Hahn Rafter, Ken Shapiro, Nigel South, Rob White, Steven Wise and Tanya Wyatt.

Time is the most prized possession of all and I have incurred many debts in its acquisition. The idea of a nonspeciesist criminology first surprised me during a six-month Fellowship from the National Endowment for the Humanities in 1988. A Liberal Arts Fellowship in 2008 at the National University of Ireland, Galway, allowed me to explore the presence of murder and nationalism in J.M. Synge's play *Playboy of the Western World*. My home institution, the University of Southern Maine, kindly awarded me a Provost's Research Fellowship in 2012 to pursue the intersection of nationalism and carnism in eighteenth-century British art. In 2013 a Visiting Fellowship at the Centre for Criminology, University of Oxford, offered me a warm and familiar atmosphere for research and gave me access to the unrivalled resources of the Bodleian Libraries.

I must also acknowledge the invaluable guidance of librarians at the Ashmolean Museum of Art and Archaeology; the Bodleian Libraries at the University of Oxford; the British Library; the Glickman Library at the University of Southern Maine; the Law School Library at the University of Maine; the Hawthorne-Longfellow Library at Bowdoin College; the Library of the London School of Economics and Political Science; and the James Hardiman Library of the National University of Ireland Galway.

When I was all at sixes and sevens with image assembly Martha Moutafis and my son Simon Beirne kindly clicked on just the right buttons. Jill Jordan-MacLean and the late Rosemary Miller offered the most competent and cheerful of office management. Krissinda Palmer worked with great diligence on the bibliography and the index. Bill Wagg and his wife Delores generously provided a quiet Nevadan refuge for me to read, write and apply some finishing touches—all held together by my wife Geraldine with her unfailing patience, wit and intelligence.

For her encouragement when we first talked about *Murdering Animals*, I am indebted to Julia Willan, my commissioning editor at Palgrave Macmillan and afterwards to her successor, Josephine Taylor and to her editorial assistant, Stephanie Carey. Sophie Richmond copyedited gently and with great skill, rescuing me from errors both large and small. Some among Palgrave's staff have assured me that no animals were harmed in the production of this book, which is dedicated to the efforts of the Animals and Society Institute and the Sea Shepherd Conservation Society, between whom any royalties will be equally divided.

Chapters 1, 5 and 7 of *Murdering Animals* appear in print for the first time here. Chapters 2, 3, 4 and 6 are more or less extensive revisions of essays that originally appeared in scholarly journals far and wide. It goes without saying, so to speak, that I alone am responsible for whatever errors remain in *Murdering Animals*, fatal or otherwise.

Piers Beirne
Merrymeeting Bay, Maine

Contents

1 **Introduction: Rights for *Whom*?** 1
Piers Beirne
This Book 4
Being Language Animals 10

2 **Theriocide and Homicide** 13
Piers Beirne
Killing Sites: Words and Things 14
Killing at a Distance 18
Killing Euphemisms 20
Homicide and Theriocide 22
The Concept of Theriocide 23
   Etymology 24
Scope 25
Intersections 33
Discussion 34
Post Mortem 36
Bibliography 42

3	**Hunting Worlds Turned Upside Down? Paulus Potter's** *Life of a Hunter*	49
	Piers Beirne and Janine Janssen	
	An Unlikely Tale	51
	A Satire on Early Modern Animal Trials?	55
	Art and Politics	58
	Hunting Worlds Upside Down	60
	Against Animal Cruelty: Montaigne, Potter and *Life of a Hunter*	62
	Bibliography	67
4	**On the Geohistory of Justiciable Animals: Was Britain a Deviant Case?**	71
	Piers Beirne	
	Rendering Animals Justiciable	74
	On the Geohistory of Justiciable Animals	85
	The British Law of Deodands	93
	In Search of Animal Trials in Britain	97
	The Trial of a Dog in Sixteenth-century Scotland	98
	The Trial of a Cock in Nineteenth-century Leeds	100
	The Trial of Farmer Carter's Dog in Chichester, 1771	101
	Animal Trials and Other Tribulations: Against Speciesist Justice	109
	Appendix 1: Animals and Crime in Lombrosian Criminal Anthropology	112
	Bibliography	128
5	**Hogarth's Patriotic Animals: Bulldogs, Beef, Britannia!**	135
	Piers Beirne	
	Let Slip the Dogs of War!	137
	Beef and Liberty! Hogarth's Consuming Passions	142
	After Hogarth	155
	Iconography: Hogarth	157
	Bibliography	162

6	**Gallous Stories or Dirty Deeds? Representing Parricide in J.M. Synge's** *Playboy of the Western World*	165
	Piers Beirne and Ian O'Donnell	
	Preamble	165
	Murder and Mayhem in Three Acts: Synopsis	166
	Riot Revisited	170
	Playboys and Parricides	173
	The 'Aran Case': William Maley's Parricide	174
	The Case of James Lynchehaun	179
	Lethal Violence in *Fin-de-siècle* Ireland	182
	The Particulars of Parricide	186
	Defending the Indefensible	187
	Finale	190
	Bibliography	194
7	**Is Theriocide Murder?**	197
	Piers Beirne	
	The Criminalization of Theriocide	198
	Legal Personhood for Animals	203
	Towards the Abolition of Speciesism	207
	Bibliography	212
Index		**215**

Notes on Contributors

Piers Beirne is professor of sociology and legal studies at the University of Southern Maine. Among his books are *The Palgrave International Handbook of Animal Abuse Studies* (2017, edited with Jennifer Maher and Harriet Pierpoint, Palgrave Macmillan); Hogarth's *Art of Animal Cruelty: Satire, Suffering and Pictorial Propaganda* (2015, Palgrave Macmillan); *Confronting Animal Abuse* (2009, Rowman & Littlefield); *Criminology: A Sociological Introduction* (2015, 6th edition, with James W. Messerschmidt, Oxford University Press). Email: beirne@maine.edu

Ian O'Donnell is professor of criminology at the School of Law in University College Dublin and Adjunct Fellow of Linacre College, Oxford. His most recent books are *Prisoners, Solitude, and Time* (2014, Oxford University Press) and *Justice, Mercy, and Caprice: Clemency and the Death Penalty in Ireland* (2017, Oxford University Press). Email: ian.odonnell@ucd.ie

Janine Janssen is head of research of the National Expertise Centre for Honour-related Violence of the Dutch Police. She is professor of violence in dependency relationships at the Expertise Centre for Safety and Criminal Justice (Expertisecentrum Veiligheid) at the Avans University for Applied Sciences in Den Bosch in The Netherlands. Email: Janine.Janssen@ziggo.nl

Raymond J. Michalowski is Arizona Regents Professor in the Department of Criminology and Criminal Justice at Northern Arizona University. Email: Raymond.Michalowski@nau.edu

List of Figures and Table

Fig. 2.1	*View and Perspective of the Menagerie from the Entrance*, engraving (Adam Pérelle, c.1670)	15
Fig. 2.2	*The Last Day of Old Smithfield Market*, engraved etching (Source: *The Illustrated London News*, 16 June 1855, p. 217)	18
Fig. 2.3	*Union Stockyards Chicago* (Source: From an original unsigned film negative, 1960–1970)	19
Fig. 3.1	*Life of A Hunter*, oil on panel, Paulus Potter, c.1647–1650	52
Fig. 3.2	*The Young Bull*, oil on canvas, Paulus Potter, c.1647	56
Fig. 3.3	*Wild Boar Hunt in a Forest*, oil on panel, Paulus Potter, c.1641	62
Fig. 4.1	*A Cat Hung Up in Cheapside, Habited like a Priest*, printed woodcut, John Foxe, 1563 (Source: John Foxe, *Acts and Monuments of the Christian Martyrs* (1563) (1776, London: H. Trapp))	72
Fig. 4.2	*De abigeatu* (On Stealing Animals), printed woodcut, Joost de Damhoudere, 1570 (Source: Joost de Damhoudere, *Praxis rerum criminalium*, 1570, Antwerp: Ioannem Bellerum, p. 374)	78
Fig. 4.3	*De damno pecuario* (On Crimes Against Mankind by Animals), printed woodcut, Joost de Damhoudere, 1570 (Source: Joost de Damhoudere, *Praxis rerum criminalium*, 1570, Antwerp: Ioannem Bellerum, p. 436)	80

Fig. 4.4	*De libello formando, seu petitione facienda in re criminali* (On Making a Petition in a Criminal Case), printed woodcut, Joost de Damhoudere, 1570 (Source: Joost de Damhoudere, *Praxis rerum criminalium*, 1570, Antwerp: Ioannem Bellerum, p. 64)	81
Fig. 4.5	*Farmer Carter's Dog Porter on Trial for Murder*, charcoal drawing, William Hone 1827 (Source: Hone 1827, 2: 100)	104
Fig. 4.6	*The Dog Killers of London & Westminster Or Licenc'd Cruelty*, engraved etching, Anon., 1760	109
Fig. 5.1	*Portrait of Mary Edwards*, oil on canvas, William Hogarth, 1742 (Source: https://commons.wikimedia.org/wiki/File:Miss_Mary_Edwards_-_Hogarth_1742.jpg)	138
Fig. 5.2	*Hogarth: The Painter and his Pug*, oil on canvas, William Hogarth, 1742	140
Fig. 5.3	*Noon* (*Four Times of the Day 2*), printed engraving, William Hogarth, 1738	145
Fig. 5.4	*Evening* (*Four Times of the Day 3*), printed engraving, William Hogarth, 1738	146
Fig. 5.5	Detail: Monkey with scrolled French menu in *Taste in High Life, or Taste à la Mode*, oil on canvas, William Hogarth, 1742 (Reproduced with permission of *La Clé des langues* (Clifford Armion, dir.) and ENS Média (Vincent Brault, photo))	147
Fig. 5.6	*A Song in Praise of Old English Roast Beef*, words and music by Richard Leveridge, c.1745 Several versions of Fielding's and Leveridge's *Song in Praise of Old English Roast Beef* are currently in circulation (for one with a ring of authenticity about it see: https://www.youtube.com/watch?v=MTH5gnluOVg) (Source: an unidentified London publisher, n.d. [c.1750])	149
Fig. 5.7	*Calais Gate*, printed engraving, William Hogarth, 1748–49 (Reproduced with permission of *La Clé des langues* (Clifford Armion, dir.) and ENS Média (Vincent Brault, photo))	150
Fig. 5.8	*Transubstantiation Satirized*, aquatint etching, William Hogarth, n.d. (Source: Samuel Ireland (1794, 1: opposite 122))	151

Fig. 5.9	*France* (*The Invasion* 1), engraved etching, William Hogarth, 1756 (Reproduced with permission of *La Clé des langues* (Clifford Armion, dir.) and ENS Média (Vincent Brault, photo))	152
Fig. 5.10	*England* (*The Invasion* 2), engraved etching, William Hogarth, 1756 (Reproduced with permission of *La Clé des langues* (Clifford Armion, dir.) and ENS Média (Vincent Brault, photo))	153
Fig. 6.1	Representing parricide (Source: Abbey Theatre Poster, 1968. Reproduced with permission of Abbey Theatre)	168
Table 4.1	Three animal trials in Britain	98

1

Introduction: Rights for *Whom*?

One winter in the late 1960s I worked as a seasonal employee in a small family-run factory and slaughterhouse—Baughan's—in Colchester, Essex. On the sides of the delivery van that ran between the factory and its retail shop in the town centre, Baughan's advertised itself as a 'High Class Pork Butchers'. Its specialty: pork pies and sausages.

My workdays at Baughan's were divided into mornings and afternoons. In the mornings I made saveloy sausages. This I did with the aid of a fearsome mechanical grinder, into the top of which I shovelled equal amounts of filling and the boiled body parts of slaughtered pigs. The filling comprised heaped onions, carrots, salt, sage and spices combined with day-old pies, bread and cakes that had been returned to the factory from the retail shop, unsold and stale. The pigs' body parts included their brains, livers, hearts, kidneys, entrails, skin, gristle and fat—nearly everything, that is, except for the animals' bones, heads, 'trotters' (feet) and 'beers' (ears), sold separately as special treats for domesticated dogs. The grinder thoroughly mixed, chopped and compressed all these ingredients—filling and animal parts, both—before ejecting the minced product onto trays to be wrapped in reddened casings fashioned from pigs' intestines. Not for nothing did Baughan's promote saveloys as 'savoury' and 'highly seasoned' pork sausages!

© The Author(s) 2018
P. Beirne, *Murdering Animals*, Palgrave Studies in Green Criminology,
https://doi.org/10.1057/978-1-137-57468-8_1

In the afternoons my job was to dress the heads of a dozen or so decapitated pigs. Armed with stout scissors and an electric razor, I had to shave the pigs' heads so as to remove all evidence of their facial hair and bristle. Suitably dressed, a celebratory green apple stuffed into each pig's gaping mouth, their heads were destined to adorn local dining tables at Yuletide and Christmas.

For a long while I suppressed all memory of my time at Baughan's the Butcher. My self-stifling in this regard was rudely broken through, however, when, nearly a decade ago, I was confronted with the image of a decapitated pig's head in a painting by the eighteenth-century English artist William Hogarth. The image appears in a detail in Hogarth's 1745 oil on canvas *The Lady's Death*. In it a skeletal dog frantically snatches a disembodied pig's head from a festive dining table. Alerted to the need for some overdue, if painful self-reflection, I discovered soon thereafter that the display of pigs' heads was an ancient English custom that had been practised in East Anglian Essex by the Saxons and perhaps even earlier by the Celtic warrior Boudica—she, the rebel queen who had led the massacre of Roman soldiers and the suspension of their imperium in Colchester and London.

As it happened, my jarring introduction to the decapitated pig's head in Hogarth's art coincided with an invitation to participate in a panel on green criminology sponsored by the United Nations (UN) at the annual meetings of the American Society of Criminology. My intention there was to provide a platform for dialogue between the nascent green movement in criminology and a variety of UN agencies which, in their everyday policy-making work, profess to promote the welfare of animals. But my plans in this regard were interrupted and then largely abandoned when, as part of my preparation for this task, I felt obliged to revisit the original wording of the UN's Universal Declaration of Human Rights. Adopted by the UN General Assembly on 10 December 1948, the first two articles of the Declaration are as follows:

1. All human beings are born free and equal in dignity and rights. They are endowed with reason and conscience and should act towards one another in a spirit of brotherhood.

2. Everyone is entitled to all the rights and freedoms set forth in this Declaration, without distinction of any kind, such as race, colour, sex, language, religion, political or other opinion, national or social origin, property, birth or other status.

Aside from questions about what human rights are or might be and about the persistent gap between their presence in a document of rights and their widespread absence on the ground, of Article 1 it must be asked: Why does the UN persist in declaring that the only beings worthy of entitlement to rights are those named *human*? If human beings are 'endowed with reason and conscience', then what might this imply for the status of humans who are moral patients, that is, those who are brain dead or in advanced stages of Alzheimer's disease or congenital analgesia? If the UN is steadfast in its view of the criteria for those who belong to the community of rights holders, then the situation of those humans who are in a coma, for example, is surely very precarious indeed. Because comatose humans are often said to have lost their reason, their conscience and their sentience, then presumably it follows that they must thereby forfeit their status as beings and as bearers of rights. On this view one has to worry whether comatose humans might be sacrificed in scientific experiments or used in blood sports.

There are numerous nonhuman animals (henceforth, 'animals') about whom it might accurately be said that their capacity to suffer pain or even to reason is no less than that of humans who are in a coma or who are of a very young age. So, why are comatose or new-born humans regarded as members of a moral community whose members act towards each other in a 'spirit of brotherhood' when animals with similar capacities are not so recognized? Moreover, in contradistinction to all other capacities, such as the capacity to suffer pain, why is the ability to reason elevated to its position as the sole criterion of rights? One answer to this question is surely that through the dogma and power of speciesism we humans tend to exclude animals from our moral community and instead to position them as insensible Cartesian automata that largely exist as our property and who may be used and abused accordingly.

Along similar lines it must be asked about Article 2 of the Universal Declaration of Human Rights: Why are animals excluded from the UN's sheltering umbrella which, as a matter of principle, is extended to 'everyone' without regard to 'race, colour, sex, language, religion, political or other opinion, national or social origin, property, birth or other status'? Why does the UN exclude animals other than humans from its seemingly inclusive embrace of everyone, as in '[e]veryone is entitled to all the rights and freedoms set forth in this Declaration … without distinction of any kind'? Isn't it about time for the UN to reconsider its self-declared privileging of human lives over and above those of all other animals? So, ultimately, the UN must be confronted with the question: Rights for *whom*?

This Book

Murdering Animals: Writings on Theriocide, Homicide and Nonspeciesist Criminology crisscrosses the intersections of animal rights theory, criminology and the history of the fine and performing arts. It is the first text in any discipline to argue that if the killing of an animal by a human is as harmful to her as homicide is to a human, then the proper naming of such a death—'theriocide'—offers a remedy, however small, to the extensive privileging of human lives over those of other animals. Whether the focus is on prose, painting, poetry or a play, each chapter addresses the killing of animals by humans, except for Chap. 6, the repeatedly threatening images of which unfold as the homicide of a father seemingly twice committed by his son. Though each of the chapters can stand alone, I hope it is not too fanciful to suggest that each also leads into the next and at strategic points dissects the others.

Chapter 2 ('Theriocide and Homicide') proceeds on the assumption that in much the same way that humans have moral rights, so also do all other sentient animas. In particular, they have the right to life, the right to respectful treatment and the right not to be treated as property. The site where animals' right to life is most extensively violated is the modern slaughterhouse. Modernist sensibilities require that, almost from the moment of its invention in early nineteenth-century France, the slaughterhouse operates according to the principles of invisibilization. Geographically, slaughterhouses have been moved away from urban areas to spaces where, behind brick and mortar and concrete, their noisy and bloody operations are hidden away. Linguistically, their killing work has been accompanied by the invention of a vocabulary of speciesist euphemisms designed to obscure their aim and characteristics.

The chapter suggests that in major respects there are structural similarities between the killing of humans and the killing of animals. Although with just one word and without too much ambiguity all those actions, lawful or otherwise, whereby one human kills another can be named homicide, there is currently no such unitary term for the killing of animals. Yet, if the killing of an animal by a human is as harmful to her as homicide is to a human, then the proper naming of such a death offers a remedy, however small, to the extensive privileging of human lives over those of other animals.

'Theriocide' is the name recommended here for those diverse human actions that kill animals. Like the killing of one human by another (e.g. homicide, infanticide and femicide), a theriocide may be socially acceptable or unacceptable, legal or illegal. The major and often intersecting types of theriocide are identified as cruelty and neglect; state theriocide; factory farming; hunting and blood sports; the trade in wildlife; vivisection; militarism and war; pollution; and climate change.

Inevitably, Chap. 2 provokes the question of whether theriocide might on occasion be tantamount to murder. This is confronted directly in Chap. 7. In between, Chaps. 3, 4, 5 and 6 operate as so many canvases that are explored to *see* how, historically and cross-culturally, theriocide and homicide are severally made and unmade in legal cultures and in works of art, literature and theatre.

Chapter 3 ('Hunting Worlds Turned Upside Down? Paulus Potter's *Life of a Hunter*', with Janine Janssen) was prompted by what is surely one of the most daunting tasks facing a nonspeciesist criminology, namely, the need to disengage discourse on animal abuse and animal cruelty from the historical dominance of human interests. The chapter's focus is a case study of *Life of a Hunter*, an extraordinary if rather obscure painting executed at some point between 1647 and 1650 by the young Dutch artist Paulus Potter (1625–54). Nowadays adorning a wall in the Hermitage museum in St Petersburg, *Life of a Hunter* boasts fourteen rectangular panels and multiple narratives. It depicts a hunter and his hounds who have been captured by the very animals who had earlier been his quarry. The hunter is put on trial by the animals, condemned to death and roasted alive. The animals are about to eat his flesh.

Life of a Hunter encourages several questions. Foremost among these are: What did *Life of a Hunter* mean to Potter and to the painting's audience? When and where did its viewpoint of an 'upside down' animal trial originate? Was its moral message encouraged by the pro-animal sentiments expressed in the essays of Michel de Montaigne?

The chapter exemplifies how the nonspeciesist turn in sociology and criminology intersects with the recent interest in matters cultural and visual. As such, one of the chapter's aims is to demonstrate how on occasion the production and consumption of a given image manage simultaneously both to reflect the prevailing cultural standards of an era and also to show the way to their erosion and possible transcendence.

Chapter 4 ('On the Geohistory of Justiciable Animals: Was Britain a Deviant Case?') examines significant, if little-known, territory in the lengthy history of human-inflicted harms to animals. Like the two previous chapters, the interrogatory form of this chapter is historical, namely, the emergence and character of fair and respectful sentiments and practices towards animals. Its focus is not on crimes committed by humans against animals, however, but on a practical outcome of the seemingly bizarre belief that animals are capable of committing crimes against humans: for several hundred years in parts of medieval and early modern Europe both secular courts and religious authorities formally prosecuted and executed animals for homicide and other misdeeds. What can be learned from the trials and tribulations of justiciable animals?

While Roman law contains some suggestive snippets about animal's blameworthiness, what remains of the doctrine and sanctions of animal justiciability are lodged in late medieval manuals of criminal law and in the records associated with criminal courts and ecclesiastical tribunals of that era. The chapter pursues two avenues of inquiry in this regard. First, it examines the ordering principles of the *Enchiridion rerum criminalium* (*Handbook of Issues in Criminal Law and Crime*) assembled by the Bruges jurist Joost de Damhoudere and first published in 1554. Second, it examine the facticity of some of the 191 animal trials reproduced and discussed by the American historian E.P. Evans in his famous book of 1906, *The Criminal Prosecution and Capital Punishment of Animals*.

Against this background the chapter contains one intriguing puzzle and pivots on another. The chapter begins with the puzzle. This is to do with the image of a cat who is seen hanging from a gibbet in Cheapside in the City of London on 8 April 1554. Her head is depicted as having been shaved in the form of a tonsure. She is garbed in the vestments of a priest. Nothing else is known of her life and death. But why was she hanged? Who hanged her? Because the setting appears formal enough, her hanging is unlikely to be an instance of popular justice: was the hanging the result of a pronouncement by a criminal court?

The chapter pivots on the question of animal trials in Britain. Did they occur there? This is a matter of some dispute. E.P. Evans insisted that there were in fact three such prosecutions: of a dog in sixteenth-century Scotland and of a dog and a cock, respectively, in eighteenth- and nineteenth-century England. Some scholars agree with Evans. Some disagree. Still others are agnostic. To resolve this issue, I draw on details contained in the records of fourteenth-century coroners' courts; on the peculiar history of the English law of deodands; and then—with as much attention as can be mustered from the scanty details—on the facticity of Evans' three British cases.

For reasons that are clarified towards the end of the chapter, the dispute about the facticity of animal trials in Britain cannot be resolved at a purely empirical level. This can only be achieved with a theoretically-grounded understanding of the characteristics and self-stated purpose(s) of animal trials. This more nuanced approach, it turns out, has considerable import for the pro-animal histories at work elsewhere in this book.

Chapter 5 ('Hogarth's Patriotic Animals: Bulldogs, Beef, Britannia!') extends my recent work on the meaning and effects of animal imagery in eighteenth-century British art. Its focus is the animal imagery and the carnist gustationary preferences of the famous English artist William Hogarth (1697–1764). Throughout his career as the self-styled 'Britophil' of British art, as social critic and as consummate polemicist, Hogarth manipulated his anthropomorphized animal images in much the same way as Punch-and-Judy puppeteers wielded their gloved crocodiles and dogs at London's annual Bartholomew Fair. Human interests always occupy the discursive centre of Hogarth's art. Even in his iconic *Four Stages of Cruelty* (1751) he deployed animal images to hammer home one point or another in his perennial grudge matches with corrupt officials, with despised contemporaries and with distasteful ideologies. In *The Bruiser* (1763), for example, Hogarth imposes his own face on a dog's body (his masculine pug, Trump) and pisses contemptuously on the title page of a poem by his bitter rival Charles Churchill; Churchill he depicts as a drunken performing bear. Several of his canvases juxtapose Shakespearean mastiffs and courageous British bulldogs, on the one hand, with the feminized lapdogs favoured by *haute couture* and by the French court on the other.

In this chapter I document Hogarth's belief that certain animal species are good to think with and even better to eat. His intense patriotism he routinely expressed not only in the animal imagery of his comic history painting—for example, in *Calais Gate, Or O the Roast Beef of Old England* (1748–49), in *France* (1756) and in *England* (1756)—but also, for instance, in his weekly bouts of drunken revelry at the get-togethers of the exclusive Sublime Society of Beef Steaks, of which he was a founding member. In these meetings he and his male friends consumed vast quantities of English roast beef and sang patriotic ballads—all the while insisting that roast beef is a dish best accompanied by lashings of francophobia and anti-popery.

In the end, I suggest, Hogarth's imaginary community of England was based mostly on myth and deceit. In this it was no different than all patriotic and nationalist projects, then and now. It hardly needs to be pointed out, or at least not here, that anthropocentrism and anthropomorphism dominate the discursive centre of the great bulk of his art. It could not have been otherwise—Hogarth died in 1764 and the concept of animal rights, as such, was not properly established until Henry Salt's *Animals' Rights: Considered in Relation to Social Progress* of 1894.

As do the previous chapters in *Murdering Animals*, Chap. 6 ('Gallous Stories or Dirty Deeds? Representing Parricide in J.M. Synge's *Playboy of the Western World*', with Ian O'Donnell) addresses lethal violence. As the other chapters also do, it engages with the importance of cultural beliefs and practices in its explanatory reach. But it differs from the other chapters in that it tries to uncover the violence by humans against one another rather than by humans against animals.

Its focus is the most famous play in the history of the Irish theatre, John Millington Synge's *Playboy of the Western World*, which has been oddly neglected in the social sciences. The chapter examines the provenance of the violence around which *Playboy*'s dizzying text swirls, namely, a tragicomic parricide seemingly twice committed. In particular, the chapter asks: is the text plausible? Though Synge's authorial intentions are not open to complete reclamation, the chapter explores first, his self-stated reliance on the actual cases of William Maley and James Lynchehaun and, second, whether the representation(s) of parricide in *Playboy* more or less accurately reflect the presence and character of parricide at the time the controversial play was being imagined and first performed in 1907. The culture wars and associated media frenzy over the play provide an ever-looming backcloth against which to interpret the meanings of intergenerational violence in a colonial society lurching towards national self-determination.

In Chap. 7 ('Is Theriocide Murder?') I argue that the claim that theriocide is or might be murder surely hinges on the well-reasoned construction of another claim, namely, that the animals whose killings are so described are beings with irrevocable moral and legal rights. These rights are enshrined in the concept of legal personhood. At a minimum, they entitle their bearers to life, to bodily liberty and to respect.

The chapter suggests that at least three questions must be raised about the granting of legal personhood to animals: (1) What arguments have been made on behalf of animals about their entitlement to legal rights? (2) What arguments might satisfy a judge or a legislature about whether animals are entitled to legal personhood? (3) How much will the acquisition of legal personhood contribute to the abolition of animal exploitation? If and only if animals are granted legal personhood does the question of whether they are capable of being murdered make any sense.

If and when this happens—and I am convinced it will happen soon—then, yes, indeed, we can begin to talk meaningfully about how we humans might be said to murder some of our fellow creatures. Which animals we are to include among those species who are capable of being murdered, I leave open for informed readers to decide …

Being Language Animals

Most of us are well aware of the need to avoid language which discriminates on the basis of race, gender, age, national origin and physical or mental disability. Discrimination harms. Sometimes it kills. Far less well recognized is discrimination on the basis of species. In our case, speciesism is the failure, intentional or otherwise, to regard species other than humans as worthy of equal consideration.

One of the main pillars of speciesism is discrimination through language. So far as is humanly possible, this book avoids the use of speciesist language. For example, though I am willing to describe a human as a *she* or a *he*, as a matter of principle I do not refer to an animal as an *it*. I also refer to 'animals who …' not 'animals that …'. Moreover, I do not refer to a human as a human *being* unless I also grant an animal the same consideration of personhood—a matter of no small concern in this book.

It is now half a century since the coining of the term 'speciesism'. Though I first wrote about the use and abuse of animals in criminology some twenty-five years ago, I must confess that I am still unable to avoid the chief speciesist construction of all, namely, the words that we use to identify humans and animals, respectively. If we use 'humans' and 'animals' to distinguish the one from the other, then we err in thinking that we humans are not animals. Much wriggling around this problem has led to the temporary popularity of terms like 'nonhuman animals', 'animals other than humans', the acronym 'aothas' and the jarring 'more than human animals'. However, none of these well-meaning, would-be replacements is able to escape the clutches of speciesism. This is so because each of them is forced to use humans as a yardstick when we speak of all the beings 'other than humans'. To speak of 'nonhuman animals', for example, involves the same sort of mistake as if we were to describe human females as nonmale humans. In other words, it is a puzzle still awaiting solution.

Regrettably, there is no easy way out of this conundrum. My continuing preference is therefore to juxtapose 'humans' with 'nonhuman animals' and then, at some suitably proximate point, to attach '(henceforth, "animals")' immediately after 'nonhuman animals'. The main title of this book is therefore *Murdering Animals*—rather than *Murdering Nonhuman Animals* '(henceforth, "animals")'—because it indicates not only that we humans are animals but also that it is we who in the pages that follow are doing the murdering.

2

Theriocide and Homicide

> *The confusion of all nonhuman living creatures within the general and common category of the animal is not simply a sin against rigorous thinking, vigilance, lucidity, or empirical authority; it is also a crime. Not a crime against animality precisely, but a crime of the first order against animals.*
> —Jacques Derrida

> *When I say that the mistreatment of animals is unjust, I mean to say not only that it is wrong of us to treat them in that way, but also that they have a right, a moral entitlement, not to be treated in that way. It is unfair to them.*
> —Martha Nussbaum

This chapter advances two claims about animals' rights. The first is that animals' chief right and the sine qua non of all their other rights is they have the right to life. As Tom Regan has put it, '[a]n animal's] untimely death is a deprivation of a quite fundamental and irreversible kind. It is irreversible because once dead, always dead. It is fundamental because

---

This is a revised and expanded version of Piers Beirne, 'Theriocide: Naming Animal Killing', *International Journal for Crime, Justice and Social Democracy*, 2014, 3(2): 50–67. © Piers Beirne.

death forecloses *all* possibilities of finding satisfaction.'[1] Actually, animals have the right not just to any life but to *their own* lives rather than to some version of what we think their lives should be. At the very least, this means that we are obliged not to kill them. The second claim, which is an aspect of their right to life but also in addition to it, is that animals have the right to be treated with respect. This means, among other things, that we must never treat them as our property.

We prefer not to think about the sites where we routinely kill animals. Yet, precisely because industrial slaughterhouses are bloody, messy, noisy and stinking places, modern sensibilities dictate that they should remain socially and geographically invisible. The bulk of this chapter aims to lay bare the speciesist language that contributes to this invisibilization. This is surely a necessary step towards piercing the indifference, the denial and the ignorance that in some combination most of us use to misdescribe, most of the time, what has been done to animals when we eat their flesh and drink their milk, when we wear their skins and fur, and when we consume products whose safety has been gauged with lethal experiments on their bodies.

The phenomenal growth in animal killing sites since approximately 1700 has been accompanied by the invention of a vocabulary of euphemisms designed to obscure their aim and characteristics. The first task of this chapter is to document this vocabulary. The second is to counter its fragile hegemony by recommending a new and more honest name—theriocide—for those diverse human actions that cause the deaths of animals. Theriocide has numerous sites and can occur one-on-one, in small groups or in large-scale institutions. Inevitably, discussion of theriocide leads to a very disquieting question: is theriocide murder?

Killing Sites: Words and Things

In 1663 the viewing of exotic animals in early modern Europe was transformed by Louis XIV's new menagerie at Versailles (Fig. 2.1). Unlike other menageries, its layout for animal spectatorship was constructed

Fig. 2.1 *View and Perspective of the Menagerie from the Entrance*, engraving (Adam Pérelle, c.1670)

neither for enforced animal-on-animal fighting nor according to the principles of a park. Rather, it was designed by the architect Louis Le Vau both as the metaphorical expression of his majesty's absolutism and of royal and aristocratic *civilité*, and also as a practical site where, under the watchful eye of the Académie des Sciences, the display of animals coincided with anatomical experimentation. (It is instructive to compare the civilized *mentalité* of the regal viewing at the Versailles menagerie with the annual 'cat feast' celebration in sixteenth-century Ypres, where the king, in a specially erected gallery, gazed down on the Place de Grève as cats and the occasional fox were placed in bags before they were thrown onto a bonfire.)[2] At the centre of the menagerie was a two-storey octagonal pavilion. On one side of the pavilion an imposing door led to a single room, the royal salon. From his salon, without being seen, the monarch could look outwards and downwards into seven enclosures. One of these was a dairy farm. Each of the six other enclosures contained an exotic species at rest—'a peaceful display'[3]—among whom were lions, tigers, wolves and raptors.

According to Michel Foucault, these spatial arrangements were a source of architectural inspiration for Jeremy Bentham's all-seeing Panopticon, 'By Bentham's time', Foucault relates in *Discipline and Punish*:

> this menagerie had disappeared. But one finds in the programme of the Panopticon a similar concern with individualizing observation, with characterization and classification, with the analytical arrangement of space. The Panopticon is a royal menagerie; the animal is replaced by man, individual distribution by specific grouping and the king by the machinery of a furtive power.[4]

Famously, of course, Bentham afterwards drew up his diabolical inspection house as a technology of power whereby, with maximum efficiency and economy, discipline and control could be imposed on isolated human individuals in prisons, workhouses, factories, asylums, schools, hospitals and leproseries. In Foucault's heavily truncated account of the cultivation of a responsible citizenry, it was from the colonization and viewing of subjugated animals that panopticism emerged as an architectural principle. It must be noted, however, that at the same time that Foucault suggests that in the Panopticon 'the animal is replaced by man', he altogether ignores the novel ways in which humans were beginning to exercise and vastly expand their dominion over the original inmates of the menagerie. At first, only a small number of exotic animals was catalogued and characterized and made ready for royal inspection in the panoptic menagerie. But new tastes were cultivated. New regimes were invented and power applied at new sites of human dominion. Most importantly, animals in hugely increasing numbers were reared in or moved to invisible sites for their transformation into edibles.

As a site reserved exclusively for the killing of animals for food, the *abattoir* was introduced in the Napoleonic era during a reorganization of slaughtering and butchery that banned private slaughterhouses and mandated that they be built far from urban centres.[5] The intention behind these relocations was that in the transformation of living beings into edible commodities there should be a disassociation between the killing of animals ('slaughter'), on the one hand, and the carving up of their bodies and the draining of their blood ('butchery') on the other.

The disassociation between the killing and the butchery of animals can also be seen in the emergence of large-scale killing sites in England. In medieval and early modern England there were numerous spaces where animals were killed for food. The social organization of these killing sites seems chiefly to have differed according to their location, their size and their degree of visibility. Among the sites were shambles, knackers' yards, slaughterhouses and individual households. A shambles or 'fleshambles' or 'shamel house', first, is of uncertain origin. It has referred to both a mess and a bloody mess where animals' blood is shed and also to a place where butchers kill animals and sell their meat (*Oxford English Dictionary* [*OED*]) and also to stalls or benches on which butchers expose meat for sale (Skeat's *Etymological Dictionary of the English Language*). Knackers' yards, second, appeared in the late sixteenth century. A knacker was probably a maker of harnesses and saddles for horses, which is confirmed in the *New Gresham Dictionary of the English Language* and which also refers to the Icelandic *knakkr* for saddle. Somewhat later, he became a person whose trade it was to buy 'worn out, diseased, or useless horses and [to] slaughter them for their hides and hoofs and for making dog's meat, etc' (*OED*). A knacker's yard was the enclosed area where horse slaughterers conducted their business.[6] The twelfth-century English 'slaughter', third, originally referred to the killing of both humans and animals, often on a large scale and with blood aplenty (Old Norse *slather*, Icelandic *slátr*). *Slautherhus* appears in fourteenth-century Middle English. About a century later it was expressed in English law as a description of the site for 'the killing of beasts … had and done in the Butchery',[7] as also were slaughter-pit, -place, -room, -shop and -yard.

Killing at a Distance

In 1700 most of London's 575,000 populace still lived either with domesticated animals or in great proximity to them. Quite apart from the emergence and rapid growth of practices of petting and animal companionship, urban dwellers often kept horses for transport and hauling and cows for milk. In their cellars they fattened pigs and kept chickens for their eggs. Barely fifty years later, the expanding production of animals as edibles began to resemble that of other commodities in a large-scale capitalist enterprise. By 1750 roughly 11,000 sheep and 1400 cattle were driven each week through London's congested streets and herded into London's medieval meat market in west Smithfield.[8] To the cattle and sheep transformed into edibles at Smithfield must be added an untold number of birds, chickens, ducks, geese, horses and pigs (Figs. 2.2 and 2.3).[9]

The forced insertion of these animals into networks of ever-expanding production and consumption must have caused London's human

Fig. 2.2 *The Last Day of Old Smithfield Market*, engraved etching (Source: *The Illustrated London News*, 16 June 1855, p. 217)

Fig. 2.3 *Union Stockyards Chicago* (Source: From an original unsigned film negative, 1960–1970)

inhabitants considerable discomfort. It is not too hard to imagine the sound, the smell and the sight of terrified animals on their chaotic journey to slaughter at Smithfield. Imagine the dreadful din: cattle bellowing, sheep bleating, pigs squealing, ducks hissing and geese honking. Aggravating this fearsome cacophony were horses who neighed and whinnied, stray dogs who barked, whimpered and whined, and cats who screeched. All these animals deposited a mass of fecal matter as they were driven along London's narrow thoroughfares. For a moment, also imagine how heavy rains exacerbated this unappetizing smell, for example, or when the terrified animals were made frantic by reckless drovers or by stray dogs.[10] Having arrived at Smithfield, those animals not taken by buyers elsewhere were killed in undrained cellars, sheds and outhouses. Exhausted horses were slaughtered in nearby knackers' yards.

Of the numerous ways in which human–animal interaction was transformed by modernity, none is more significant than the new institutions of factory farming. The technical genius of those large-scale institutions lay in their simple disassociation between the rearing and the killing of animals. Spatially and linguistically, their twofold strategy has from the first been to conceal the fact that they transform animals' flesh into edibles and their skins into clothing and other by-products, such as fat used for candles and glue and even whales' 'blubber' for light and heating. On the one hand, this large-scale animal killing was and is deftly hidden from the citizenry ('[it] should be exercised in remote places', advised Blackstone in 1765).[11] Tanneries, fish cleaners and slaughterhouses were moved to rural areas or their sounds and odours otherwise masked in order to satisfy the pained sensibilities of polite and educated society. As Keith Thomas gently puts it: 'The concealment of slaughter-houses from the public eye had become a necessary device to avoid too blatant a clash between material facts and private sensibilities.'[12] On the other hand, because of the division of labour within slaughterhouses, then and now, about only a tiny fraction of workers can it be thought that they participate in, or even see, the actual moment of an animal's death—'killing at a distance'.[13] No one stands accused in these deaths. No one is deemed guilty. There is no need for forgiveness.

Killing Euphemisms

In addition to the enclosure and invisibilization of slaughterhouses, several other strategies have helped to hide the messy business of killing animals for food. For example, no longer do cookbooks recommend in grotesque detail the techniques for softening and slow roasting of the flesh, while alive, of eels, geese, ducks and pigs. Fishes, hares, pigs and rabbits are far less often served at table with their heads and other recognizable features still attached. Ears, eyeballs, feet, tails, liver, heart, tongue and kidneys are less often considered delicacies.

Other sops to squeamish sensibilities include the abeyance of any vernacular deemed too coarse and uncouth or too close to the bone. With the advent of modernity one finds the renaming of offending plants and animals, for example. For plants, exit: black maidenhair, pissabed, mare's fart, priest's ballocks and prick madam.[14] For rendered animals, enter: 'beef', 'mutton', 'veal', 'pork', 'poultry', 'bacon', 'sausage', 'pâté' and 'terrine'.

The variety of ways that we kill animals seems without limit. Animals can be boiled, cooked, crushed, drowned, electrocuted, ensnared, exterminated, harpooned, hooked, hunted, injected with chemicals, netted, poached, poisoned, run over, shot, slit, speared, stoned, strangled, stuck, suffocated, trapped and vivisected. However, operating in tandem with the strategic invisibility of animals in slaughterhouses is the increasing elusiveness of their deaths in various discourses of lethality. Euphemisms rule. Varying according to such factors as the social class of the hunters and the species of the hunted, many hunting discourses, for example, describe the dead bodies of 'game' as the 'catch', 'bag', 'yield', 'take' and 'harvest'. Speciality hunting often requires speciality language. Among the euphemisms for the killing of foxes, for example, hunters refer to the imminent killing or the moment of killing of their quarry as 'to account for', 'bowl over', 'break up', 'bring to book', 'chop', 'deal with', 'punish', 'crush' and 'roll over'. Heads of killed foxes are named 'masks', their paws 'pads' and their tails 'brushes'. Animals dissected and killed during scientific experiments and vivisection: 'sacrifices', 'subjects', 'objects' and 'products'. Animals killed by the military: 'collateral damage'. Animals 'humanely' killed and 'put to sleep' and 'euthanized' in 'shelters': 'pest control' and 'nuisance avoidance.'

Some killing euphemisms do duty in different discourses. Among these are 'cull', 'catch', 'crop'—both 'live' and 'dressed'—'harvest' and 'sacrifice'. 'Cull', for example, is used by ecologically-minded hunters to refer to the killing and 'removal' of weaker animals in a herd or to police and 'eliminate' undesirable predators which threaten more desirable species. In this capacity 'cull' competes with 'animal population control', 'artificial selection', 'nuisance wildlife management', 'selective breeding' and 'game management'. Sometimes, as well, culling or 'putting down' is Orwellian newspeak for the killing of cattle infected with bovine spongiform encephalopathy (BSE). A 'harvest' also refers to the killing of fish or to the number of animals killed, as does a 'strike'. When the harvest is coupled with or intersects self-stated ecological practices, human actions are termed 'sound' or 'responsible' or 'ethical' or 'sustainable'. When human intervention practices lead to the killing of an entire species, such as famously happened to mammoths and to passenger pigeons, for example, animals are said to become 'extinct'; a more apt term for such extinctions might be 'speciescide'.

The recitation of these euphemisms is intended as a step on the path towards greater honesty in how we talk about our killing of animals. This I begin to do by juxtaposing how we talk about humans killing humans, on the one hand, with how we describe humans killing animals on the other.

Homicide and Theriocide

In their approach to homicide most law and criminology texts begin their subject matter with a short definition like 'homicide is the killing of one human being by another'. Homicide: Latin *homo* (man[kind]) + *cædere* (to cut, strike, kill or murder). This definition is then illustrated with historical examples. These tend to be picked from seventeenth- and eighteenth-century commentaries on the English common law by jurists like Coke and Blackstone. Next might follow an outline of the concepts of *actus reus* and *mens rea*. At some point, fine distinctions must be made between lawful and unlawful homicide and between one level of culpability and another—murder, manslaughter and further subdivisions (first and second degrees and so on). Is the -cide illegal? Did the offender intend to commit it? A murder is a homicide in which the offender has what lawyers call criminal intent, malice aforethought or a guilty state of mind. Not all homicides amount to murder, of course. Some homicides occur in self-defence, others are accidental, some are face-to-face and still others occur at a distance. Some are self-inflicted. Sometimes those who are prosecuted for homicide are described as having acted like animals.

Within the forms of homicide, there are twenty or so types of murder and manslaughter. Each is named in short form as a '-cide' word. Most -cide words identify consanguinity between offender and victim—matricide, patricide, sororicide, fratricide and so forth. A few are based on status or role encumbency, such as regicide, tyrannicide and the recent clinicide and gendercide. If they are committed multiple times, some murders are then termed multiple murders and subdivided according to whether they occur in one place (mass murder, genocide) or over time (serial murder). Perhaps our ideal text will end with a chapter or two on murder in other times, places and cultures. Across time, a question might be raised as to whether there are more or less murders than there used to be. Across cultures, are there more murders in some places and times than in others?

Animals other than humans, however, are not typically regarded as beings or persons who can be murdered. Animals' master status in law is that of property. An animal is not a she or a he. Animals are things. They are *its*. They altogether lack agency. Animal narratives are *it* narratives. Somewhat surprisingly, therefore, it turns out that there are numerous -cide words in our language that already refer to animals killed by humans. Among them are avicide, bovicide, ceticide and macropocide. Some of these animal -cide words are more aggressively speciesist than others. This is the case with besticide, pesticide and verminicide, for example, each of which also refers to a lethal mix of chemical agents and which, though their content and object are subject to considerable cultural variation, can result in arachnicide, herpicide, insecticide, lupicide, muricide, rodenticide, serpenticide, talpicide and vulpicide.

Note that with just one word and without too much ambiguity, all those actions whereby one human kills another can be named homicide. Examples: 'homicide rates in Australia, the UK and the US are at 40-year lows' or 'homicide has been a daily fact of life in Mesopotamia since the 2003 invasion'. For the killing of animals there is no such unitary term. To remedy this absence I propose the name 'theriocide'. As it happens, this chosen usage of theriocide is in the good company of other recent neologisms, each of which expresses opposition to human dominion over animals—speciesism, misothery and animal sexual assault, in particular. In what follows I outline the definition, etymology and scope of theriocide.

The Concept of Theriocide

Theriocide refers to those diverse human actions that cause the deaths of animals. Like the killing of one human by another (e.g. homicide, infanticide and femicide), a theriocide may be socially acceptable or unacceptable, legal or illegal. It may be intentional or unintentional. It may involve active maltreatment or passive neglect. Theriocides may occur one-on-one, in small groups or in large-scale social institutions. The numerous sites of theriocide include one-on-one acts of cruelty and neglect; state theriocide; factory farming; hunting and blood sports; the lethal trade in wildlife; vivisection; militarism and war; pollution; and human-induced climate change.

Etymology

Theriocide is the killing of an animal by a human. It combines the ancient Greek θηρίον (an animal other than a human) and the Latin *cædere*. θηρίον, first, is a prosaic variant of θηρ, which seems originally to have meant a beast of prey. Later, θηρ was extended to other animals, probably including wild and domesticated animals and metaphorical monsters. *Cædere* denotes the action of cutting or felling or killing. It is the source of the French word *abbatoir*, where the felling of trees is used as a euphemism for both the rendering of animals to a horizontal position and also the site of their slaughter. Homologically, living trees are felled and become wood while living animals are slaughtered and become meat.

It is almost impossible to know exactly when and why many words are invented. To my knowledge, the term 'theriocide' has been used four times before.[15] In my own case, in 2007, theriocide was inserted as a concept into a critical assessment of evidence on the progression thesis, namely, the claim that there is a link between animal cruelty and subsequent violence between humans. My argument, which still stands, was to welcome the scholarly and activist interest in understanding individualized cruelty to animals but also to problematize a widespread reluctance to investigate institutionalized cruelties where animals suffer theriocide on a much more despicable and scandalous scale.

Later in the same year, quite coincidentally, the rabbinical scholar Christophe Nihan used 'theriocide' as his translation of the Hebrew phrase for 'wrongful animal killing'.[16] Nihan's choice of theriocide stemmed from his interpretation of the strictures in Genesis 9: 4–6 and Leviticus 17: 3–4 against the shedding of human and nonhuman blood.

These rules entailed, on the one hand, that any wrongful killing of humans was condemned by God (i.e. Yahweh) as homicide and was subject to divine sanction. On the other, the judgment of an animal's death as wrongful killing—as 'theriocide', that is—was limited to the profane sacrifice of three species of domestic quadrupeds, namely, oxen, sheep and goats.[17] (It is unclear in both Genesis and Leviticus, and also in Nihan's account, whether or not the unlawful killing of animals was intended to be regarded as lesser and lower-key derivations of homicide laws.)

Etymologically speaking, at least two sorts of objection may be made to my employment of theriocide in lethality discourse. Purists might object, for example, that theriocide is a hybrid and therefore inferior to constructions with simpler pedigrees. But stuffiness towards hybrids has been waning of late. None of us shudders very often or, at least, not for that reason, when we use words like television or criminology.

Moreover, two other constructions may be mentioned: 'zoocide' and 'animalicide'. Against zoocide: on the one hand, though the ancient Greek *zoon* means a living being, including an animal—as opposed to a plant, *phyton*—the verb it is cognate with (*zao*) is also used for human life. In other words, zoocide locks us into a Wittgensteinian vicious circle that ironically privileges humans. On the other hand, though 'zoo' has the apparent advantage that it is very well known as the name of a site where animals are incarcerated and used as objects of spectacle and entertainment, it is overloaded with cultural baggage. Against animalicide: this entails one of the same problems as zoocide, namely, that it at once refers both to humans and to animals other than humans. Worse still, animalicide would be an anthropocentric derivation from the Sanskrit origin of the word animal, namely, that which is to be feared.

Scope

A brief rehearsal of the sheer enormity of the nine major sites in which animals are killed now follows. No prioritization is implied by their order of presentation.

1. One-on-one Acts of Cruelty and Neglect In recent years it has been chiefly because of a preoccupation with one-on-one cases of animal cruelty and neglect that the topic of animal abuse has been propelled into public discussion. Theriocide in one-on-one situations and in small groups has been extensively investigated of late by criminologists and sociologists. It has been shown, for example, that the killing of companion animals by physical and sexual abuse often occurs disproportionately in various situations of family violence.[18]

Consider also that the object of anti-cruelty legislation is not always the welfare of animals. Historically and still today, it is human dominion, vanity and private profit that mostly lie behind these instruments. Why is it that the development of anti-cruelty legislation almost never deters would-be offenders and that it has almost always been accompanied by a massive increase in the number of legal and socially acceptable theriocides at large-scale killing sites? This problem is precisely what I have examined in the three concrete examples of the English-imposed *Act of Plowing by the Tayle* (1635) in Ireland, the prosecution of animal cruelty in the Puritan Massachusetts Bay Colony between 1636 and 1683 and the Cromwellian Protectorate's *Ordinance for Prohibiting Cock-Matches* (1654).[19] On the surface each of these legislative devices was intended to reduce animal cruelty: respectively, to horses in Ireland used to plough; to cattle in Puritan Massachusetts; and to cockerels and gamecocks in mid-seventeenth-century England. At the same time, the cultural matrix in which each occurred was much broader than its self-stated legislative intent: in Ireland the *Act of Plowing by the Tayle* was one small weapon among many forcefully used by the English to impose their cultural norms (on animal husbandry, on the ideal war horse, on efficient horse furniture and so on) and their search for economic profit, and to extirpate the backward customs of the barbaric Irish; in post-1636 Massachusetts, the criminalization of some forms of animal abuse (read: the abuse of cattle) at a time when the raising of cattle was absolutely crucial to the very survival of the colonial outpost; and in 1654 England the empowered puritans, many of whom loved to attend cockfights, were less concerned to suppress cruel blood sports than they were to quash the public drunkenness and disorder that frequently attended these entertainments.

Against old-fashioned teleological and Whiggish accounts of the history of anti-cruelty legislation I note, in passing, that there is an urgent need in North and South for new nonspeciesist, postcolonial histories of anti-cruelty legislation from the late eighteenth century to the present.

Animal cruelty and neglect is also found extensively in many of the other major sites of theriocide. These individualized cases surely deserve profound attention and condemnation. But we should be even more attentive to the fact that the vast majority of theriocide occurs in large-scale institutions. These occur silently, invisibly and with little recognition.[20]

2. State Theriocide State theriocide is committed by local and national states and by international governmental organizations.[21] Like other forms of theriocide, it can occur in numerous ways. State theriocide can be legal or illegal, intentional or unintentional. It can happen in times of war or peace. It can occur directly or indirectly and by acts of commission or omission.

The state commits theriocide directly when either it or its appointees kill animals, such as in the course of using animals to test the effectiveness of weapons manufactured by private companies. This is also an example of how the state colludes in *state-corporate theriocide*. Another example is the tragic loss of many lives in a fire at a large chicken processing plant in Hamlet, North Carolina in 1991: the fire was caused by the lax or nonexistent enforcement of safety standards in a climate of profit-seeking capitalism.[22] State officials and state regulatory agencies, greased with bribes or other favours, sometimes look the other way when confronted with illegalities.

The state also commits theriocide when it 'culls' some species in what it usually says is in the public interest. For example, according to APHIS (the USDA's Animal and Plant Health Inspection Service), in 2015 it killed or euthanized 31 bobcats, 60 feral cats, 44 feral dogs, 16 peregrine falcons, 102 foxes, 22,388 Canada geese, 11 feral goats, 332 mountain lions, 300 house mice, 8825 raccoons, 5081 striped skunks, 17,355 brown tree snakes, 56,840 feral swine and 415 grey wolves. In one year, in total, APHIS admitted to having killed or 'euthanized' 2,744,010 animals and another 1,149,415 members of nameless 'invasive' species; it also 'dispersed' 21,962,997 others.[23] Beyond its mathematical precision in the presentation of these staggering numbers, APHIS provides no clear reasons for these killings, though the first two interests itemized in its mission statement are the protection of agriculture and property; another is intervention when it perceives conflict arising between wildlife and the human population.[24]

State theriocide can also occur indirectly. This happens whenever the state encourages or permits or partners with non-state individuals or corporations or other bodies to kill animals. This it does when the US Department of Agriculture permits, licenses and regulates the massive slaughter of animals on factory farms and through vivisection. It also kills animals indirectly when it licenses private shelters to euthanize animals who are homeless, elderly, unwell, unwanted or deemed dangerous to humans. The same is true when the state licenses individuals to hunt and kill animals (Departments of Fish and Wildlife); licenses exterminators to kill 'pests' and 'vermin' (typically, Departments of Agriculture, of Environmental Protection and of Consumer Services/Fraud); and licenses supermarkets and restaurants to sell animal edibles (Departments of Food Safety, of Food and Drug Administration, and the Centers for Disease Control and Prevention). Between states and corporations, moreover, there are often powerful and willing intermediaries—for example, Dr Temple Grandin, whose disturbing equation for success with the architecture of slaughterhouses I translate as 'Animal Science + Autism = Humane Slaughter'.[25]

3. Factory Farming According to its annual summary by the United States Department of Agriculture (USDA), the number of slaughtered 'red meat' livestock includes 33 million cattle, 772,100 calves, 113.2 million hogs, and 2.18 million sheep and lambs.[26] For cattle and hogs, at least, while each year since 1950 the 'head count' of both has been increasing, the number of slaughterhouse plants has been steadily declining, with Nebraska, Iowa, Kansas and Texas now accounting for 49 per cent of commercial killing. To these totals for 2015 must be added a staggering 8,822,695,000 chickens, 232 million turkeys and an unknown number of other species, including geese, guinea fowl, ostriches, emus, rheas and squabs.[27] Also add a significant number of animals condemned pre- or post-mortem by federal inspectors because they have been mishandled in the course of being raised or transported for slaughter or at slaughterhouses, or have acquired diseases in the process, among which are tuberculosis, leukosis, septicaemia, aissacculitis, synovitis, tumours, bruises, cadaver contamination and overscald.[28]

In addition, around the world roughly 90 billion marine animals are killed each year for human consumption.[29] In 2015, 9.9 billion pounds of fish and shellfish were landed in the US. Recreational saltwater anglers caught an additional 345 million fish.[30] To these numbers must be added the enormous amount of imported fish and crustaceans, and the production of salmon, trout and catfish in aquaculture and hatcheries.

4. Hunting and Blood Sports Theriocides also include those deaths where humans train and employ certain animals to kill other animals. (No, this is not a prelude to advocacy for the policing of natural relations.) These theriocidal practices have been and are enormously popular in some societies. They include blood sports such as bear-, badger-, bull- and horse-baitings; dog- and cock-fighting; the use in hunting of dogs for waterfowl, bears and foxes, for example; falcons for small edible animals and rodents; and worms and other bait for fish.

These theriocides are rarely conceived and experienced by their human participants as naked cruelty or even as harmful. Rather, beginning with the emergence of sportization practices in the seventeenth century, they are rule-bound practices that ironically and perversely specify codes of honour, etiquette, fair play and other civilities. Their sites are legion. Among them are ballads, poems and novels; pronouncements from pulpits; hunting and animal husbandry manuals; statutory and other juridical instruments; and the sustainability mantras and practices of many environmentalist organizations.

Nowadays, a claim commonly found on the internet is that hunters kill around 200 million animals in the US each year.[31] This number is not supported by any reliable data. Motivated perhaps by long-standing anxieties about declining hunting licenses and revenues therefrom, there are considerable official government data on the age and gender of hunters and fishers, but little or no information about the species and numbers of animals killed.

By adding state-level data on hunting licenses, the US Fish and Wildlife Service estimates that of the 13.7 million hunters that 'took to the field' in 2011, 11.6 million hunted big game, 4.5 million hunted small game, 2.6 million hunted migratory birds and 2.2 million other animals.[32] Perhaps through licensed hunters' self-report data on the average number of animals killed per hunter, a rough guess could be determined for the total number of animals that they kill. However, to this total must at a minimum be added the untold number of animals illegally killed by poachers. Moreover, it must be asked: among the species of scavenger should we count shoppers who walk the aisles in supermarkets in search of neatly wrapped packages of animal flesh?

5. The Lethal Trade in Wildlife The abduction, kidnapping and killing of wildlife may be either legal or illegal, with a combined monetary value estimated at $165–80 billion annually.[33] It is widely estimated that illegal trafficking in wildlife is the second largest and fastest growing illegal trade worldwide. It is said to be worth $6–20 billion annually. Although the exact number of animal killings is unknowable, the illegal trade in live animals and in body parts threatens perhaps one-third of the world's species. Note how difficult it is to draw sharp boundaries between wild animals and domesticated animals.[34]

6. Vivisection No one knows how many theriocidal procedures are administered to animals imprisoned in research laboratories. The US government, for example, does not even count rodents and birds as animals in its annual estimates of animals used in scientific research (education, product safety testing and experimentation, including medical research). Tom Regan has estimated that each year in the US, 'somewhere between 25 and 50 million may not be an unreasonable estimate. Worldwide, the figure must run into the hundreds of millions.'[35] In the UK, one estimate is that as many as 3.7 million experiments per year are conducted on animals.[36]

7. Militarism and War In-depth information on the amount and the species used and killed by the military-industrial complex is not plentiful. Two recent book-length exceptions are the two volumes of original essays edited by Ryan Hediger and by Anthony Nocella, Colin Salter and Judy Bentley.[37] Both books offer good-faith but nevertheless unverifiable estimates of animals used and killed by the military-industrial complex now and over time, in peace and in war. The former book contains essays on a wide range of topics, including the militarization of bees; the use of canine soldiers by the US military and of 200,000 dogs used as guards by the Nazis in the Holocaust; the ecology of exterminism (E.P. Thompson's bold term for nuclear cold war); wars of images, symbols and other representations; and the military uses of animals in zoos and animals represented on war memorials. The latter provides an overview of the military-animal and industrial-animal complex, several chapters on how animals such as horses, dogs and homing pigeons have been used and killed in a variety of wars over time, and an activist thrust towards peace and the elimination of war.[38]

One unexplored effect of militarism and civil war is the killing or displacement of animals during and after forced human migration. A tsunami in 2011 led to the Fukushima Daiichi nuclear power plant meltdown, which resulted in the evacuation of at least 158,000 people from Japan's Fukushima prefecture. Two months afterwards, the Japanese government ordered the killing of all surviving livestock in the exclusion area by lethal injection. This decision helped quell the fears of contaminated beef exports from Japan in the wake of the disaster. Elsewhere, Syrian refugees have been consistently reported to have resorted to the eating of dogs, cats, kittens and donkeys as a result of the ongoing conflict.[39] The effects of habitat destruction, fragmentation and pollution as a result of forced migration are serious threats to wildlife. Refugee camps often occupy areas which were previously unused by humans, depriving wild animals of critical land for predation, procreation, foraging and migration. Furthermore, in the effort by refugees to supply camps with adequate fuel and material goods, and to accommodate their subsistence animals, the land surrounding refugee camps may be degraded through deforestation and erosion.

8. Pollution The killing of animals through pollution is ubiquitous and multifaceted (cattle themselves contribute to pollution through the production of methane gas). Pollution may occur through the generation, transport and disposal of hazardous, nuclear and radioactive waste. Pollution may infiltrate soil, water, air and space.

Oil pollution, for example, is a high-profile and enormously damaging problem that ought to have become only a rare risk by the start of the twenty-first century. Yet, in April 2010 the Gulf of Mexico and the coast of Florida were flooded by crude oil that spilled out from BP's Deepwater Horizon oil rig. By the time BP's faulty well was capped three months later, the Gulf waters were polluted by 210 million US gallons of oil. While the media offered chilling images of oil-soaked birds, the long-term effects of the BP disaster on marine eco-systems and on coastal fauna and flora are still unknown but perhaps devastating.[40] In 2012, after the nuclear disaster in Fukushima, Japan, the government banned the sale of 36 species of fish in which radiation levels were found to be especially high.

Note that, while pollution is an endemic by-product of unregulated industrial production, euphemisms rule here as well: instead of catastrophes there are 'accidents', 'spills', 'leaks' and 'meltdowns'.[41]

9. Climate Change Once upon a time Big Tobacco used to deny that its products caused cancer even when—or especially when—it was familiar with the contrary scientific evidence. So too, nowadays, ExxonMobil and other multinational corporations deny that its activities are *inherently* dangerous to the environment even when they have known for a decade or longer the scientific consensus about the harmful effects of burning fossil fuels. The long-term existence of all life on planet Earth is seriously threatened by human-induced climate change, and, in particular, by global warming. In multiple locations in the air, on the land and in the sea, anthropogenic climate change is recognized as a major threat to the survival of thousands of species over the next century.[42]

At times, greenhouse gases have contributed to climate change through active collusion between powerful governments and corporations in a globalized world of national inequalities.[43] Currently, humans release 40 gigatons of carbon dioxide annually into the atmosphere.[44] The short-term results of this greenhouse-gas pollution include ocean acidification, dead or deteriorating coral reefs, calcified plankton, and declining and threatened populations of larger animals. One somewhat contentious study has found that, given current trends of CO_2 emissions, 55 per cent of common plant species and 35 per cent of animal species are likely to see their living space halved by 2080. The most at-risk animal species are amphibians and reptiles, especially in sub-Saharan Africa, Central America, Amazonia and Australia.[45] The most publicized at-risk species tend to be exotica/flagship/charismatic/mega-species such as whales, walruses, polar and panda bears, tigers, leopards, elephants and rhinos. Another study, synthesizing 131 published studies, has found that, given a business-as-usual trajectory between 2080 and 2100, climate change will render 16 per cent of all species extinct, with disproportionate extinctions occurring in South America, Australia and New Zealand.[46]

Intersections

Their interconnectedness is a major characteristic of the sites of theriocide. As a site of theriocide, militarism and war, for instance, intersects with pollution and state-corporate theriocide. One of militarism's major effects is environmental degradation, including space junk, contaminated military bases, the dumping of jet and other fuels, overboard ship discharges, and the use of bombs and toxic weapons such as Agent Orange. All this activity kills animals either directly or indirectly by degrading or destroying their habitat. Militarism intersects with other sites, as well, such as vivisection. Thus, animal experimentation is practised in the US by both the Department of Defense and the National Aeronautics and Space Administration.[47] Military experiments and military training exercises are conducted with the use of birds, cats, dogs, dolphins, ferrets, fish, goats, mice, pigs, rabbits, rats, and sheep and—until quite recently—with primates, including 4000 monkeys at the Oregon National Primate Research Center.

Militarism intersects with factory farming, as well. While no procurement figures are available for meat consumption by national militaries, the roughly 3 million frontline personnel and reservists in the US military must keep numerous slaughterhouses at work providing three square meals of meat and potatoes per day. Moreover, if Carol Adams' arguments in *The Sexual Politics of Meat* are any indication, then the crude, in-your-face masculinities associated with the military are also an indicator of higher-than-average meat consumption per capita therein. In their turn, factory farming regimes intersect with pollution. Among the inevitable products of these loosely regulated regimes are disease-causing pathogens, such as salmonella. Fish, in particular, are at great risk from pollution spawned by slaughterhouse sludge. For example, in North Carolina an eight-acre hog-waste lagoon burst in 1995, spewing 25 million gallons of sludge into the New River and killing 10 million fish. In 2011, an Illinois hog farm discharged 200,000 gallons of sludge into a creek, killing over 110,000 fish.[48]

The magnitude of theriocide in these nine sites is hard to grasp. Some species are in the process of disappearing even before we know that they exist. A proper specification and accounting requires that we surmount some difficult methodological and conceptual obstacles. As an example of the former: in respect of theriocide in factory farming, there must be an independent authority for enumeration that is not complicit in the killing process, as is the USDA (which is responsible for overseeing the 'humane killing' procedures of the Animal Welfare Act). As such, using USDA data to measure the incidence of slaughterhouse theriocide is rather like relying on internal police department inquiries in order to measure the extent and seriousness of police brutality.

Discussion

In addition to its other virtues, such as clarity, parsimony and utility, a good definition should encourage criticism. Not unexpectedly, each part of my definition of theriocide is contentious. Among numerous issues, consider very briefly just four:

1. What is an animal? In my definition above the opening sentence states that '[t]heriocide may be defined as those diverse human actions that cause the death of an animal'. A minefield of issues lurks here. To start with, what species should be included in the class of animals? In responding to this question, should we employ some Linnaean/Lamarckian taxonomy or phylogenetic scale? Perhaps there will be near universal agreement for the inclusion of all mammals. But what of invertebrates? Insects? Bivalves? Should a similarly respectful line of questioning also be accorded to plants?

   At the forefront of existing conceptual problems is surely the question of which species should be included in any tally of lethality. Elephants, cattle *and* mosquitoes? Fish, shrimp *and* molluscs? At the moment, to the question 'How much theriocide is there?' we arrive dangerously close to the answer: as much as we would like there to be. Jacques Derrida's advice on this conundrum: '"Animals" … I interrupt my nomenclature and call Noah to help insure that no one gets left on the ark.'[49]

   Suppose at the end of this discovery process the lowest common denominator of animalhood is found to be sentience (the ability to feel pain and pleasure). How is this capacity to be measured? Some will perhaps want to draw a dividing line somewhere between a shrimp and a mollusc or between a mollusc and a mosquito. But, does it matter, in terms of what we call the swatted death of the latter—*she*? *he*? *it*?—whether the mosquito we killed was biting us or not? Is the killing in self-defence? Possibly. If bites to one's self are not allowable as a defence, then should we just grimace and turn the other cheek?

2. How long is the chain of causation? Theriocide refers to 'human actions that *cause* the death of an animal' (italics added). Now consider a package of cow's flesh ('beef') bought and sold in a supermarket. Suppose we can agree that a theriocide was committed in a slaughterhouse when a stun gun bolt applied by a worker to her head killed the cow whose flesh was afterwards transformed into an edible. Whether we think such an act is socially and ethically acceptable or not is not relevant to the question: who was responsible for killing the cow? Was it the person who wielded the stun gun? Or slaughterhouse owners?

Supermarket owners? Transporters? Advertisers? Consumers? Similar lines of interrogation about the length and the links in the chain of causation surely apply to responsibility for theriocide not only in factory farming but also to each of the other eight sites listed above.

3. Should socially acceptable animal killings be considered theriocide? Of course they should. In research where human–animal studies intersect the social sciences, especially psychology, it is a commonplace that analysis of the link between animal abuse and interhuman violence must proceed on the basis of what is regarded as socially unacceptable behaviour. In this scenario the study of animal sexual assault is acceptable because the action is not; whereas the study of vivisection is not worthwhile because what goes on in scientific laboratories is for the good of mankind. But such distinctions are little more than speciesist positions dressed up in the vocabulary of value-free social science. The social construction of some actions as acceptable and others as unacceptable must surely itself be problematized as one of the key objects of inquiry about theriocide. Dare I say it, but a killing is a killing is a killing, no matter whether it is regarded as acceptable or not.

4. Can theriocide be blameless? Can it be legal? The socially acceptable answer to these questions is: only if it is socially acceptable. But the strong language in point 3 above also applies here. In particular, though they have severe consequences for those so labelled, of course, the labels of legality, illegality and delinquency are nevertheless manufactured categories with no ontological reality. As such, legality is irrelevant to the determination of theriocide. Indeed, it is a matter of great interest why some animal killings attract the condemnation of law and others do not. Why is most theriocide defined as neither criminal nor abusive?

Post Mortem

If the killing of an animal by a human is as harmful to her as homicide is to a human, then the proper naming of this death offers a remedy, however small, to the extensive privileging of human lives over those of other animals. The term 'theriocide' is intended to do just this. Rather than misdescribe our killing of animals with speciesist euphemisms, we should acknowledge our participation in animals' deaths and name them as such.

Sociologically, not all deaths are equal. More happens with some deaths than with others. The deaths of the rich, the powerful and the famous are more likely to be reported and publicized than those of the disadvantaged, for example. Moreover, a homicide generally attracts more attention than other types of death—death by suicide, by accident, by act of God or from natural causes, for example. So, also, the death of a rich and powerful homicide victim garners more attention than if the victim is disadvantaged. The media coverage, the public indignation and the use of police resources all tend to be greater, moreover, when a high-status individual is killed by a member of a social, racial or religious minority.

When the disadvantaged are killed, their deaths are less likely to be reported to authorities, less likely to be investigated and less likely to be reported in the media.[50] In speciesist societies so it is, too, with the killing of animals. Because the lives of animals are valued much less highly than human lives, theriocides tend to draw much less attention than homicides; meanwhile the bodies of homicide victims are always assigned for examination by a forensic pathologist or other medical examiner. While human 'corpses' garner respect for the dead and are honoured with religious, familial and other ceremonial rites, the overwhelming majority of animal bodies ('carcasses') are disposed of invisibly, silently and without inspection or record.[51]

Just as they vary in the incidence and rates of murder and rape so, too, some societies are more prone to theriocide than others. In the US, for example, roughly 8000 animals will have been slaughtered for human consumption in the time it takes to read this one page. Each year approximately 1.2 million dogs and 1.4 million cats are killed in animal shelters in the US, allegedly for homelessness or aggression; 41 per cent of cats and 31 per cent of dogs who enter shelters are said to be euthanized.[52]

Because these theriocides are regarded as neither illegal nor wrongful, let alone as *real* harms, they and most other theriocides are hardly ever seen as newsworthy (though Chap. 7, 'Is Theriocide Murder?', begins with some notable exceptions to these attitudes). On those rare occasions when animals kill humans—when they crash into our vehicles or when they bite us with poisonous fangs and large teeth, use their sharp claws or when they transmit diseases to us—it is *our* deaths that are accompanied by media attention, moral panic, medical advice and dire warnings about the dangers animals pose to public, that is, human, safety. At the sight or the sound of a theriocide most of us respond with some mixture of denial, indifference, embarrassment, pity and compassion. Some express anger, outrage or revulsion. Still others experience pleasure or joy.[53]

Inevitably, this chapter leads to a very disquieting question, which is confronted in Chap. 7: 'Is theriocide murder?'

Notes

1. Regan (2004: 202).
2. On the Ypres custom see Cohen (1993: 107).
3. Sahlins (2012: 243); see further Senior (2004). Derrida recounts a visit to the menagerie by Louis XIV in 1681 when the Sun King deigned to bestow his presence on the ceremonial dissection of an elephant. Somewhat incongruously with the direction of much else of his discussion of animal exploitation in *The Beast and the Sovereign*, Derrida proceeds to describe as '*sad* … the decline of the menagerie under Louis XV and Louis XVI and its inglorious end during the Revolution' (2009: 275, my emphasis).
4. Foucault (1978: 203). Bentham himself suggested in a letter written in Crecheff in White Russia, however, that he had borrowed the idea of the Panopticon from several drawings of an inspection house executed ('Samuel Bentham … *renit*') by his brother Samuel (Bentham 1787: 65). A year earlier, in 1786, while he was manager of Potemkin's estate, Samuel Bentham designed workshops and a panoptical factory to guard the undisciplined overseers of peasant workers. The precise inspiration for Samuel Bentham's own design remains a mystery. See also the ironic postscript identified in note 50 below.
5. Vialles (1998: 15, 22–26). See also Lee (2008).
6. My colleague Ian O'Donnell has kindly informed me that the word 'knacker' is used in modern-day Ireland as a derogatory term for a member of the Travelling Community.
7. 1487, Act 4, *Hen. V11*, c.3.
8. Dodd (1856: 90). See also Jones (1976: Chap. 4) and MacLachlan (2007).

9. See further Beirne (2013: 11–12).
10. See further Beirne (2013: 53–54). In his *Commentaries on the Laws of England* Blackstone (1765–69, III, Chap. 13: 217) recorded that animals' 'stench' could be cause for actionable nuisance:

> [I]f a person keeps his hogs, or other noisome animals, so near the house of another, that the stench of them incommodes him and makes the air unwholsome, this is an injurious nusance, as it tends to deprive him of the use and benefit of his house. A like injury is, if one's neighbour sets up and exercises any offensive trade; as a tanner's, a tallow-chandler's, or the like.

None of the numerous royal and statutory proclamations aimed to reduce or eliminate animal slaughter; their intention was always to reduce noise, smell, blood and offal.
11. Blackstone (1765–69, III, Chap. 13: 217).
12. Thomas (1983: 300).
13. Pachirat (2011: 138–39).
14. Thomas (1983: 83–85).
15. Beirne (2007: 63, 2009: 17, 182), Nihan (2007: 407–08, 413 n.76) and Schwartz (1996: 7, 31). I have used the term 'serial theriocide' as shorthand for a series of fatal sexual assaults on horses and cattle in England and Wales; for two decades of pigeon poisonings in Central Park in New York City; and for the decade-long killing of dogs along bicycle and jogging paths in affluent expatriate areas in Hong Kong (Beirne 2009: 17, 182).
16. Nihan (2007: 408).
17. Nihan (2007: 407–08, 413 n.76), See also Milgrom (2008: 1456–57).
18. For example, see the numerous chapters on animal abuse, cruelty and neglect in Maher, Pierpoint and Beirne (2017) and Brewster and Reyes (2016). The death of animals through neglect is still relatively unexplored, though Nurse (2017) does much to remedy this silence.
19. See respectively, Beirne (2009: 21–68, 48–49) and Beirne (69–96).
20. For example, in the US roughly 2.4 million chickens are killed each day for American consumers, as are 650,000 turkeys and 72,000 ducks (USDA 2016a, b).
21. In employing the term 'state theriocide' I have leaned on both (1) Raghnild Sollund's (2017) analysis of the speciesist interventions by the Norwegian state in the failed suppression of certain forms of the illegal

wildlife trade there and (2) the existing concepts of state-organized crime and state-corporate crime in critical criminology (for example, see Kramer and Michalowski 2012; Lynch, Burns and Stretesky 2010; Bisschop 2015).
22. On the state-corporate collusion that caused the fire see the detailed analysis of Aulette and Michalowski (1993).
23. APHIS (2016).
24. APHIS (2016).
25. Dr Temple Grandin has been praised by PETA (People for the Ethical Treatment of Animals), by the American Meat Institute and by Oliver Sacks in his well-known interview with her in *An Anthropologist on Mars*. Grandin herself and others have said that 50 per cent of all cattle slaughtered in the US and Canada are killed according to her architectural principles and designs. However, there are great philosophical difficulties raised by her claim that it is her disability that allows her to 'think in pictures' and to understand or empathize with animals. Moreover, there are serious ecofeminist concerns with the self-declared scientific objectivity and logic of her approach to animal welfare, which is situated in a masculinist and speciesist binary.
26. USDA (2016a: 8). Derrida has compared human genocide with the large-scale rearing and killing of animals for food, which is 'over the past two centuries … *unprecedented*' (2002: 394–95); see further Taylor and Fraser (2017).
27. USDA (2016b: 5).
28. USDA (2016b: 12–17). For discussion of the harms inherent in factory farming see, for example, Taylor and Fraser (2017), Pachirat (2011) and Fitzgerald (2010).
29. This is the rough estimate by the animal rights group ADAPTT (2017).
30. National Oceanic and Atmospheric Administration (2016: 4–5).
31. On hunting illegalities in the UK see Squires (2017) and Nurse (2013).
32. US Fish and Wildlife Service (2012).
33. Sollund (2013: 72), Wyatt (2013: 9) and Sollund and Maher (2015: 1). On the importance of renaming animal 'trafficking' as the abduction and kidnapping of animals see Sollund (2011: 438, n.3, 2015: 163, 163n) and Goyes and Sollund (2016: 88). See discussions by Maher and Wyatt (2017) and (Sollund 2017) on animals and animal body parts seized in the course of their abduction and Boekhout van Solinge (2010) on the effects of deforestation on wildlife habitat destruction.
34. See Peterson (2013: Chaps. 4 and 5).

35. Regan (2007: 118).
36. Sorenson (2014a: 33).
37. Respectively, Hediger (2013) and Nocella et al. (2014). See also Hediger (2017) and Fichtelberg (2015).
38. For a discussion of the military–beef nexus during the Second World War, see Adams (2010: 52), who notes how US government rationing policies reserved a consistent supply of meat for American soldiers, who were the epitome of masculine men at that time. For a discussion of the couplet of nationalism and carnism, see Chap. 4 below.
39. See further Beirne and Kelty-Huber (2015).
40. Walters (2013: 140–01) and White (2013).
41. Walters (2013: 137). On the relative lack of publicity regarding environmental pollution, see Lynch, Stretesky and Hammond (2000), Brisman, South and White (2015), Lynch, Barrett, Stretesky, Long, Jarrell and Ozymy (2015) and Lynch et al. (2017).
42. Cahill et al. (2012: 1). See also IPCC (2016), Agnew (2013) and White (2013).
43. Lynch, Burns and Stretesky (2010) and Kramer and Michalowski (2012).
44. Le Quéré et al. (2015).
45. Cahill et al. (2012) for a list of currently endangered and critically endangered species worldwide see the International Union for Conservation of Nature (2017).
46. Urban (2015: 571–73).
47. Sorenson (2014b). See also Singer (1975: Chap. 2).
48. National Resources Defense Council (2013); see also Gray and Hinch (2015: 104) and Bristow and Fitzgerald (2011).
49. Derrida (2002: 402).
50. An ironic postscript to the comments on brothers Samuel and Jeremy Bentham's eighteenth-century panoptical design (see note 4 above) is provided by a petition from Animal Aid, the UK animal rights organization. The petition urges the mandatory use of CCTV in slaughterhouses: 'Installing CCTV in slaughterhouses would monitor workers to prevent animal cruelty, help with training staff, and record any instances of animal abuse for use in prosecutions' (2013).
51. On the variety of reactions to animals' deaths see further Taylor (2013).
52. American Society for the Prevention of Cruelty to Animals (2017).
53. See further Taylor's (2013) enlightening essay on the complexity of our responses to animals' deaths. See also Dooren (2014).

Bibliography

Adams, Carol J. (2010). *The Sexual Politics of Meat: A Feminist-Vegetarian Critical Theory.* New York: Continuum.

ADAPTT. (2017). 'Animal Kill Counter.' Available http://www.adaptt.org/killcounter.html. Accessed 3 Mar 2017.

Agnew, Robert. (2013). 'The Ordinary Acts that Contribute to Ecocide: A Criminological Analysis.' In: Nigel South and Avi Brisman (eds.), *The Routledge International Handbook of Green Criminology.* London: Routledge, 58–72.

American Society for the Prevention of Cruelty to Animals. (2017). 'Shelter Intake and Surrender: Pet Statistics.' Available www.aspca.org/aanimal-homelessness/. Accessed 31 Jan 2017.

Animal Aid. (2013). 'Make CCTV mandatory for slaughterhouses!' Available http://www.thepetitionsite.com/881/159/121/make-cctv-mandatory-for-slaughterhouses. Accessed 23 June 2013.

Anonymous. (1849). 'Smithfield Cattle Market,' *The Farmer's Magazine* (2nd series) 20: 142–3.

APHIS. (2016). 'Animals Dispersed/Killed or Euthanized/Removed or Destroyed/Freed,' *United States Department of Agriculture.* Available aphis.usa.gov.

Aulette, Judy Root and Raymond Michalowski. (1993). 'Fire in Hamlet: A Case Study of a State-Corporate Crime.' In: Kenneth D. Tunnell (ed.), *Political Crime in Contemporary America: A Critical Approach.* New York: Garland, 171–206.

Beirne, Piers. (2007). 'Animal Rights, Animal Abuse and Green Criminology.' In: Piers Beirne and Nigel South (eds.), *Issues in Green Criminology: Confronting Harms AgainstEnvironments, Humanity and Other Animals.* Cullompton: Willan, 55–83.

Beirne, Piers. (2009). *Confronting Animal Abuse.* New York: Rowman & Littlefield.

Beirne, Piers. (2013). 'Hogarth's animals,' *Journal of Animal Ethics*, 3(2): 146–75.

Beirne, Piers and Caitlin Kelty-Huber. (2015). 'Animals and Forced Migration,' *Forced Migration Review*, 49: 97–8.

Bentham, Jeremy. (1787). 'Panopticon; Or, the Inspection-House.' In: J. Bowring (ed.), *The Works of Jeremy Bentham.* 11 vols. Edinburgh: William Tait, 65–6.

Bisschop, Liesolot. (2015). 'Facilitators of Environmental Crime. Corporations and Governments in the Port of Antwerp.' In: Judith van Erp, Wim Huisman, Gudrun Vande Walle and Joep Beckers (eds.), *The Routledge Handbook of White-Collar and Corporate Crime in Europe*. London: Routleddge, 246–59.

Blackstone, William. (1765–69) (1778). *Commentaries on the Laws of England*. Oxford: Clarendon Press.

Boekhout van Solinge, T. (2010). 'Deforestation Crimes and Conflicts in the Amazon,' *Critical Criminology*, 18: 263–77.

Brewster, Mary P. and Cassandra L. Reyes. (2016). *Animal Cruelty: A Multidisciplinary Approach to Understanding*. Durham, NC: Carolina Academic Press.

Brisman, Avi, Nigel South and Rob White. (2015). 'Toward a Criminology of Environment-Conflict Relationships.' In: Brisman, South and White (eds.), *Environmental Crime and Social Conflict: Contemporary and Emerging Issues*. Burlington, VT: Ashgate, 1–38.

Bristow, Elizabeth and Amy J. Fitzgerald. (2011). 'Global Climate Change and the Industrial Animal Agriculture Link: The Construction of Risk,' *Society and Animals*, 19(3): 205–24.

Cahill, Abigail E., Matthew E. Aiello-Lammens, M. Caitlin Fisher-Reid, Xia Hua, Caitlin J. Karanewsky, Hae Yeong Ryu, Gena C. Sbeglia, Fabrizio Spagnolo, John B. Waldron, Omar Warsi and John J. Wiens. (2012). 'How Does Climate Change Cause Extinction?' *Proceedings of the Royal Society B*. Available http://rspb.royalsocietypublishing.org/content/early/2012/10/15/rspb.2012.1890.full. Accessed 23 June 2015.

Cohen, Esther. (1993). *The Crossroads of Justice: Law and Culture in Late Medieval France*. Leiden: E.J. Brill.

Cudworth, Erika. (2015). 'Killing Animals: Sociology, Species Relations and Institutionalized Violence,' *The Sociological Review*, 63(1): 1–18.

Cusack, Carmen M. (2013). 'Feminism and Husbandry: Drawing the Fine Line between Mine and Bovine,' *Journal for Critical Animal Studies*, 11(1): 24–45.

Derrida, Jacques. (2002). 'The Animal That Therefore I Am (More to Follow),' *Critical Inquiry*, 28(2): 369–418. Translated by David Wills.

Derrida, Jacques. (2009). *The Beast & the Sovereign*. 1 vol. Edited by Michael Lisse, Marie-Louise Mallet and Ginette Michaud. Translated by Geoffrey Bennington. Chicago: Chicago University Press.

Dodd, G. (1856). *The Food of London: A Sketch*. London: Brown, Green and Longmans.

Dooren, Thom van. (2014). 'Mourning Crows.' In: Garry Marvin and Susan McHugh (eds.), *Routledge Handbook of Human-Animal Studies*. London: Routledge, 275–89.

Dunayer, Joan. (2004). *Speciesism*. Derwood, MD: Ryce Publishing.

Fichtelberg, Aaron. (2015). 'Resource Wars, Environmental Crime, and the Laws of War: Updating War Crimes in a Resource Scarce World.' In: Avi Brisman, Nigel South and Rob White (eds.), *Environmental Crime and Social Conflict: Contemporary and Emerging Issues*. Burlington, VT: Ashgate, 177–95.

Fitzgerald, Amy J. (2010). 'A Social History of the Slaughterhouse: From Inception to Contemporary Implications,' *Human Ecology Review*, 17(1): 58–69.

Foucault, Michel. (1978). *Discipline & Punish: The Birth of the Prison*. Translated by Alan Sheridan. New York: Vintage.

Goyes, David Rodríguez and Ragnhild Sollund. (2016). 'Contesting and Contextualising CITES: Wildlife Trafficking in Colombia and Brazil,' *International Journal for Crime, Justice and Social Democracy*, 5(4): 87–102.

Gray, Allison and Ron Hinch. (2015). 'Agribusiness, Governments and Food Crime.' In: Ragnhild Sollund (ed.), *Green Harms and Crimes: Critical Criminology in a Changing World*. Basingstoke: Palgrave Macmillan, 97–116.

Haraway, Donna J. (2008). *When Species Meet*. Minneapolis: University of Minnesota Press.

Hediger, R. (ed.). (2013). *Animals and War. Studies of Europe and North America*. Leiden: Brill.

Hediger, Ryan. (2017). 'Animal Abuse in War.' In: Jennifer Maher, Harriet Pierpoint and Piers Beirne (eds.), *The Palgrave International Handbook of Animal Abuse Studies*. Basingstoke: Palgrave Macmillan, 475–94.

Humane Society of the United States. (2013). 'Common Questions About Animal Shelters.' Available http://www.humanesociety.org/animalcommunity/. Accessed 2 Nov 2013.

Intergovernmental Panel on Climate Change. (2016). *Climate Change: Fifth Assessment Synthesis Report*. Available http://www.ipcc.ch/report. Accessed 27 Oct 2016.

International Union for Conservation of Nature. (2017). 'Redlist.' Available http://www.iucnredlist.org. Accessed 9 Feb 2017.

Jacques, M. and C. Gibbs. (2013). 'Confined Animal Feeding Operations,' *CRIMSOC: The Journal of Social Criminology*, Autumn: 10–63.

Jones, P. (1976). *The Butchers of London. A History of the Worshipful Company of Butchers of the City of London*. London: Secker & Warburg.

Kramer, Ron and Raymond J. Michalowski. (2012). 'Is Global Warming a State-Corporate Crime?' In: Rob White (ed.), *Climate Change from a Criminological Perspective*. New York: Springer, 71–88.

Le Quéré, C., R. Moriarty, R.M. Andrew et al. (2015). 'Global Carbon Budget 2014,' *Earth Systems Science Data*, 6: 235–63.

Lee, Paula Young. (2008). 'Siting the Slaughterhouse: From Shed to Factory.' In: Lee (ed.), *Meat, Modernity, and the Rise of the Slaughterhouse*. Durham: University of New Hampshire Press, 46–70.

Lynch, Michael J., Paul Stretesky and Paul Hammond. (2000). 'Media Coverage of Chemical Crimes, Hillsborough County, Florida, 1987–97,' *British Journal of Criminology*, 40(1): 112–26.

Lynch, Michael J., Ronald G. Burns and Paul B. Stretesky. (2010). 'Global Warming and State Corporate Crime: The Politicization of Global Warming under the Bush Administration,' *Crime, Law and Social Change*, 54(3): 213–39.

Lynch, Michael J., Kimberly L. Barrett, Paul B. Stretesky, Michael A. Long, Melissa L. Jarrell and Joshua Ozymy. (2015). 'Crime as Pollution? Theoretical, Definitional and Policy Concerns with Defining Crime as Pollution,' *American Journal of Criminal Justice*, 40(4): 843–60.

Lynch, Michael J., Michael A. Long, Paul B. Stretesky and Kimberly L. Barrett. (2017). *Green Criminology: Crime, Justice and the Environment*. Oakland, CA: University of California Press.

MacLachlan, Ian. (2007). 'A Bloody Offal Nuisance: The Persistence of Private Slaughterhouses in Nineteenth-Century London,' *Urban History*, 32(2): 227–54.

Maher, Jennifer and Tanya Wyatt. (2017). 'Abuse in International Trade in Animals and Animal Parts.' In: Jennifer Maher, Harriet Pierpoint and Piers Beirne (eds.), *The Palgrave International Handbook of Animal Abuse Studies*. Basingstoke: Palgrave Macmillan, 179–99.

Maher, Jennifer, Harriet Pierpoint and Piers Beirne. (eds.). (2017). *The Palgrave International Handbook of Animal Abuse Studies*. Basingstoke: Palgrave Macmillan.

Milgrom, Jakob. (2008). *Leviticus 17–22*. Translated and Introduced by Milgrom. New Haven, CT: Yale University Press.

National Academy of Sciences. (2013). *Abrupt Impacts of Climate Change: Anticipating Surprises*. National Academies Press. Available http://www.nap.eduhttp://www.nap.edu. Accessed 22 Oct 2013.

National Oceanic and Atmospheric Administration. (2016). 'Fisheries of the United States. 2015.' Available https://www.st.nmfs.noaa.gov/Assets/commercial/fus/fus15/documents/FUS2015.pdf. Accessed 20 Jan 2017.

National Resources Defense Council. (2013). 'Pollution from Livestock Farms.' Available http://www.nrdc.org/water/pollution/ffarms.asp. Accessed 2 Sept 2013.

Nihan, Christophe. (2007). *From Priestly Torah to Pentateuch: A Study in the Composition of the Book of Leviticus*. Translated by Möhr Siebeck. Nehren: Laupp & Göbel.

Nocella, Anthony J. II, Colin Salter and Judy K.C. Bentley. (eds.). (2014). *Animals and War: Confronting the Military-Animal Industrial Complex*. Lanham, MD: Lexington Books.

Nurse, Angus. (2013). *Animal Harm: Perspectives on Why People Harm and Kill Animals*. Farnham: Ashgate.

Nurse, Angus. (2017). 'Animal Neglect as Abuse.' In: Jennifer Maher, Harriet Pierpoint and Piers Beirne (eds.), *The Palgrave International Handbook of Animal Abuse Studies*. Basingstoke: Palgrave Macmillan, 89–108.

Pachirat, Timothy. (2011). *Every Twelve Seconds: Industrialized Slaughter and the Politics of Sight*. New Haven, CT: Yale University Press.

Peterson, Anna. (2013). *Being Animal. Beasts and Boundaries in Nature Ethics*. New York: Columbia University Press.

Regan, Tom. (1983). (2004). *The Case for Animal Rights*. Berkeley, CA: University of California Press.

Regan, Tom. (2007). 'Vivisection: The Case for Abolition.' In: Piers Beirne and Nigel South (eds.), *Issues in Green Criminology: Confronting Harms Against Environments, Humanity and Other Animals*. Cullompton: Willan, 114–39.

Sahlins, Peter. (2012). 'The Royal Menageries of Louis XIV and the Civilizing Process Revisited,' *French Historical Studies*, 35(2): 237–67.

Schwartz, Baruch J. (1996). 'The Priestly Account of the Theophany and Lawgiving at Sinai.' In: M. Fox, V. Hurowitz, A. Hurvitz, M. Klein, B. Schwartz and N. Shupak (eds.), *Texts, Temples, and Traditions: A Tribute to Menahem Haran*. Winona Lake, IN: Eisenbrauns, 103–34.

Senior, Matthew. (2004). 'The Ménagerie and the Labyrinthe: Animals at Versailles, 1662–1792.' In: Erica Fudge (ed.), *Renaissance Beasts: Of Animals, Humans, and Other Wonderful Creatures*. University of Illinois Press, 208–32.

Serpell, James (1996). *In the Company of Animals*. Oxford: Basil Blackwell.

Singer, Peter. (1975). (1990). *Animal Liberation*. New York: Avon.

Sollund, Ragnhild. (2011). 'Expressions of Speciesism: The Effects of Keeping Companion Animals on Animal Abuse, Animal Trafficking and Species Decline,' *Crime, Law & Social Change* 55(5): 437–51.

Sollund, Ragnhild. (2013). 'Animal Trafficking and Trade: Abuse and Species Injustice.' In: Reece Walters, Diane Westerhuis and Tanya Wyatt (eds.),

Emerging Issues in Green Criminology: Exploring Power, Justice and Harm. Basingstoke: Palgrave Macmillan, 72–92.

Sollund, Ragnhild. (2015). 'With or Without a License to Kill: Human Predator Conflicts and Theriocide in Norway.' In: Avi Brisman, Nigel South and Rob White (eds.), *Environmental Crime and Social Conflict: Contemporary and Emerging Issues*. Burlington, VT: Ashgate, 95–121.

Sollund, Ragnhild. (2017). 'Routine Theriocide of Animals Seized in Traffic.' In: Jennifer Maher, Harriet Pierpoint and Piers Beirne (eds.), *The Palgrave International Handbook of Animal Abuse Studies*. Basingstoke: Palgrave Macmillan, 453–74.

Sollund, Ragnhild and Jennifer Maher. (2015). 'The Illegal Wildlife Trade: A Case Study Report on the Illegal Wildlife Trade in the United Kingdom, Norway, Colombia and Brazil,' *European Union Action to Fight Environmental Crime*. Available www.efface.eu. Accessed 8 Feb 2017.

Sorenson, John. (2014a). 'Animals as Vehicles of War.' In: Anthony J. Nocella II, Colin Salter and Judy K.C. Bentley (eds.), *Animals and War: Confronting the Military-Animal Industrial Complex*. Oceania: Institute for Critical Animal Studies, 19–36.

Sorenson, John. (2014b). 'Terrorism, Corporate Shadows, and the AETA: An Overview.' In: Jason Del Gandio and Anthony J. Nocella II (eds.), *Terrorization and Dissent: Corporate Repression, Legal Corruption and the Animal Enterprise Terrorism Act*. Lantern Books, 161–74.

South, Nigel and Tanya Wyatt. (2011). 'Comparing Illicit Trades in Wildlife and Drugs: An Exploratory Study,' *Deviant Behavior*, 32(6): 538–61.

Squires, Peter. (2017). 'Sports Shooting and Animal Abuse: The Ambiguities of 'Country Sports'.' In: Jennifer Maher, Harriet Pierpoint and Piers Beirne (eds.), *The Palgrave International Handbook of Animal Abuse Studies*. Basingstoke: Palgrave Macmillan, 289–311.

Stretesky, Paul B., Michael A. Long and Michael J. Lynch. (2014). *The Treadmill of Crime: Political Economy and Green Criminology*. Abingdon: Routledge.

Taylor, Chloë. (2013). 'Respect for the (Animal) Dead.' In: Jay Johnston and Fiona Probyn-Rapsey (eds.), *Animal Death*. Sydney: Sydney University Press, 85–101.

Taylor, Nik and Heather Fraser. (2017). 'Condoned Animal Abuse in the Slaughterhouse: The Language of Life, the Discourse of Death.' In: Jennifer Maher, Harriet Pierpoint and Piers Beirne (eds.), *The Palgrave International Handbook of Animal Abuse Studies*. Basingstoke: Palgrave Macmillan, 179–99.

Thomas, Keith. (1983). *Man and the Natural World: Changing Attitudes in England 1500–1800*. Oxford: Oxford University Press.

Toynbee, Jocelyn. (1973). *Animals in Roman Life and Art*. London: Thames & Hudson.
United Nations Office on Drugs and Crime. (2011). *Transnational Organized Crime in the Fishing Industry. Focus on: Trafficking in Persons, Smuggling of Migrants, Illicit Drugs Trafficking*. Vienna: United Nations.
Urban, Mark. (2015). 'Accelerating Extinction Risk from Climate Change,' *Science*, 348(6234): 571–73.
US Department of Agriculture. (2016a). 'Livestock Slaughter. 2015 Summary,' *National Agricultural Statistics Service*. Available http://usda.mannlib.cornell.edu/usda/current/LiveSlauSu/LiveSlauSu-04-20-2016.pdf. Accessed 20 Jan 2017. (2017 Now Available).
US Department of Agriculture. (2016b). 'Poultry Slaughter. 2015 Summary,' *National Agricultural Statistics Service*. Available http://usda.mannlib.cornell.edu/usda/current/PoulSlauSu/PoulSlauSu-02-25-2016.pdf. Accessed 20 Jan 2017.
US Fish and Wildlife Service. (2012). *National Survey 2011*. Available http://wsfrprograms.fws.gov/Subpages/NationalSurvey/2011Survey.htm. Accessed 2 Aug 2013.
Vialles, Noëlie. (1998). *Animal to Edible*. Translated by J.A. Underwood. Cambridge: Cambridge University Press.
Walters, Reece. (2013). 'Air Crimes and Atmospheric Justice.' In: Nigel South and Avi Brisman (eds.), *The Routledge International Handbook of Green Criminology*. London: Routledge, 134–49.
White, Rob. (2013). *Environmental Harm: An Eco-Justice Perspective*. Bristol: Policy Press.
Wyatt, Tanya. (2013). *Wildlife Trafficking: A Deconstruction of the Crime, the Victims and the Offenders*. Basingstoke: Palgrave Macmillan.

3

Hunting Worlds Turned Upside Down? Paulus Potter's *Life of a Hunter*

Piers Beirne and Janine Janssen

> *It was in Plato (was it not?) that I came across the inspired adage, 'Nature is but enigmatic poetry,' as if to say that Nature is intended to exercise our ingenuity, like a painting veiled in mists and obscured by an infinite variety of wrong lights.*
> —Montaigne

The seventeenth-century Golden Age marked a transformation in some of the key aspects of human–animal relationships in Dutch society. It was a multifaceted realignment that entailed an upwardly spiralling vicious cycle of the construction of menageries, for example, and the rise of scientific experimentation and of pet keeping. Attached to these new fashions was the emergence of a demand for artistic representations of landscapes populated with animals. A chief characteristic of this art was the tendency to depict lifelike horses and sheep at pasture or grazing in a meadow. Nicolaes Berchem, Willem van de Velde, Aelbert Cuyp, Paulus Potter and Philips Wouwerman all laboured on this task. This is not to

---

This chapter is a revised version of an essay by Piers Beirne and Janine Janssen that originally appeared in *Tijdschrift over Cultuur & Criminaliteit*, 2014, 4(2): 15–28.

© The Author(s) 2018
P. Beirne, *Murdering Animals*, Palgrave Studies in Green Criminology, https://doi.org/10.1057/978-1-137-57468-8_3

imply that when viewers looked at pictures of landscapes they made no association between what they saw on a canvas and what they saw in life: horses, oxen and cows in a meadow were probably associated with wealth and fertility, for example, dogs with loyalty and the interior of a stable with Christmas.[1] Cattle were also represented in political prints in the Netherlands. This was done in order to refer, for example, to the importance of the dairy industry in the creation of the considerable wealth in the Low Countries. As such, it was not uncommon for political processes to be expressed in images of wheeling and dealing at cattle markets.[2]

Although at first sight their representational accuracy seems their chief quality, paintings that depicted animals often had a variety of symbolic meanings. Indeed, in addition to their novel appearance in Golden Age lifelike landscapes, animals also frequently appeared in a second tendency favoured by certain Dutch and Flemish painters. This was the genre painting devoted to subjects from everyday life, by artists such as Adriaen van Ostade and the Flemish artists David Teniers and Pieter Brueghel the Elder and Jan Brueghel the Elder. Known for their rowdy scenes, these painters portrayed common folk going about their daily business in ordinary places such as taverns, surgeries, cobbler shops and meetinghouses. There was much irreverence in these scenes, with ale aplenty and much urine spilled.

The placing of animal heads on human bodies—and vice versa—was used especially in works of social commentary and political satire in Flemish art.[3] A famous example of this satyr satire,[4] set in the context of contemporary debates about the nature of the five senses, is Jan Brueghel the Elder's and Peter Paul Rubens' *Allegory of Sight* (1617). This depicts a monkey, holding spectacles, peering at a painting. What the artists thereby seem to suggest is that, with or without spectacles, monkeys look but are incapable of seeing. A monkey could never comprehend such an image, so the argument goes, because only humans have the ability to think rationally and to see clearly. Yet another example is a painting by Jan Brueghel the Younger, *Satire on Tulip Mania* (c.1640). Brueghel's *Satire* lampoons the speculative bubble around tulip investing—which had burst in 1637, leaving many speculators ruined. It depicts the tulip investors as monkeys who, needless to say, lack adequate or proper intelligence; see also Brueghel's *Persiflage of the Tulipomania* (c.1630), which depicts a monkey urinating on two tulips.[5]

This chapter tries to understand *Life of a Hunter*, an extraordinary painting executed at some point between 1647 and 1650 by the young Dutch artist Paulus Potter (1625–54). The 411 mm × 809 mm/16.18″ × 31.8″ canvas has been described by Goethe as 'a poem in paint' and by the eminent art historian Martin Kemp as 'among the most remarkable of all animal "histories" from any period'.[6]

An Unlikely Tale

To anyone interested in the historical development of sentiments that are at once against cruelty and pro-animal, *Life of a Hunter* is a confrontational centuries-old shocker. It depicts a hunter who has been captured by animals, condemned to death, roasted alive and then no doubt consumed by the very creatures who had earlier been his quarry. *Life of a Hunter* provokes several all-too-obvious questions, first and foremost among which is: What did *Life of a Hunter* (Fig. 3.1) mean to Potter and to the spectators of his era?

In order to begin to piece together the meaning of *Life of a Hunter* one has to enter its world through the prism of the ancient Greek myth of Diana and Actaeon. This particular myth was popularized by the Roman poet Ovid in his narrative poem *Metamorphoses*. It goes as follows. A young man named Actaeon, the grandson of Cadmus, is hunting deer in a forest. While engaged in this pursuit, he unwittingly stumbles across Diana, the goddess of the hunt. She, naked and chaste, is attended by an escort of nymphs while she bathes in a spring. The nymphs try to shield the embarrassed Diana from the gaze of the lovestruck Actaeon. As punishment for his transgression, Diana throws water at Actaeon, deprives him of speech and turns him into a stag with huge antlers (the ten points of which later came to represent the Christian commandments). Actaeon-as-deer flees the scene, afraid. Eventually, he is chased down by his own dogs and fellow hunters. Actaeon the deer is not recognized as Actaeon the man. Encouraged by his unsuspecting friends, fifty of his own hunting dogs rip Actaeon to pieces.

As they have been handed down from one storyteller to another and travelled from one culture to another, the plot and the cast of characters

Fig. 3.1 *Life of A Hunter*, oil on panel, Paulus Potter, c.1647–1650

in Ovid's myth of Diana and Actaeon have been endlessly reimagined. At times, Ovid's creation has been conflated with and then blended into new myths and legends, notably those surrounding the grisly deaths of Catholic martyrs. Painters and sculptors, too, have represented one or another version of Ovid's myth, most famously, perhaps, *The Death of Actaeon* (c.1562) by Titian. One of the most dramatic paintings of the Ovidian myth is the anonymous mural *The Legend of St Eustace* (c.1480). Set on a wall panel in Canterbury cathedral in Kent, in southeastern England, this complex painting has a convoluted narrative, each of whose several scenes lurches forwards or sideways and then disappears into other stories. At the bottom of the painting is an image of the stony-faced Roman general Placidus, in the service of the second-century emperor Trajan. While out hunting deer, Placidus has a vision—he sees the crucified Christ between the antlers of a large stag. At once persuaded to convert from paganism to Christianity, Placidus adopts the new name Eustace.

His new faith puts Eustace to several tests, including, ultimately, an order by the emperor Hadrian that after a Roman military victory he must perform a customary pagan sacrifice. Refusing Hadrian's demand, Eustace, his wife and his sons are entombed alive by their executioners in a bronze bull. They are then roasted to death.

Paulus Potter's *Life of a Hunter* tells the tale of a well-heeled gentleman who likes to hunt and to kill game and exotic animals. In ten of the panels, each set around the margins of the painting, the well-outfitted hunter is depicted in the act of hunting, shooting with gun or bow, trapping and spearing his chosen prey.[7] Moving downwards on the right, across the bottom and ascending to the left, we gaze successively at the hunter's pursuits. Some of these are quite explicit; some Potter borrows from *De natura animalium* (c.1800 b.p.), a miscellany of facts about animals and humans, genuine or supposed, collected by the Roman historian and sophist Aelian. As follows, they are:

- The lower-right panel represents a bull at the moment he is set upon by four of the hunter's dogs. The bull vigorously resists their lunges and their fangs. But from this picture one cannot tell whether the hunter's intention is to kill the bull or to bait him and thus allow him to escape for another occasion. Perhaps, instead, the baiting is in fact an exercise in softening the bull's flesh prior to feasting on him.

- In other panels of *Life of a Hunter*, aside from shooting at what appear to be indigenous deer and boars, the hunter is also portrayed in search of exotic quarry. In the lower-middle panel, for example, he tries to kill two lions. In this endeavour he is assisted by a turbaned Indian archer and by hunting dogs. One of the dogs is mauled by a lion and heaved into the air. In the lower left a lion tries to pull the hunter from his horse. Other scenes portray the hunter variously trying to capture a bear, a troop of monkeys and a leopard.

- In the scene at the top centre the hunter displays a freshly caught hare. This animal he has managed to kill with the use of two greyhounds (dogs who were often specially trained for hunting small prey).

- In two of the top panels Potter begins to draw the viewer into the heart of the story. In these panels the myth of Diana and Actaeon is merged with the legends of St Eustace and of St Hubertus, the seventh-century bishop of Liège and the patron saint of hunters in that region. In the right-hand panel, the naked Diana, accompanied by her female escorts, has been seen bathing by Potter's seventeenth-century hunter. He is visible in the distance, fleeing the scene and weighed down by a rack of deer's antlers as punishment for his transgression.

- In the top left-hand scene the hunter is entranced by the vision of a stag between whose antlers there appears a crucifix. (Though Potter's art began with certain of the numerous animal symbols associated with Christianity, these aspects had dwindled or else were disguised during the early 1640s as the artist tried to represent real animals in his work.) The hunter has dismounted from his horse and is caught in the act of genuflecting before the stag. In the lower section of this panel appear the initials 'C.P.' These surely signify Cornelis van Poelenburgh (c.1594–1667), the well-known Utrecht painter who specialized in biblical or mythical narratives superimposed on Mediterranean landscapes.[8] One assumes that this Ovidian characterization must have actually been painted by van Poelenburgh rather than by Potter himself.

- In the two-panel panorama at the centre of *Life of a Hunter*, the tables have been turned on the hunter. Animals have captured him and his two dogs. But instead of indulging in the sport of hunting and killing, they have put the hunter on trial. Presumably, he is charged with the serious crime of having hunted, killed and eaten animals. To the right, a lion presides over the affair. A fox records the proceedings. Officers of the court include a stag, a bear and two wolves, who surround the hunter, and a boar, a fox and an elephant, who stand guard and watch. The hunter himself, standing, arms tied behind his back, bows his head in recognition of the court's authority.

- In the final panel the hunter's dogs have been strung up on a tree limb. They dangle, limp and expired, hanged by a noose around their necks. A third dog awaits a similar end. To the left, the naked hunter is roasted on a flaming spit. Nearby lies his gun, on the ground and impotent. A goat and a bear baste the hunter, turning him over the fire. The animals dance and prance and howl with joy.

A Satire on Early Modern Animal Trials?

What did *Life of a Hunter* signify to Paulus Potter? When and where did its viewpoint originate?

Potter doubtless possessed a talent for the representation of animals from an early age. It can be said with confidence that the majority of his animal images are landscape paintings in which he gave animals the most prominence, while the presence of humans is limited to the odd farmer or milkmaid. At work in The Hague, he lived only a few metres from meadows, so he did not have to walk far in order to see cattle, for example. Indeed, the animal paintings undertaken in his studio were inspired by sketches he had made during his walks in the outdoors.[9] From 1643 onwards, he only depicted the animals and people whom he had encountered or imagined he had encountered in his immediate geographic vicinity.

In the course of his short life Potter pictured animals in almost one hundred paintings and in even more drawings and etchings. (He died of tuberculosis in Amsterdam in 1654, aged 29.) Among his most notable works are *Wild Boar Hunting in a Forest* (1641), *The Young Bull* (1647), *Cattle and Sheep in a Stormy Landscape* (1647), *Figures with Horses by a Stable* (1647), *Cows Reflected in the Water* (1648) and *The Bear Hunt* (1649). In each of these pictures animals are the chief focus. Each of their titles reflects the fact that, for whatever reason and endowed with whatever authorial intent, Potter's enduring artistic interest was the representation of animals and of our relationships with them.

In trying to explain why Potter paid such frequent and detailed attention to animals, some art historians have suggested that perhaps he simply had or knew that he had greater talent for painting animals.[10] In other descriptions of the stylistic development of his work, it has been said that he started to depict animals in order to connect the foreground of his compositions to their backgrounds. Thus, some animals he pictured as staring far off into the distance, while others look the viewer directly in the eye. In so doing, it has sometimes been claimed, Potter managed to present animals as individuals with distinct personalities.[11] This certainly seems to be the case with his best-known work, *The Young Bull* (c.1647, Fig. 3.2). If one enters The Hague's Mauritshuis museum and stands in front of this grand painting—it measures a whopping 235 cm × 339 cm (92.7″ × 133″)—it is easy to recognize the painter's attempt to portray a lifelike young bull. The animal makes eye contact. One can also admire the nice touches of flies around the bull's head and the small frog on the ground.

But *Life of a Hunter* has a special place in Potter's *oeuvre*. It screams out, so to speak, for further interpretation. It has the look of a cartoon. Its exotic animals are not well executed. Reading backwards from completed canvas to Potter's intentions—a hazardous journey even in the best

Fig. 3.2 *The Young Bull*, oil on canvas, Paulus Potter, c.1647

of circumstances—one must believe that the work of the Flemish painter and engraver Theodoor Galle was a major source of inspiration for *Life of a Hunter*. Galle's engraving *The Revenge of the Animals* (c.1600), for example, shows the trial and roasting of a hunter and his dogs by a variety of animals, including hares, boars, deer, a lion and a fox.[12] Moreover, Galle's *Discovery of America* (c.1630, after a drawing of 1575 by Jan van der Straet in Flanders) depicts Amerigo Vespucci newly arrived on American soil. It is pre-eminently a work of propaganda for the European expansion that depicts the feminized and subordinate America with a symbolic accompaniment of indigenous fauna and even, in the background, a spit over which indigenes are portrayed as cannibals roasting their human food.[13]

Noticing a few minor similarities between *Life of a Hunter* and Galle's two earlier engravings, of course, tells us very little about the meaning(s) attached by either Galle or Potter to their respective creations. All three depict animals (both human and other). Two prominently depict animals conducting a trial of human hunters. Is it possible that the major narrative of *Life of a Hunter* is a satire on the early modern practice of prosecuting animals for their crimes, such as pigs who had been winterized indoors and who happened to roll over in the middle of the night and smother a human infant? Although no animal trials were recorded in the Netherlands, in E.P. Evans' haphazard compendium *The Criminal Prosecution and Capital Punishment of Animals* (1906) at least five such cases have been identified there.[14] Perhaps Potter was aware of the details of these proceedings. One trial is said to have happened in 1571 in Middelburg. In this proceeding a bull was prosecuted after he had killed a woman by stabbing her in the stomach with his horns. How the bull was executed is unknown, though his head was displayed in public and his flesh was divided among the poor and those in prison. Another trial took place in Leiden in 1595, as a result of which a dog was hanged for having bitten a child.[15]

Why did Potter depict animals who put a hunter on trial, convict him, execute him and hang his dogs? If *Life of a Hunter* actually does represent Potter's satiric view of such animal trials, then it is short on evidence. It therefore leaves us in the dark as to its meaning. We don't even know whether Potter knew of these trials or, if he did, what his opinion of them might have been.

Art and Politics

The small handful of Anglophone art historians who have examined *Life of a Hunter* seem to agree that it is an allegory of the chaotic political situation in the mid-seventeenth-century Dutch Republic. Perhaps Potter's message in *Life of a Hunter* is the not-too-veiled threat of what might happen to an afflicted people when they rise up against a bellicose leader.[16] It is no accident, so this view goes, that Potter executed *Life of a Hunter* at the very time when the states, especially Amsterdam, were already sceptical and fast becoming restless over the expensive military ambitions of the young Stadholder, Prince Willem II. Potter's putative warning: He who treats his fellow creatures aggressively risks similar treatment in return! Thus, interpreting the scene at the top-centre panel of *Life of a Hunter*, Martin Kemp speaks of the 'calm and judicious hunter … who looks directly out at the spectator [and] has been identified as a portrait of Count Johan Maurits'.[17] Moreover, from the left distance the hunter is being rapidly approached by a messenger—a vignette interpreted to signify news of an invitation for Maurits to lead Holland out of its political quagmire. As it happened, no such invitation was made and the office of Stadholder was left open.

An inevitable corollary of the interpretation above is the suggestion that, clearly designed and rapidly executed, *Life of a Hunter* was directly commissioned in 1650 by Johan Maurits to stand as 'a kind of allegorical manifesto, speaking of his intention to rule with moderation'.[18] Clearly, something more needs to be said about how in this case a commission for a work of art by Paulus Potter might or might not be able to influence its content and production. Let us offer two comments on this, one leaving considerable room for speculation, the other closing it altogether.

First, the occupation of painter, if performed skilfully and with an eye to consumer preference, might have led to upward social mobility in the society of the Dutch Golden Age.[19] It is probable that the painting of animals carried little social prestige, especially at a time when the upper echelons of Dutch society—the nobility, the landowners and the emergent bourgeoisie—were beginning to commission and collect painted representations of themselves. Individual or group portraiture, though dull, might have been more profitable and more enviable work than animal depictions. But perhaps paid commissions did not much matter to Potter as he came from a well-to-do family of glassmakers and married into a family of wealthy builders. It is worth adding that Potter's prospective father-in-law, van Balckeneynde, at first opposed his daughter Adrianna's marriage to young Paulus because he had chosen to represent animals rather than humans in his paintings.[20] As it happened, friends and high-placed contacts came to Potter's rescue and assured van Balckeneynde that Potter was a talented and well-respected artist. Soon enough, Potter was introduced by van Balckeneyde to the social elite in The Hague. With their deep pockets they were well placed to bid for Potter's time and brushwork. (Indeed, Potter is known to have once received a commission from Princess Amalia van Solms—the wife and widow of Stadholder Frederik Hendrik of Orange—though the finished canvas created a minor scandal and was rejected after the artist placed a urinating cow in the composition.)

Unfortunately, as is the case with many other Dutch paintings, it is usually unclear with Potter's art if the terms of a particular commission demanded a specific content or style agreed on with the artist in advance. Although, according to art historians, *Life of a Hunter* was probably commissioned by a person in Johan Maurits' circles, it must be said that, because of his growing reputation and increasing wealth, Potter was likely not altogether dependent on commissions and so sometimes was able to paint what he pleased. Yet it is a second, quite different issue that leads us to believe that Potter did not paint *Life of a Hunter* because of a commission from the circle of Johan Maurits. Convention generally has it that the date of production of *Life of a Hunter* was 'c.1650'.[21] This is a big and risky 'c[irca]', however, because the website of the Hermitage museum—which owns and exhibits the painting and for some unknown reason chooses to entitle it *The Punishment of the Hunter*—claims that it dates back to 'c. 1647'.[22] But if 1647 is accepted as accurate and 1650 is in error, then the earlier date is critical to the painting's meaning because Frederick Henry of Orange died in 1647. By then, because of his pursuit of freedom of religion, his encouragement of trade and industry and his construction projects, he had managed to restore some respect for the House of Orange. Within a few years his son William II would squander much of that good reputation. Of course, neither this nor any other turn of events could possibly have been foreseen in 1647.

Hunting Worlds Upside Down

If Potter actually did produce *Life of a Hunter* as early as 1647, then still a different interpretation of its meaning is required. In trying to understand *Life of a Hunter*, we began with the grisly death of Actaeon, who was ripped to pieces by his own hunting dogs after he had been transformed into a stag. The ancient Greeks termed such an inversion of normal everyday practices *adynaton* ('impossible').

Moving fast forward, now consider the dynamic, self-styled World Upside Down tradition ('WUD') that began with twelfth- and thirteenth-century stories of half-animal/half-human characters and which circulated as burlesque at carnivals and in plays and taverns throughout much of Europe.[23] Often responding to natural disasters or to perceived social injustices, cheaply produced woodcut WUD prints expressed the hopes and aspirations of the downtrodden for the overturning of existing social hierarchies, especially those in politics and in relations between men and women. Sometimes, such WUD prints were altogether serious. Here their meaning is fairly explicit—as when they depict role reversals in families, with women assuming dominant roles (weapon-toting wives, for example) or children instructing parents. At other times, they were chiefly comical—when their visual puns took the form of nonsense, re-worked proverbs or satire. Here, their meaning is much harder for us to fathom. The animals who were represented in WUDs were often of the comical sort: animals with objects—for example, hay chasing after a donkey; or animals with other animals—such as mice hunting cats; or animals with humans—for example, coachmen pulling a horse and carriage.

WUD prints had been familiar fare in the Netherlands since at least 1485, when van der Meer produced a new Dutch version of the epic tale of Reynaert, the wily half-human half-animal fox who was put on trial before King Lion for raping the she-wolf Hersent. The Dutch had no difficulty construing Reynaert's adventures as comedic criticism of the goings-on of life at court. During the Dutch Revolt (1568–1648) against Spanish rule Reynaert's story gained a following when, depicted as reading aloud a list of complaints at a trial, he was popularly imagined to be criticizing cruel and unjust rule.[24] In a singular piece of scholarship on WUDs by David Kunzle, Potter's *Life of a Hunter* is identified as a WUD.[25] It certainly *looks* like a WUD. Just as *Life of a Hunter* is, many WUDs are grid-like with a minimum of twelve panels and as many as twenty-five. Potter's had fourteen. Most of the sixty or so broadsheet WUDs examined in Kunzle's essay have inscribed at their footers *mundus inversus, mondo alla rovescia, monde à l'envers, mundo al revés, verkehrte welt* or *omgekeerde wereld*. But there is no '*omgekeerde wereld*' attached to Paulus Potter's *Life of a Hunter*. Perhaps it is, after all, an artistic if impenetrable comment on the state of Dutch politics. Nevertheless, there are no obvious textual clues that we can use to pierce its silence in this respect.

If it can be agreed that *Life of a Hunter* is a WUD, then one should also examine whether Potter intended his creation to be a satire or a comedy or a combination of both, as many creations by Hieronymous Bosch and by Pieter Brueghel pointedly were, for example. Perhaps *Life of a Hunter* is a satire. But if so, then what is its object—Dutch politics or animal trials or the ethical dilemmas of hunting practices? If *Life of a Hunter* is a comedy, then at what does it poke fun—a foolish hunter caught by his prey, perhaps, or the notion that animals are able to converse and follow legal procedure? There is no obvious answer to such questions.

We might also ask if *Life of a Hunter* is a WUD that expresses Potter's contempt for hunting and for other forms of animal cruelty. (It cannot be denied: on first inspection, we expected—hoped, even—that *Life of a Hunter* would turn out to be an unheralded marker in the history of anti-cruelty sentiments!) If found to be so, then Potter might well have been voicing that very same oppositional sentiment in *Wild Boar Hunt in a Forest* (1641; see Fig. 3.3) and in *The Bear Hunt* (1649). That is, these two fierce and gory artworks might represent *both* glorification of the hunt *and* a measure of sympathy for the hunted. Or does this suggest a choice between a lust for hunting and the laying down of arms? Indeed, one could be led to suspect that, owing to Potter's tendency to favour the depiction of animals in such a lifelike way and in graphic detail, without explicit symbolism, his labours reflect a deeply held respect or admiration for his fellow creatures and an interest in animals in themselves and for their own sakes. Though perhaps this is a bit of a stretch.

Fig. 3.3 *Wild Boar Hunt in a Forest*, oil on panel, Paulus Potter, c.1641

Against Animal Cruelty: Montaigne, Potter and *Life of a Hunter*

Were our tentative interpretation of *Life of a Hunter* to be correct, then Paulus Potter's painting would become an important visual marker in the lengthy trajectory of arguments against animal cruelty which arose with the works of Erasmus, Thomas More, Montaigne and the Calvinist Jean de Léry. Each of these thinkers described the killing of animals as cruel, especially when it involved a pleasurable spectacle, as it did with hunting. But it was Michel de Montaigne's essays (composed in late sixteenth-century France) which were most influential. In his famous essay of 1580 on cruelty, Montaigne had suggested not only that we humans wrong animals when we hunt and kill them but also that those who grow accustomed to the slaughtering of animals are more likely to proceed to the killing of humans.[26] 'There is,' Montaigne urged, 'a certain respect, a general duty of humanity, not only to beasts that have life and sense, but even to trees and plants'.[27] In another essay (his epistemologically sceptical 'Apology for Raymond Sebond'), he had even opposed and contradicted the ingrained belief that we humans are superior to all other animals: 'The natural distemper of Man is presumption … When I play with my cat, how do I know that she is not passing time with me rather than I with her?'[28] In his essay 'Of Cruelty' Montaigne repeats the Pythagorean dictum that 'I think 'twas slaughter of wild beasts that first stained the steel of man with blood.'[29]

Through the Calvinist precept that humans have a God-given obligation to act with care towards our fellow creatures, Montaigne's strictures against animal cruelty quickly travelled elsewhere—to England and to the Netherlands, in particular. Montaigne's essays, which had themselves been considerably influenced both by the teachings of Rotterdam's Erasmus and by the recent history of the turbulent relationship between the southern and the northern Netherlands, were undoubtedly influential in the Netherlands during Potter's era.[30] Indeed, strong evidence for Montaigne's popularity is lodged in Dutch library auction catalogues published in the seventeenth century; one study has found that, between 1601 and 1700, Montaigne's name appears in 38 per cent of 211 auction catalogues of private libraries in the Netherlands.[31] Although we are not privy to precisely which texts were owned and read by painters like Potter, it is known that there was a Dutch tendency to emblematize Montaigne's essays. The painter Pieter van Veen, for example, was especially interested in the animals described in Montaigne's 'Apology for Raymond Sebond' (in a collection of 191 illustrations by van Veen, eighty-seven referred to the *Apology* and nineteen depicted animals as their subject, including an illustration of Montaigne's famous question about the possible subjectivity of the playing cat).[32]

One of us has argued elsewhere that it must have been unclear to seventeenth-century Protestants exactly what message they should or could glean from Calvin's writings on animals.[33] In Calvin's boundary-marking *Institutes of the Christian Religion* (1541–59), for example, the faithful are pointed not in one but in several directions. Consider two. On the one hand, animals are part of God's creation. We humans are therefore obliged to treat them with respect: '[God] sustains, nourishes, and cares for, everything he has made, even to the least sparrow.'[34] On the other hand, the *Institutes* unequivocally demand obedience to the Old Testament injunctions about the hierarchical Great Chain of Being. This means that because humans are by nature superior to beasts, the labour, skin and flesh of the latter are at our disposal as and when we should need them.

At the same time, especially, in his *Commentaries*, Calvin seemed to leave a door open for more refined discussion, flatly stating that 'the bodies of dumb beasts ... and donkeys and men come from the same clay', and that 'men are required to practice justice even in dealing with animals ... a just man cares well for his beasts.'[35] Almost needless to say, however, the attempt to read backwards from actions to motives was a treacherous path for seventeenth-century Protestants. So it is also for us.

Though we might not wish to go quite as far as Martin Kemp does when he suggests '[t]he whole of the Dutch painter's canvas has a very Montaignean feel to it',[36] aspects of Potter's *Life of a Hunter* nevertheless do encourage that interpretation. But to go further than this would in our view surely risk anachronism. Potter's painting expresses a moment of transition in cultural attitudes towards human–animal relationships: its restricted vision of animal cruelty is not against animal abuse *tout court* and its inversion of two major links in the accepted Great Chain of Being is very far from being altogether pro-animal.

There is work still to be done, clearly, on how Montaigne's ideas about animal suffering travelled from one society to another and on how different societies received them differently. At least one of the major sub-plots of this chapter—the influence of early modern animal trials—is the point of entry into the next chapter. The book moves from examining Potter's *Life of a Hunter* in the Netherlands to the perplexing image of a cat hanging from a gibbet in mid-sixteenth-century London. Does this image indicate the presence of animal trials in Britain? If so, is their eventual decline tied to the emergence of the humane influence of Montaigne on seventeenth-century English puritanism?

Notes

1. Chong (1988: 56–82), Davids (1989: 35) and Wolloch (2006: Chap. 6).
2. Chong (1988: 73–82).
3. Antal (1962: 61–62).
4. The English artist William Hogarth must have looked long and hard at the paintings of Egbert van Heemskerck the Elder (c.1634–1704), who had migrated from Holland to London around 1675, living close by the Hogarth family's residence in West Smithfield during William's childhood. See in particular van Heemskerck's *Quaker Meeting* (c.1680) and his humorous satire *Midnight Magistrate* (c.1690). The latter depicts a trial in which a monkey magistrate presides in a case against a young female cat, while animals and hybrids observe. The presence of several hybrid constables and a concerned owl make the scene eerily reminiscent of Hogarth's *Cruelty in Perfection* (1751). Hogarth also made extensive use of satyrs and other hybrids as instruments of political and social satire in eighteenth-century London (for example, in his *South Sea Scheme*, 1721); see further Beirne (2013: 142–46).
5. See also *De Allegorie van Prins Maurits en Johan van Oldenbarnevelt* (c.1620), a painting by the brothers Herman and Cornelis Saftleven of Groenestijn castle near Baarn. In *De Allegorie* the Republican van Oldenbarnevelt, who appears as a wise owl, is chased from his castle by a mounted knight. This warrior is meant to be Maurits, Prince of Orange, which is quite a message in itself. Moreover, in the foreground are two crested fowls. These birds likely symbolize noblemen whom it was hoped would not intervene in the acute conflict over state governance (leading to van Oldebarnevelt's death).
6. Respectively, Goethe (cited in Walsh, Buijsen and Broos 1994: 127) and Kemp (2007: 101).
7. In his history of the emergence of the first fully fledged animal paintings, in the seventeenth-century Netherlands, Wolloch credits as one of the chief facilitating agents the growing habit of keeping exotic and domesticated animals, which may have led to 'the observation of animals by artists and encouraged the interest in animal painting' (2006: 173).
8. On van Poelenburgh's contribution to *Life of a Hunter* see further Walsh et al. (1994: 127–28) and Kemp (2007: 101–02).
9. Buijsen and Dumas (1998: 227).
10. For example, see Buijsen and Dumas (1998: 225).
11. Arps-Aubert (1932: 11).

12. See also Walsh et al. (1994: 129–30).
13. In by far the most complete study of Potter, Amy Walsh has documented that '[t]he interest in the "savage" was particularly strong during the 1640s when, among other studies, Jan Maurits commissioned Albert Eeckhout to document with paintings the appearance and activities of the Indians of Brazil' (1985: 334, n.88). See further Joppien (1979: 302ff).
14. Five Netherlandish animal trials are described in Stokvis (1931); see also Praag (1932).
15. Fuchs (1957: 5–8). It is worth mentioning that quite close by, in thrifty Flemish Ghent, after a judicial sentence of death had been passed on a cow: 'she was slaughtered and her flesh sold as butcher's meat, half of the proceeds of the sale being given as compensation to the injured party and the other half to the city treasury for distribution among the poor' (Evans 1906: 169).
16. The English physician John Keys reported that Henry VII once commanded some of his own hunting dogs to be hanged after they had assaulted 'the valiaunt Lyon king of all beastes. An example for all subjectes worthy remembraunce, to admonishe them that it is no advantage to them to rebell against ye regiment of their ruler, but to keepe them within the limits of Loyaltie' (Keys 1576: 26). This story is also recounted by Walsh, who comments: 'the context of the application of the image is important for its interpretation. In this case our interpretation of the image as a statement against the military is indicated by Potter's orientation toward peaceful means in his other contemporary works' (1985: 408).
17. Kemp (2007: 103–04).
18. Kemp (2007: 103–04).
19. van Deursen (2010: 91–98).
20. Houbraken (1753: 126).
21. This assertion is made, for example, by Walsh et al. (1994: 133–35).
22. This claim by the Hermitage is available at: http://www.hermitagemuseum.org/ (accessed 20 January 2014).
23. Two excellent accounts of the WUD tradition are provided in Kunzle (1978) and in Stallybrass (1991).
24. An interesting explanation for Reynard's upside-down trial is given by the Reijnaart Association, available at: http://www.reynaertgenootschap.be. See further Varty (2003) and van Dievoet (1975).

25. Kunzle (1978: 55–56). Moreover, upside-down pictures were not completely unknown in Holland at this time; see the anonymous *Wild Animals Taking Their Revenge on Hunters and Hunting-dogs*, for example, in Walsh et al. (1994: 130).
26. Montaigne (1580: 187–88).
27. Montaigne (1580: 191).
28. Montaigne (1576: 16–17). For an excellent discussion of Montaigne's essay 'Of Cruelty' see Erica Fudge (2006: 76–79). Against the rival interpretations of Quint (1998) and Hallie (1977), she insists that Montaigne 'treats animals as moral patients, as beings that suffer … [and] he writes that "I do not see a chicken's neck wrung, and I cannot bear to hear the scream of a hare in the teeth of my dogs"' (Fudge 2006: 78). For the easy and unfair criticism that Potter failed to understand anything about the mental life of animals, see John Ruskin (1894: 275–76).
29. Montaigne (1580, 10: 187).
30. Ellerbroek (1948: 49–54).
31. Smith (2007: 5–7).
32. Kolfin and Rikken (2007: 253).
33. Beirne (2009: 46).
34. Calvin (1541–59, I, XVI, 1: 197–98).
35. Calvin (n.d.: 294 and 329).
36. Kemp (2007: 115). At the same time, we have to disagree with Amy Walsh's awkward rejection of a Montaignean influence or theme in Potter's *Life of a Hunter*. She *both* dismisses Kunzle's (1978: 55ff) claim that 'Potter's painting reflects the artist's humanitarian concern for the plight of the animals' (1985: 407, n.114) *and* admits 'Potter stresses … the stoic concepts of moderation, simplicity, and naturalness, all of which are found more perfectly in the animal' (1985: 414).

Bibliography

Antal, Frederick. (1962). *Hogarth and His Place in European Art*. New York: Basic Books.

Arps-Aubert, Rudolf von. (1932). *Die Entwicklung des reinen Tierbildes in der Kunst des Paulus Potter*. Halle: Eduard Klinz Buchdruck-Werkstätten.

Beirne, Piers. (2009). *Confronting Animal Abuse*. New York: Rowman & Littlefield.

Beirne, Piers. (2013). 'Hogarth's Animals,' *Journal of Animal Ethics*, 3(2): 133–62.

Buijsen, Edwin and Charles Dumas. (1998). *Haagse schilders in de Gouden Eeuw. Het Hoogsteder Lexicon van alle schilders werkzaam in Den Haag 1600–1700*. Den Haag and Zwolle: Kunsthandel Hoogsteder & Hoogsteder and Waanders Uitgevers.

Calvin, John. (1541–1559). (1960). *Institutes of the Christian Religion*. Edited by John T. McNeill. Translated by Ford Lewis Battles. 2 vols. Philadelphia: Westminster.

Calvin, John. (n.d.). (1958). *Commentaries*. Translated by Joseph Haroutunian. Phildelphia, PA: Westminster.

Chong, Alan. (1988). 'In 't verbeelden van Slachtdieren,' Associaties en betekenissen, verbonden aan het Hollandse veestuk in de zeventiende eeuw.' In: C. Boschma, J.M. de Groot, G. Jansen, J.W.M. de Jong and F. Grijzenhout (eds.), *Meesterlijk vee. Nederlandse veeschilders 1600–1900*. Zwolle: Uitgeverij Waanders, 56–86.

Davids, K. (1989). *Dieren en Nederlanders. Zeven eeuwen lief en leed*. Utrecht: Matrijs.

Deursen, A. Th. van. (2010). *De Gouden Eeuw compleet*. Amsterdam: Uitgeverij Bert Bakker.

Dievoet, Guido van. (1975). 'Le Roman de Renart et Van den Vos Reynaerde, témoins fideles de la procédure pénale aux XIIe et XIIIe siècles.' In: E. Rombauts, A. Welkenhuysen and G. Verbeke (eds.), *Aspects of the Medieval Animal Epic*. Louvain: Leuven University Press, 43–52.

Ellerbroek, G.G. (1948). 'Notes sur la fortune de Montaigne en Hollande,' *Neophilologus*, 32: 49–54.

Evans, Edward Payson. (1906). *The Criminal Prosecution and Capital Punishment of Animals*. New York: E.P. Dutton. (Reprinted in 1987, London: Faber and Faber).

Fuchs, J.M. (1957). *De hond aan de galg*, Amsterdam: Querido.

Fudge, Erica. (2006). *Brutal Reasoning: Animals, Rationality, and Humanity in Early Modern England*. Ithaca, NY: Cornell University Press.

Hallie, Philip P. (1977). 'The Ethics of Montaigne's De la cruauté.' In: Raymond C. La Charité (ed.), *O Un Amy! Essays on Montaigne in Honor of Donald M. Frame*. Lexington, KY: French Forum.

Houbraken, Arnold. (1753). (1976). *De groote schouburgh der Nederlantsche konstschilders en schilderessen*. Amsterdam: B.M. Israël BV.

Joppien, R. (1979). 'The Dutch Vision of Brazil: Johan Maurits and his Artists.' In: E. van den Boogaart with H.R. Hoetink and P.J.P. Whitehead (eds.),

Johan Maurits van Nassau-Siegen 1604–1679; A Humanist Prince in Europe and Brazil. The Hague: The Johan Maurits van Nassau Stichting, 297–376.

Kemp, Martin. (2007). *The Human Animal in Western Art and Science*. Chicago: University of Chicago Press.

Keys, Johannes. (1576). *Of English Dogges, the Diversities, the Names, the Natures, and the Properties*. Translated by Abraham Fleming. London: Richard Johnes. Available http://www.projectgutenberg.org. Accessed 22 Nov 2017.

Kolfin, Elmer and Marrigje Rikken. (2007). 'A Very Personal Copy: Pieter van Veen's Illustrations to Montaigne's *Essais*.' In: Paul J. Smith and Karl A.E. Enenkel (eds.), *Montaigne and the Low Countries (1580–1700)*. Leiden: Brill, 247–61.

Kunzle, David. (1978). 'World Upside Down: The Iconography of a European Broadsheet Type.' In: Barbara A. Babcock (ed.), *The Reversible World: Symbolic Inversion in Art and Society*. Ithaca: Cornell University Press, 39–94.

Montaigne, Michel de. (1576). (1987). *An Apology for Raymond Sebond*. Translated by M.A. Screech. London: Penguin.

Montaigne, Michel de. (1580). (1910). 'Of Cruelty.' In: *Essays of Montaigne*. Translated by Charles Cotton. 10 vols. New York: Edwin C. Hill, 4: 162–93.

Praag, A. van. (1932). 'Het strafproces tegen dieren,' *Themis*, (93): 345–75.

Quint, David. (1998). *Montaigne and the Quality of Mercy: Ethical and Political Themes in the Essais*. Princeton, NJ: Princeton University Press.

Ruskin, John. (1894). *Modern Painters*, vol. 5: *Of Leaf Beauty – of Cloud Beauty, of Ideas of Relation*. New York: Estes and Lauriat, 275–76.

Smith, Paul J. (2007). 'Montaigne and the Low Countries – Synopsis – and New Perspectives.' In: Paul J. Smith and Karl A.E. Enenkel (eds.), *Montaigne and the Low Countries (1580–1700)*. Leiden: Brill, 1–15.

Stallybrass, Peter. (1991). 'The World Turned Upside Down: Inversion, Gender and the State.' In: V. Wayne (ed.), *The Matter of Difference*. Ithaca: Cornell University Press, 201–17.

Stokvis, Benno J. (1931). 'Bijdrage tot de kennis van het wereldlijke direnproces in de noordelijke Nederlanden,' *Tidschrift voor Strafecht*, 41: 399–424.

Varty, Kenneth. (ed.). (2003). *Reynard the Fox: Social Engagement and Cultural Metamorphoses in the Beast Epic from the Middle Ages to the Present*. New York: Berghahn Books.

Walsh, Amy. (1985). *Paulus Potter: His Works and Their Meaning*. Unpublished Ph.D dissertation, Graduate School of Arts and Sciences, Columbia University.

Walsh, Amy, Edwin Buijsen and Ben Broos. (1994). *Paulus Potter: Paintings, Drawings and Etchings*. Mauritshuis, The Hague: Waanders Publishers.

Wolloch, Nathaniel. (2006). *Subjugated Animals: Animals and Anthropocentrism in Early Modern European Culture*. Amherst, NY: Humanity Books.

4

On the Geohistory of Justiciable Animals: Was Britain a Deviant Case?

> *He that kills another's ox, sins, not through killing the ox, but through injuring another man in his property. Wherefore this is not a species of the sin of murder but of the sin of theft or robbery.*
> —Aquinas, *Summa Theologica*

On 8 April 1554 a cat was hanged on a gibbet in Cheapside in the City of London. A funeral director, Henry Machyn, gave an account of the hanged cat: 'somebody unknown hanged a cat on the gallows beside the cross in Cheap, habited in a garment like to that the priest wore that said mass; she had a shaven crown, and in her fore feet held a piece of paper made round, representing the wafer.'[1] A few more details of the situation of the hanged cat are provided in John Foxe's *Acts and Monuments of the Christian Martyrs*:

Chapter 3 is a quite different project from those that originally appeared in Beirne (1994) and Beirne (2011).

© The Author(s) 2018
P. Beirne, *Murdering Animals*, Palgrave Studies in Green Criminology,
https://doi.org/10.1007/978-1-137-57468-8_4

a cat with hir head shorn, and the likenes of a vestment cast over hir, with hir fore feet tied togither, and a round peice of paper like a singing cake betwixt them, was hanged on a gallowes in Cheape, neere to the crosse, in the parish of S. Mathew, which cat being taken downe, was caried to the Bish. of London, and he caused the same to be shewed at Pauls crosse, by the preacher D. Pendleton.[2]

A woodcut illustration, *A Cat Hung Up in Cheapside, Habited like a Priest* (Fig. 4.1), accompanies the description of the feline's execution in Foxe's *Acts and Monuments,* whose pages have been said to show that '[m]ost of the martyrs … were executed following an orderly judicial process'.[3] Whatever the precise setting represented in this startling image, it appears that the macabre event took place next to or even in the courtyard of a mid-sixteenth-century London mansion (perhaps an official or

Fig. 4.1 *A Cat Hung Up in Cheapside, Habited like a Priest*, printed woodcut, John Foxe, 1563 (Source: John Foxe, Acts and Monuments of the Christian Martyrs (1563) (1776, London: H. Trapp))

a state building). Those in attendance are two clerics who oversee the hanging and several spectators whose garb identifies them as well-to-do citizenry. But nothing else has yet been uncovered about the particular circumstances of the unfortunate cat's hanging. Was the cat's hanging preceded by prosecution in a court of criminal law?[4]

This chapter tries to settle an unresolved issue in the geohistory of justiciable animals, namely, that of the facticity of animal prosecutions in Britain (I use the term 'justiciable' [medieval Fr. *justisable*] as shorthand for the subjection of animals to the discursive practices of a criminal court with its panoply of censures and sanctions). In his path-breaking book *The Criminal Prosecution and Capital Punishment of Animals* of 1906, the American historian E.P. Evans reported that of 191 animal trials in late medieval and early modern Europe a mere three took place in Britain: a dog in sixteenth-century Scotland and a dog and a cock, respectively, in eighteenth- and nineteenth-century England. While there is little dispute about the occurrence of animal trials in several societies in northern and western Europe, scholars nowadays are about evenly divided on their presence in Britain. Some, such as Harriet Ritvo and Keith Tester, claim that animal trials were common in Britain, at least from Elizabethan times up to the Victorian era. Others, such as Erica Fudge and Laurie Shannon, have denied this claim, insisting that no such trials ever took place in Britain or, indeed, anywhere else in the British Isles.[5] Clearly, Evans' claim—though they were uncommon, animal trials did occur in Britain—runs counter to both groups of scholars who have taken a position on their facticity.

In order to resolve this issue I begin by identifying the legal doctrine and criminal procedure attached to animal trials known to have been conducted in continental Europe. This is done with a view, next, to uncovering two other major dimensions of their geohistory, namely, their periodicity and their geographical location. For reasons that will eventually become clear, it turns out that the question of whether or not animal trials were conducted in Britain cannot be resolved at a purely empirical level. This apparent difficulty opens up an alternative perspective on what animal trials might be, which has considerable import for a pro-animal or green history such as the one intended here.

Rendering Animals Justiciable

> If an ox gore a man or a woman that they die, then the ox shall be surely stoned, and his flesh shall not be eaten; but the owner of the ox shall be quit. (Exodus 21: 28)

> What view should be held about wolves who on occasion snatch people and children from their cradles and eat them? (*Malleus maleficarum*)

In late medieval and early modern Europe vast swarms of insects and other animals suffered the curse of an anathema or a writ of excommunication for having caused humans thirst, disease, starvation and death. At the same time, emerging first in and around Burgundy and Paris in the late thirteenth century and appearing immediately thereafter in other jurisdictions, hundreds of quadrupeds were formally prosecuted for homicide. Most were convicted and executed. While there was some overlap in the jurisdictions and functions of the ecclesiastical courts and the secular courts, in general it was the former that issued maledictions against harmful, or potentially harmful, wild animals, plagues, vermin and pests, while it was the latter which tried domesticated animals.

The most notorious of these animal prosecutions was that of a homicidal sow who had been hanged in 1386 in Falaise, a Normandy town north of Paris. According to a nineteenth-century transcription of the matter-of-fact language of the official quittance of the case:

> This original receipt of January 9th, 1386, was attested to by Guiot de Montfort, notary of Falaise, and given by the executioner of this town, for the sum of ten sols and ten deniers tournois. This money was pay-ment for dragging to a place of justice and then hanging in Falaise, a sow, aged 3 years or thereabouts. The sow had eaten the face of the 3-month-old infant, son of Jonnet le Maux, who was in a cradle, so that he died. Also, the sum of ten sols tournois for a new glove so that the executioner could perform the hanging. This quittance is given by Regnaud Rigault, Vicomte of Falaise. The executioner declares that he is content with the sum and will absolve the King and the Vicomte of any further obligation to him.[6]

In trying to excavate the meaning of this fourteenth-century executioner's quittance and of other contemporary records of animal justiciability, one is immediately confronted with some thorny questions of epistemology and method. What are the protocols for understanding the social practices of another period or culture whose standards of rationality and criteria of proof differ from our own? In terms of the attribution of a criminal intent to animals, for example, some early French legal texts describe an offending animal as a Latinate *auctor criminis*,[7] yet it is not at all clear how meaningful it would be to transfer ancient concepts like *auctor* into their seemingly obvious early modern and modern equivalents, such as 'subject of law' and 'malefactor'. Risking similar frustration, we might also ask: how much importance should be attached to the beliefs of pre-Cartesian jurists about such concepts as human-ness and the construction of human–animal boundaries?

Most likely because such questions have no easy answer, the meaning of bygone animal trials has been a topic of lively debate for the past century and more. Anthropologists, legal philosophers and historians of law, especially, have worried whether the trials should be understood as irrational and superstitious practices or as instances of tough justice and rough humour.[8] To complicate matters further, Paul Friedland has shown how, just like a children's game of telephone or Chinese whispers, successive generations of historians have altered and exaggerated the details of the sow's trial and hanging in Falaise almost beyond recognition.[9] Friedland is persuasive in arguing that the punishment of animals 'made perfect sense at the time' and, moreover, 'the only thing that was extraordinary about the Sow of Falaise … was what later historians made of it'.[10]

In what follows I subscribe to the view that no matter how absurd or harmful the beliefs underlying the animal trials might on first inspection seem to us, in order to understand or make sense of them we must initially try to make them appear as rational as possible. Indeed, to those bygone clerics and lawyers who prosecuted animals for murder and who defended them, as well, there could not have been anything irrational or bizarre about the trials. The criminal prosecution of a homicidal animal must surely have been undertaken as a necessary and rational practice. It was seen as a duty ordained by God. Most likely, it was understood as a spectacular way of overcoming the enormity of a murder and of helping the community to heal.[11] One of the desirable effects of an animal trial must presumably have been to convey to law-abiding animal owners a warning about proper supervision of their charges. Thus, in a French case of 1567, where a pig was executed for having killed an infant in Senlis, the judge warned the inhabitants of the village '*not to permit the like to go unguarded* on pain of an arbitrary fine and of corporal chastisement in default of payment'.[12]

Both prosecuting and defence lawyers invested animal prosecutions with roughly the same gravitas as they did the criminal prosecution of humans. This can be inferred not only from what they said and did in the courtroom but also from the considerable expenditures that had to be met by the local communities in which the trials were held. Significant payments had to be made for the extraction of evidence to those skilled in the art of torture; to attorneys for presenting and debating evidence and to experts and other witnesses for recounting an animal's transgressions; to magistrates who adjudicated and delivered verdicts and to clerics and aldermen who assisted them; and to scribes and notaries for recording all the proceedings. Other substantial expenses were for food and shelter for accused animals and for rope to bind them while awaiting trial and execution; stipends for gaolers; monies for carriages or carts for carrying animals between prison and their place of execution; payments to hangmen; and monies for the eventual removal of the corpses of executed animals from the gallows tree.

When the incidence of animal trials was at its height—in sixteenth- and seventeenth-century continental Europe—the judges and lawyers who staffed the criminal courts routinely sought guidance from the ordering principles of the *Enchiridion rerum criminalium* (*Handbook of Issues in Criminal Law and Crime*). Compiled by the Bruges jurist Joost de Damhoudere (1507–81) and first published in 1554 in Flemish in Louvain, the *Handbook* summarizes the proper procedure and courtroom conduct for each stage of the process of criminal justice, among which were preliminary investigation; the reading of criminal charges; the use of torture to procure evidence; punishment for malefactors; and petitions for clemency and pardons. No mere scholastic exercise, the *Handbook* had as its chief aim the vigorous suppression of crime by means of practical instruction. Quickly becoming the standard textbook on criminal law in western and northern Europe, Damhoudere's *Handbook* was translated from its original Latin into French, Dutch and German, at least, and eventually released in more than thirty editions. Its authority was enormous.[13]

Damhoudere's *Handbook* marshalled supporting authority with references drawn not only from Ulpian's third-century *Edicts* and the monumental eleventh-century *Institutes* (also known as the *Corpus Iuris Civilis* or the *Justinian Digest*) but also from biblical injunctions, medieval theology, and canon and customary law.[14] Its advice extended to a broad array of crimes, both extraordinary and run-of-the-mill. Among them were homicide, assault, insurrection and buggery, as also were incest, adultery, theft, the dumping of waste onto public streets, and the use of deceptive weights and measures by merchants.

The *Handbook* condenses the status of animals into two more or less discrete categories in criminal law. The first is distilled from the master status of animals in civil law, namely, animals-as-property. In this regard, like bales of hay or bottles of wine, animals can be damaged, stolen or otherwise misappropriated.[15] By way of illustration of animals-as-property, Damhoudere's script is interspersed with woodcut images of animals as the objects of theft. One particular image (Fig. 4.2), for example, depicts with great gusto thieves who are caught in the act of stealing cattle, sheep and geese.

Animals' second status in criminal law Damhoudere identifies as their potential or actual *justiciability*. '[A] man is not always injured by another man …', he states, but '[sometimes] … animals [*bestiae*] can cause the harm.'[16] Whether in any given set of circumstances an animal is or is not rendered justiciable hinges on how 'active' they were in the chain of events preceding the crime (the *'actus reus'*). Thus, when animals are involved in actions that cause harm and injury, they are not to be held responsible if the harm was caused by negligence or carelessness on the part of their owners or of those entrusted with their supervision.[17] For example: if a mule upsets its load onto someone because it had stumbled on rough ground or because it had been overburdened by the negligence of its driver, no action would lie against the animal. Again: if a horse kicked out because it had been worried by the cruelty of the man who was riding it, no action would lie against the animal. Rather, proceedings

Fig. 4.2 *De abigeatu* (On Stealing Animals), printed woodcut, Joost de Damhoudere, 1570 (Source: Joost de Damhoudere, *Praxis rerum criminalium*, 1570, Antwerp: Ioannem Bellerum, p. 374)

could be brought for wrongful injury or damage against the person who had hit or wounded the horse. In such cases it was humans who were justiciable and it was they who were to be be tried and punished.

In the *Handbook* the justiciability of animals is seen to flow from the fact that on occasion they are capable of being more 'active' than mere property. Justiciable animals can be either domesticated or wild[18]—the *Handbook* instantiates foxes, bears, lions and wolves as examples of the latter. In outlining this other involvement the *Handbook* relies on the authority of the *Edicts* and the *Institutes* to the effect that domesticated quadrupeds commit '*pauperies*' when, acting against their natural disposition (*contra naturam*), they harm the person or property of a citizen who is not their owner.[19] One chapter in the *Handbook*—'*De damno pecuario*' ('On Crimes Against Mankind by Animals'; see Fig. 4.3)— depicts several animals inflicting fatal physical injuries on humans in a rural village.[20] A pig is shown biting an infant's leg. The pig's face has a devilish look about it. In a manner that has been proverbial since the time of the Hittites, an ox is caught in the act of goring.[21] With an agonized look a prostrate man tries in vain to defend himself from the ox's attack. A large dog is about to inflict mayhem on a flock of sheep. In the background, overlooking the village, a rough-hewn gallows looms, threateningly. Four or five birds fly overhead—directly above the gallows—though the image does not clarify whether they are meant to be fast-moving geese unaware of the carnage below—or escaping it, perhaps—or circling crows awaiting a feast.

These statements of animal justiciability (of animals-as-criminals) are especially effective in the illustration 'On Making a Petition in a Criminal Case' (Fig. 4.4).[22] This image shows a criminalized dog and her handcuffed owner petitioning the court for clemency. This sight is so powerful precisely because it reveals how matter-of-fact and unexceptional the criminalization of animals must have seemed to those who lived in the sixteenth century. Were the dog and her master to be unsuccessful in their petition(s), then their executions would be by the court's choice of hanging, strangling, beheading, knocking on the head, burning, stoning or interment while alive.[23] (Whether or not these proceedings would have been recorded for posterity is not known.)

Remarkably, neither the *Edicts* nor the *Institutes* ever indicated that animals themselves should be put on trial and punished when they had committed *pauperies* because, from the perspective of Roman law, animals and other things were incapable of rational thought (i.e. the type of thinking engaged in by humans). In such cases the remedy for aggrieved

Fig. 4.3 *De damno pecuario* (On Crimes Against Mankind by Animals), printed woodcut, Joost de Damhoudere, 1570 (Source: Joost de Damhoudere, *Praxis rerum criminalium*, 1570, Antwerp: Ioannem Bellerum, p. 436)

parties lay in a noxal *actio de pauperie*. By this action owners of animals who had committed *pauperies* could be held liable for harm caused by their things, that is, by their animals and by their slaves. Owners of such animals were obliged either to hand them over to those whom their animals had harmed or else to pay monetary damages to the aggrieved

On the Geohistory of Justiciable Animals... 81

Fig. 4.4 *De libello formando, seu petitione facienda in re criminali* (On Making a Petition in a Criminal Case), printed woodcut, Joost de Damhoudere, 1570 (Source: Joost de Damhoudere, *Praxis rerum criminalium*, 1570, Antwerp: Ioannem Bellerum, p. 64)

party.[24] What happened thereafter to offending animals is generally not recorded, though one has to assume that in cases where their offences involved physical harm to humans, their lives would often be considerably at risk of termination.

If Roman law was largely silent about appropriate punishments for offending animals—generally more interested, as it was, in legal reasoning about intent and responsibility than in constructing formulae for penalties—then Damhoudere's *Handbook* takes—or seems to take—animal justiciability to another level. To Damhoudere, justiciable animals are guilty animals if they 'instigate [*instigatio*] harm through their own ill will and voluntary malice [*ex propria, & ultronea militia*]'. Thus: 'if anyone's horse, ass, pig, ox, dog or similar domestic animal harmed, injured or even killed another [person] from its own natural badness and not from someone's instigation, the owner of the animal that caused the harm should in no way be held to blame or punished'.[25] Damhoudere's guidelines suggest that, whether or not animals possess the same sort and degree of intent as humans (and he comes perilously close to stating that they do), the absence of intent does not absolve them from liability for having caused wrongful death. To put Damhoudere's anthropomorphic logic another way, irrespective of their mental state, animals who commit homicide should be tried, convicted and punished for their actions. The Lord of All Creation demands it. Earthly justice must follow suit.

The procedure dictated by Damhoudere's *Handbook* was of course only one element in a complex interaction of juridical and other factors that determined if and when homicidal animals actually were tried, convicted and punished for their actions. The penal style of some jurisdictions would have been more amenable to animal prosecutions than those of others (not all animals who killed humans were prosecuted for their misdeeds). In this regard, how often animals were held to be justiciable for homicide would rather haphazardly have hinged on local custom,[26] in which decade of what century the offence was committed and also, especially in France, on which of the overlapping royal, urban, seigneurial and ecclesiastical courts was the one of jurisdiction. Indeed, Friedland has summarized the complexities of French legal history and its uneven development through the intermingling of diverse penal styles and traditions[27]:

France's complex legal history … [w]as the product of a gradual layering of separate penal traditions on top of one another. In this sense, France's history is not very different from that of the rest of western Europe. On the decayed foundations of Roman law was layered a theory and practice of penal compensation, payback, and the righting of wrongs; on top of this were layered Catholic practices of atonement, expiation, public apology and forgiveness, expulsion, reincorporation, and redemption; and on top of these was yet another layer of Roman law, and a preoccupation with deterring crime in the public interest, with malicious intent, and with exemplary deterrence.

Homicide was not the only crime for which animals could be prosecuted. In this respect something must be said about how the dogma and the policing institutions of Roman Catholicism were wielded against animals. To late medieval and early modern theologians the harming of humans by animals was seen as a dire rupture of the hierarchical Great Chain of Being. The God of Judaeo-Christendom ruled alone at the summit of this hierarchy and below Him were His earthly representatives from church and state. Below them were the multi-tiered social strata of feudal and early modern societies. Animals were at the bottom of the chain. Dividing phylogenetic and other taxonomies increasingly classified animals, in their turn, as higher or lower (the very lowest of which were unpopular species termed 'vermin' and 'pests'). The thirteenth-century theologian Thomas Aquinas reasoned that if the lower animals are God's creatures and are employed by Him for His purposes, then it would be blasphemous for us to curse them. The sole justification for trying and punishing animals, Aquinas believed, was that the guilty ones are agents of Satan. In the same way that the devil was able to penetrate the bodies and minds of humans, so also could he enter those of animals. The disposition of such cases, Aquinas concluded, should not be seen as culminating in the punishment of animals but in the hurling of them at the devil, who makes use of irrational creatures to our detriment.[28]

If and when it was required, biblical support for animal prosecutions could easily be extracted from a plethora of Hebraic commands: for example, in Exodus 21: 28 that goring oxen should be killed by stoning; in Genesis 9: 5 that animals must be held accountable for the shedding of human blood; in the cursing of the serpent in the Garden of Eden in Genesis 3: 14–15; and in David's cursing of the rocks and mountains of Gilboa in 2 Samuel 1: 21. When lower animals killed higher animals, so went the reasoning, they were to be executed not because they were morally guilty but because they threatened to turn the fragile hierarchy of God's creation upside down.

For certain crimes—bestiality (*'offensa cujus nominatio crimen est'*), sorcery ('witchcraft') and heresy, in particular—the guidelines in Damhoudere's *Handbook of Issues in Criminal Law and Crime* were employed in concert with more specialized texts, such as the 1486 *Malleus maleficarum* ('The Hammer for Sorceresses' or 'The Hammer of Witches'). In use until the late eighteenth century, *Malleus maleficarum* implicated animals as guilty victims at several stages of the fearsome inquisitorial process against sorcery. Citing support from Augustine and Aquinas, especially, *Malleus maleficarum* pontificated on three 'animal questions' within the larger project of suppressing sorcery: (1) whether, through the art of conjuring, sorceresses work on humans by turning them into the shapes of beasts (snakes, frogs and wolves); (2) how sorceresses change humans into the shapes of wild beasts; (3) and how sorceresses inflict various forms of harm on domestic animals (horses, cows and donkeys).[29]

The categorical proximity of sorcery and bestiality accusations is nicely displayed in one case of unknown date, when a certain Françoise Sécretain was burned alive because she had had carnal knowledge of domestic animals—a dog, a cat and a cock—and because she admitted she was a witch and her animals were actually earthly forms of the devil.[30] In a case of 1474, Basle magistrates sentenced a cock to be burned at the stake 'for the heinous and unnatural crime of laying an egg'.[31] In this case, and in others like it, it was widely believed that the *oeuf coquatri* was the main ingredient in witch ointment and, when hatched by a snake or a toad, monsters such as basilisks would emerge, hide in a dwelling and destroy its inhabitants with their death-darting eyes. In such cases it was the practice for both human and animal to be executed, usually by fire but sometimes by beheading or hanging. Their bodies, with all legal documents and pieces of evidence, were then buried together. Like the animals who were damned for harming humans or who were implicated in sorcery, animals in cases of bestiality were seen as having ruptured the divine order of the universe. Thus, Exodus 22: 19: 'Whosoever lieth with a beast shall surely be put to death,' the 'whosoever' here referring to both men (Leviticus 20: 15) and to women (Leviticus 20: 16).

It is tempting to read backwards from the actions and discourse of early theologians and lawyers in order to discern their possible motives and intentions in prosecuting animals for crime. However, even if we could correctly identify and understand the subjective purposes that underlay the emergence of animal trials, we would still not have explained either why they arose in the particular geographical locations that they did or why, during the mid-eighteenth century, they abruptly declined and then apparently disappeared altogether. To what is known about the geohistory of justiciable animals this chapter therefore now turns.

On the Geohistory of Justiciable Animals

Much of our knowledge of the geohistory of animal trials comes straight from the century-old archival research of E.P. Evans (1831–1917). A one-time professor of modern languages at the University of Michigan, Evans was a member of that extinct Victorian species whose intellectual interests were encyclopaedic and which, in his case, encompassed history, languages, literature, oriental studies and considerably more than a passing acquaintance with the new British movement in animal rights. Only after he had laboured with great dedication for four decades—among the judicial records held in Munich's Royal Library and in monastic and municipal libraries and vaults in Berlin and elsewhere—was Evans' book *The Criminal Prosecution and Capital Punishment of Animals* (henceforth, *CPCPA*) published in 1906 in London.

So pivotal a role does *CPCPA* occupy in the small English-language literature on the geohistory of justiciable animals that most enquiry has been unusually dependent on its findings. To these latter, therefore, this chapter now turns.

CPCPA has a glitzy façade. Its uneven and somewhat rambling structure is ornamented throughout by a sarcastic disdain for medieval jurisprudence and monastic monition. Because their pronouncements were full of comical *non sequiturs* and sheer nonsense, Evans therefore invites us to join him in laughing at the subtleties and quiddities of the lawyers and theologians who spent serious time on such silly questions as whether pigs, donkeys and other beasts were capable of the mental state necessary to be convicted of crime ('*mens rea*', for which read: evil intent/malice aforethought/guilty state of mind). In so doing he often comes across as a Victorian missionary smugly conveying religious truth to ignorant and unruly natives. He refers disparagingly, for example, to 'the childish disposition to punish irrational creatures and inanimate objects, which is common to the infancy of individuals'.[32]

CPCPA's historical narrative is woven around descriptions of animal trials to indicate retrospectively not only the comical stupidity of earlier beliefs about animals but also the awful abuse—'intolerable tyranny'—humans exert over our fellow creatures. Once one has pierced grinding his sarcasm, Evans' concerns can be understood as more complex than their manner of presentation suggests. Though its concepts are not always altogether coherent, *CPCPA* was nevertheless a sophisticated work influenced both by its author's compassion for animal suffering and his sympathy for the emerging British movement for animal rights. Every page of *CPCPA* clamours against the mistreatment of animals.[33] The cognitive mistakes of anthropomorphizing lawyers might have been the source of endless mirth to Evans had it not been for their dreadful practical consequences: 'Medieval jurists and judges did not stop to solve intricate problems of psycho-pathology … The puzzling knots, which we seek painfully to untie and often succeed only in hopelessly tangling, they boldly cut with executioner's sword.'[34] At some point, therefore, the pen must become mightier than the sword.

Reading *CPCPA*, one eventually learns how ultimately indebted both Evans and we ourselves are to Bartholomé de Chassenée, a distinguished French jurist whose chronicles of animal trials were first published in 1531. Evans relates that Chassenée had made his own reputation at the

French bar as counsel for an unspecified number of rats, who were prosecuted in the ecclesiastical court of Autun between 1510 and 1530 for having feloniously eaten and wantonly destroyed local barley.

> On complaint formally presented by the magistracy, the official or bishop's vicar, who exercised jurisdiction in such cases, cited the culprits to appear on a certain day and appointed Chassenée to defend them. In view of the bad repute and notorious guilt of his clients, Chassenée was forced to employ all sorts of legal shifts and chicane, dilatory pleas and other technical objections, hoping thereby to find some loophole in the meshes of the law through which the accused might escape, or at least to defer and mitigate the sentence of the judge. He urged … that inasmuch as the defendants were dispersed over a large tract of country and dwelt in numerous villages, a single summons was insufficient to notify them all; he succeeded, therefore, in obtaining a second citation, to be published from the pulpits of all the parishes inhabited by the said rats.[35]

So keen was Evans to popularize Chassenée's forgotten sixteenth-century records that his exhaustive treatment at times comes across as a simple recitation of Chassenée's materials, one animal trial predictably and grotesquely following another. Though some of his French sources—Chassenée among them—tended to report animal prosecutions only if the accused had been found guilty, Evans notes that not all animal prosecutions led to convictions.[36] In a case of 1457 in Savigny, for example, a sow and her six piglets were prosecuted for having murdered and partly devoured a child aged five, Jehan Martin. Although the sow was sentenced to death and later hanged, the piglets were acquitted on account of their youth and their mother's bad example.[37] In a case in Vanvres in 1750 a female ass was acquitted in the bestiality trial of Jacques Ferron. Even though the human defendant was convicted and hanged, the ass was acquitted on the grounds that she was the victim of violence and had not participated in her master's crime 'of her own *free-will*'.[38] This verdict was also influenced by a *curé*'s testimony that he had known the animal for four years and knew her to be virtuous. On rare occasions, moreover, the condemned were even offered pardons or clemency (see Fig. 4.4).

CPCPA goes to some length to identify which animal species were formally prosecuted for what crimes and the date and geographical location of their trials. In an appendix following the main body of the text, *CPCPA* provides a chronological list of 191 animal trials. A few words are attached to each trial about 'sources of information', 'types of animal', 'places' and 'dates'. These apparently allow reconstruction of several major aspects of the geohistory of animal trials.

The judicial notices of indictment—some of the originals are reproduced in *CPCPA*—refer to crimes such as murder committed by bees, bulls, horses and snakes; fraud by field-mice disguised as heretical clerics; infanticide by pigs; theft by foxes; and the causing of famines by locusts, weevils and rodents. Judicial proceedings for other crimes were instituted against numerous other species, including cocks, cows, dolphins, donkeys, doves, eels, goats, mice, moles, mules, oxen, rats, snails, wolves, worms, beetles, caterpillars, flies, grasshoppers and termites. *CPCPA* refers to a string of cases in which men and the occasional woman were convicted of having sex with a variety of animal species; these included cattle, equines, pigs and sheep. In accusations of bestiality combined with witchcraft, goats were the animals most often abused by humans.

Between the ninth and the nineteenth centuries animal defendants included not only domesticated and wild animals but also insects, other vermin[39] and even the occasional transmogrified creature.[40] Of 191 prosecutions 63 were of 'vermin' (insects, rats and mice), proceedings against whom would have been conducted by the ecclesiastical courts. Some of these affairs would have been long and drawn out since the date of their successful conclusion must of necessity have been frequently postponed. In the remaining 128 cases, most of which would have been prosecuted in the secular courts, the most common species were pigs (36 cases, 28.1 per cent), followed by equines (33, 25.7 per cent), cattle (11, 8.5 per cent) and dogs (9, 7 per cent).

Two other major aspects of the geohistory of animal trials—their periodicity and their geographical location—can also apparently be reconstructed from *CPCPA*. The first legal proceeding against an animal, we learn, was conducted in the year 824—an ecclesiastical excommunication of moles in the Valle d'Aosta, a region of north-west Italy bordering

France and Switzerland; the first trial and hanging of a quadruped was in 1266—a homicidal pig in Fontenay-aux-Roses. The prosecution of quadrupeds fanned outwards to all of northern France, as far west as Normandy and Brittany, and afterwards to Belgium, Holland, Germany, Italy and Switzerland. Animal prosecutions seem to have been concentrated in the fifteenth (36 cases), sixteenth (57) and seventeenth (56) centuries. The last trial, according to an unverified report in the *New York Herald* in 1906—published just before *CPCPA* went to press—was of a dog in Delémont in Switzerland.[41] *CPCPA*'s list of animal trials also suggests that some societies held more animal trials than others, with the great majority concentrated in the south and the east of France and in adjacent regions of Italy, Germany and Switzerland. *CPCPA* also documents the existence of animal trials, with diminishing frequency, in Belgium, Denmark, Portugal, Russia, Spain, Britain, Portugal, Turkey, the former Yugoslavia and the New World (one case in Brazil,[42] one in Canada[43] and one in colonial Connecticut.[44])

Cautions must now be issued on the adequacy of *CPCPA*'s findings, in particular, and on the understanding of the geohistory of justiciable animals in general. To begin with, it is true that in some as-yet-unknown number of *CPCPA*'s 191 animal trials, Evans was able to consult actual notices of indictment and execution. Some of these *CPCPA* reproduces in their original Latin, French and German. But how carefully did Evans monitor the veracity of his numerous secondary sources, prominent among which were nineteenth-century French compilations of the odd, the unusual and the sensational, and a scattershot of French, Italian and German academic articles and newspaper reports? As yet, we do not know. Perhaps, when deploying this unusual mix of fact and fiction, Evans threw caution to the wind—just as, over the centuries, others had already done (in the notorious case of the homicidal sow in Falaise, for example).[45]

It must be said that there was often no attempt by medieval and early modern courts to preserve their records. Sometimes there were no records to preserve, either because no scribe had documented them or because a judge ordered that all documents should be burned and buried with the cadavers and corpses of the condemned. It is therefore likely that in a majority of cases, any documents associated with the basic facts, legal arguments, verdict, sentencing and execution were destroyed as soon as possible. Of those records that were not immediately destroyed many, if not most, have probably not survived the ravages of time, wars, fire, natural disasters and the gnawing of rodents (even the gnawings of rodents would sometimes have been devoured by the gnawing of other rodents). In any event, doubtless just like those records that, for whatever reason, have disappeared, surviving records state only a bare minimum of details (in one short paragraph the animal, the name of their murdered victim and the sentence).

CPCPA has been brought harshly to task for not having adequately explained the presence of 'animal trials' in some locations and their absence in others, or else for implicitly misunderstanding their nature. For example, J.J. Finkelstein has chided Evans for failing to appreciate the true significance and complexity of animal trials. After the most thorough reading of ancient texts—such of those of Mesopotamia and the Babylonian king Hammurabi—he stresses that, far from being an invention of early cultures, animal trials never took place there. He suggests that existing data offer only meagre evidence of the existence of non-occidental animal trials, with all the specific examples illustrating not the trial and punishment of animals but the responsibility of owners for damage and death caused by their animals.[46] For Finkelstein, therefore, the animal trials were not an atavistic relic but a product of the cosmological and legal universe of medieval and early modern occidental societies.

A related problem is whether animal trials existed in the occident *before* the medieval period in Europe. According to W.W. Hyde, it is known that the ancient Persians considered animals as responsible beings and punished them for their misdeeds. Yet only in classical Athens is there reliable evidence of animal trials in the ancient world.[47] Their existence in Athens is known from descriptions of relevant legal procedures in texts such as Aristotle's *Constitution of Athens* and Plato's *Laws*. In the Athenian Prytaneum—the unifying single hearth of the city—a special court was convened to try unknown murderers, inanimate objects like stones and beams, and animals who had caused the death of humans. These three categories of malefactor it was thought necessary to prosecute formally in cases of wrongful death because—in reasoning similar to that underlying the *lex talionis*—an unavenged murder would disturb the moral equilibrium and the physical health of the community, the wrath of the Furies would be aroused and the soul of the deceased would be unable to find rest.[48]

The very terms of this interesting dispute have been strenuously challenged by Esther Cohen. To Evans, to Hyde and to Finkelstein she retorts that one cannot settle in purely empirical terms the question of whether animal trials existed in pre-medieval Europe or outside the occident. To Cohen this issue largely hinges on what counts as an animal trial. Adroitly wielding the sensitive anthropological analyses of law of the 1960s and 1970s, she argues that to deny the extra-occidental existence of animal trials is to view the conflict and dispute resolution mechanisms of other, perhaps technologically less developed societies, through *our* cultural and legal prisms. Simply because, when trying to resolve the harms caused by animals, non-occidental societies do not apply the institutional arsenal of western law does not mean that by *their* standards they do not prosecute animals for their misdeeds. 'In fact many non-literate, nonwestern societies prosecuted and punished offending animals,' Cohen points out, 'albeit less formally than the Europeans, for their entire judicial structure was conceived in a different form.'[49]

Somewhat following Cohen's lead, it must now be said that the question of whether or not animal trials existed in Britain (or in Normandy or Bruges) cannot be resolved at a purely empirical level. This is so not least because a proper accounting requires a theoretical understanding of the basic characteristics of animal trials. For example, whether or not the first animal trial was conducted in 824 in the Valle d'Aosta and the last in 1906 or 2016 or some other year very much and with great consequence hinges on how an animal trial is defined. The very same definitional issue surely also applies to whether there were precisely 191 animal trials in medieval and early modern Europe as portrayed in Evans' list—with three cases in Britain—or 19 or 19,111. Do the defining characteristics of animal justiciability lie in some Weberian-like construct whose legal thought can be categorized as formal and rational, and whose institutions are staffed and enforced by a professional cadre of judges, lawyers, bailiffs and gaolers? Instead, might animal trials and animal justiciability also consist in institutions or processes of 'conflict resolution' that are less formal and more ad hoc and impromptu?

To pile these difficulties onto another, while Evans answered in some detail his own question of which animal species were formally prosecuted and for what crimes, he failed altogether to juxtapose the situations of those animal species that were formally prosecuted with those that were not. We might ask: why were pigs prosecuted so often, dogs quite rarely and cats almost never? It is not that surprising that pigs were prosecuted more often than other species because there were many of them in the medieval and early modern landscape. In addition, they were often allowed to run free in towns and villages. Wintry or stormy weather, however, dictated that they be brought indoors. Given their close proximity in this situation, the sheer size and weight of some pigs—up to 800 lbs/363 kg—must sometimes have caused considerable harm, especially to sleeping infants and children. For the same reasons, equines (horses, donkeys and mules) and cattle also suffered more than their fair share of prosecutions.

At the same time, of the pigs and equines who were known to have harmed humans, some were prosecuted and some were not. How did these two groups differ in their social situations? Though justiciable, some of the animals who had harmed humans must have been disposed of as soon as they were rounded up and with no thought of ever putting them on trial. When they were deemed dangerous or a nuisance many animals were dispatched with little ado. In late thirteenth-century England, for example, City of London officials appointed slaughterers to find and kill all pigs found wandering in public; pigs so killed became the property of the slaughterer unless the owner paid him four pence per pig for the bodies.[50] In such cases, the slaughterer acted as a one-man judge, jury and executioner. Similar cleansing operations would surely have occurred throughout continental Europe, especially in the much feared cases of 'mad-dogs' and 'foaming dogs'.

Moreover, to some unknown degree, *CPCPA*'s claim to have uncovered the trials' geographical locations reflects the initiative of local historians who happened to have been interested in the genealogy of animal trials in their region and who, for whatever reason, had access to trial records, and who then uncovered, documented and publicized some of their proceedings, which were later to be appropriated by Evans as building blocks for *CPCPA*'s architecture. It is therefore reasonable to assume that the relevant judicial and ecclesiastical records of some of the regions not known to have had animal trials are still waiting to be unearthed.

To put these difficulties another way, there is no doubt that *CPCPA*'s chronological list of animal trials is a vulnerable edifice.[51] In his foreword to the 1987 reissue of *CPCPA* Nicholas Humphrey states that '[n]o one, I gather, has challenged any of Evans' facts relating to the trials as such'. At the very least, *CPCPA* is open to simple, case-by-case scrutiny and confirmation or disconfirmation by addition and subtraction.[52] This is perhaps what Humphrey means when he adds that *CPCPA* 'has been caught out in one or two minor historical inaccuracies'.[53] With this grudging admission of *CPCPA*'s minor failures, we are now reasonably well positioned to examine the facticity of animal trials in Britain. It is time to cross the border marked by La Manche/the English Channel and head directly for Britain.

The British Law of Deodands

Beginning with the imposition of Norman law in the late eleventh century, the importance of animals is routinely documented at all levels of British society. (Somewhat ironically, such discourses were communicated on pages that were stitched together with animal sinews and bound with the skins of cattle and goats to form books.) On the stages of everyday social life, animals' ubiquitous presence is reflected in official records of interpersonal disputes over fences, wills, contracts and an emergent case law of private wrongs. Moreover, the medieval and early modern records of mercantile and craft guilds and in those of menageries, husbandry manuals, manorial provisioning, aristocratic feasts and wedding banquets are rich and diverse sources of animal images; they also appear in bestiaries, heraldry, liturgical brasses and misericord wood carvings.

The records of guilds and of mercantile trading companies confirm the huge volume of animals used in the development of commodity markets in cattle, fish and woollens.[54] Official state papers, law books and court records also show that animals were used in the course of numerous aspects of British state formation. Among these official practices, especially, were the deployment of animals at home and abroad by the military (as edibles and for transportation, and as cavalry in battle) and by the state in emerging horse-powered postal and espionage systems. Parliamentary statutes and ordinances, judge-made common law and the regulations of borough and local authorities produced an arsenal of fierce new strategies for reining in and eliminating animals who were believed to have caused humans harm and nuisance.[55]

Though many of the non-legal strategies employed in Britain for the killing of bothersome animals were doubtless also used throughout continental Europe, in its legal doctrine England was unique in its development of the 'deodand' (Latin *deo dandum*: 'needing to be given to God'). From at least the mid-thirteenth century, when Bracton's *De Legibus et Consuetudinibus Angliae* first documented the rules of deodand, the English eyre and assize courts developed the Anglo-Saxon doctrine of *noxae deditio* ('surrender of the one who harms'). A leading rationale of the deodand was stated by the great jurist Coke as follows: 'Deodands [apply] … when any moveable thing inanimate, or beast animate, doe move to, or cause the untimely death of any reasonable creature by mischance … [shall be] grounded upon the law of God.'[56]

In cases where an animal was thought to be responsible for a human's death, the coroner of jurisdiction would assemble a jury of local citizens who would discuss the facts. He and they would then deliver a verdict. In cases where an animal was thought to be the prime mover, the animal's owner was compelled by law to give her assessed value in coin to the royal exchequer—or, in the City of London, to the Sheriff—which was then obliged to donate the sum for some avowedly charitable or pious purpose. A good example of the law of deodands at work is a coroner's inquest in London on 19 May 1321[57]:

> On the Death of Johanna, Daughter of Bernard de Irlaunde Friday after the Feast of St. Dunstan, it happened that Johanna daughter of Bernard de Irlaunde, a child one month old, lay dead of a death other than her rightful death, in a shop held by the said Bernard of Philip "Balum" in the parish of St. Michael, in the Ward of Queenhithe. On hearing this, the aforesaid Coroner and Sheriffs proceeded thither, and having summoned good men

of that ward and of the three nearest Wards, viz. Vintry, Castle Baynard and Bredstrete, they diligently enquired how it happened. The jurors say that when in the preceding Thursday, before the hour of Vespers, the said Johanna was lying in her cradle alone, the shop door being open there entered a certain sow which mortally bit the right side of the head of the said Johanna. At length there came Margaret, wife of the said Bernard and mother of the said Johanna, and raised the cry and snatched up the said Johanna and kept her alive until mid-night of the said Friday when she died of the said bite and of no other felony. Being asked who were present, they say No one except the said Margaret; nor do they suspect anyone thereof except the bite aforesaid. The corpse of the said Johanna viewed on which no hurt appeared. The sow appraised by the jurors at 13½d, for which Richard Costantyn, the Sheriff, will answer.

From the vantage point of English law and custom what is most remarkable about the resolution of the case of infant Johanna is how unremarkable deodands must have seemed at the time of their operation. Moreover, of the eighteen cases of deodands recorded in the *Coroners Rolls of the City of London A.D. 1300–1378*, nearly a third involved animals. Besides the case of Johanna, cited above, the remainder of such cases were as follows:

- *On the death of Petronilla daughter William de Wyntonia* (29 August 1301). Petronilla was playing in a street in Cripplegate when a strong horse, ridden by Hugh Picard, struck her on her right side with its right fore-foot. Blue and badly bruised, the girl died of her wound the next day. The horse was valued at one mark, which was handed to the Sheriff.[58]
- *On the death of Agnes de Cicestre*, 14 February 1330. Two carters taking two empty carts out of the City were 'urging their horses apace' so that one cart collapsed and the other fell on Agnes. She died immediately. Both carts and their belongings and both horses (one blind of both eyes) were deodand. Total value to be handed to the Sheriff, 28s. ½d.[59]
- *On the death of John le Stolere*, 9 May 1338. Ralph de Mymmes, a groom aged 12, was delivering water in a cart pulled by two horses. One of the cart's wheels ran over John le Stolere, a pauper and mendi-

cant, as he sat in the street relieving nature. Stolere died immediately. The cart and horses, &c, were appraised at 20s., for which the Sheriff will answer.[60]

- *On the death of Peter de Bermondeseye, 'portour'*, 25 July 1339. Peter was riding a grey horse owned by Robert Cros, in the water of the Thames near Oystergate wharf. The jurors found that, though no one had frightened the horse, Cros fell off his mount and was drowned. The horse was valued at 5s. and handed over to the Sheriff.[61]

Deodands were in force not only in England but also elsewhere in the British Isles for several centuries. For example, until at least the end of the seventeenth century deodands were enforced in the Isle of Man. Thus, in the parish of German, a bull who in 1694 killed John Cain, of Lhergy Dhoo, was forfeited as deodand to the manorial lord.[62] In Scotland and Ireland forfeiture by deodand was a legal remedy available to an aggrieved party through which a human plaintiff sought compensation from an offending animal's owner. The Scottish system of escheats was similar to the English law of deodands, although in Scotland the 'nearest relation of the person killed or damaged might bring an action for damages … and each relation might come in turn'.[63] In Ireland, pigs, hens and cats were the subject of civil proceedings in cases where they had trampled, eaten or otherwise destroyed another's property. Even in a case where a sounder of pigs belonging to a rich Ulster landowner, Mugnae, had killed the son of Maine, the remedy was distraint and the penalty was a fine and the forfeiture of Mugnae's pigs.[64]

E.P. Evans was obliged to perform some fancy footwork to argue *both* that there were three animal trials in Britain *and* that in neither origin nor purpose did the law of deodands differ much from the animal prosecutions of continental law. In this particular context, doubtless with Bracton in mind, he instantiated the confiscation or destruction of homicidal beams, blocks and rafters in Schleswig and similar cases in Bavaria, Lüneburg and Marseille.[65] At the same time, he relied on an American folklorist, W.W. Newell, who was able to connect rat-rhyming practices in seventeenth-century Ireland and Scotland and nineteenth-century New England (in Boston and Maine) with the writs of excommunication against noxious animals served in medieval France and Germany.[66] It might be added that both Ben Johnson's *Poetaster Or, His Arraignment* and Shakespeare's *As You Like It* refer to the ditty 'Rhime them to death, as they do Irish rats in drumming tunes.' The rhyme used to be written as a letter politely asking nuisance rats to leave, then folded and smeared with butter and molasses and posted in the offending rats' holes, in the hope that the rats would desist and move elsewhere. There is also evidence in Ireland of a belief, held at least until 1820, that witches ('eye-biters') can cause children and cattle to fall suddenly sick and that the remedy was to seek the powers of bardic rhymers.[67]

But it is likely that Evans was mistaken in his finding that English deodands were very similar to the continental animal trials.[68] From the several deodand cases described above it is clear that in none of them did the English law of deodands render animals justiciable. In juridical terms, at least, the only three issues facing a coroner's court in this regard were (1) whether someone had died 'a death other than his rightful death' (*ex alia morte quam recta morte sua*); (2) whether an animal had contributed to this death; and (3) objective determination of the animal's assessed value and to whom the payment should revert: to the monarch, to a sheriff or to some worthy cause, among whom sometimes were impecunious relatives of the deceased.

It is a distinct possibility that the English law of deodands and the similar Scottish system of escheats, on the one hand, and the continental system of animal trials on the other, were alternative legal forms that were also mutually exclusive. If the presence of the one implied the necessary absence of the other, then the existence of deodands and escheat suggests that *CPCPA*'s two dogs and one gamecock would not also have been defendants in formal criminal trials in either England or Scotland. This chapter will attempt to resolve this issue now.

In Search of Animal Trials in Britain

What evidence might law books and other documents yield about the possible presence of animal trials in medieval and early modern Britain? To pose this question in another way, what can be discovered about the three British cases that appear in the weighty chronological list of 191 animal trials in *CPCPA*'s appendix? Nowhere else in *CPCPA* are the British cases mentioned. As such, none of their potentially spectacular details is spelt out by Evans in order to instantiate some point about law as a discourse, or about human ignorance or indifference to animal suffering. What might these textual silences in *CPCPA* tell us about the nature of Evans' knowledge of the three trials? Unfortunately, his investigative principles are not known. What criteria did he employ to place a suspected animal trial on his list? These are not self-evident. Given the absence of other avenues, the only way to proceed is by beginning with *CPCPA*'s textual references to each of the three British cases. In so doing perhaps some light can be thrown on the question of whether criminal prosecutions of animals were actually conducted in Britain (Table 4.1).

The Trial of a Dog in Sixteenth-century Scotland

Evans claims a dog was prosecuted in sixteenth-century Scotland.[69] But the sole authority he provides for this case is a reference to an essay of 1854 by Charles Louandre. A French historian of sorcery and the occult, Louandre himself had stated simply that 'in the sixteenth century, a demonic [*sorcier*] dog was burned in Scotland'.[70] But Louandre provided no documentation whatsoever for this claim, including whether or not the dog's death was the result of a formal judicial sentence.

It is fairly safe to say that no such trial happened. So why did both Evans and Louandre agree on the trial's authenticity? There is no clear

Table 4.1 Three animal trials in Britain

	Animal	Date	Place	Source of information
(1)	Dog	c.1500–49	Scotland	Louandre: 'L'Épopée des Animaux'
(2)	Gamecock	Nineteenth century	Leeds, England	*Allg. Deutsche Strafrechts-zeitung*, 1861, No. 2. Also Pertile: 'Gli animali in Giudizio'
(3)	Dog	1771	Chichester, England	A Report of the Case of Farmer Carter's Dog. Amira 1891, p. 559

Source: Evans (1906: 277, 286, 285)

answer to this question. But two possibilities suggest themselves. One derives from a passage in William Shakespeare's *Merchant of Venice* of 1598, where Gratiano harangues Shylock:[71]

> O be thou damn'd, inexecrable dog, And for thy life let justice be accus'd! Thou almost mak'st me waver in my faith, To hold opinion with Pythagoras That souls of animals infuse themselves Into the trunks of men: thy currish spirit Govern'd a wolf, who, hang'd for human slaughter, Even from the gallows did his fell soul fleet, And whilst thou lay'st in thy unhallow'd dam, Infus'd itself in thee; for thy desires Are wolfish, bloody, starv'd, and ravenous.

Despite what this passage seems to imply, there is no known record that the execution of a wolf in England or Scotland was ever accompanied by the pomp and ceremony of formal law. Indeed, while it was customary for farmers to kill wolves and dogs and to parade their hanged carcasses on fences if they had killed sheep or chickens or other valuable domesticated animals, actually wolves had been trapped almost to extinction in sixteenth-century Scotland and England. Moreover, written and first performed in 1598, Shakespeare's *Merchant of Venice* was set not in Scotland but in Italy. It must also be said that in Shakespeare's text the murderous and hanged wolf (Latin: *lupus*; Spanish: *lopez*) represents not a canine but, instead, the playwright's punning and possibly anti-semitic stab at Rodrigo Lopez (1525–94)—a doctor of Portuguese-Jewish ancestry who had been physician-in-chief to Queen Elizabeth and who was tried for treason and convicted of trying to poison his monarch. Afterwards, in June 1594, Lopez was taken to Tyburn, where he was castrated, hanged, disembowelled and quartered in front of a noisy crowd that just might have included a curious Shakespeare.[72]

Another possibility is that Louandre's claim for a dog prosecuted in sixteenth-century Scotland resulted from a confusion over an incident involving the apparent trial and hanging of a treasonous dog in seventeenth-century Restoration Scotland. These events took place in 1671 in the context of the conviction of the Earl of Argyll for refusing to swear under the *Test Act* that in all temporal and spiritual matters he was a good Protestant and a loyal subject of King Charles II. The *Act* required, in particular, that anyone holding an office of public trust should take an oath declaring the illegality of the National Covenant and the Solemn League and Covenant; Scots officials included Lords of Session, members of the College of Justice, exchequer commissioners, sheriffs, stewards and their staff, burgh magistrates and councillors, and justices of the peace and their clerks.[73]

Later, upon Argyll's conviction and death sentence, angry popular protests erupted in Scotland. Believing that Argyll had been wrongly convicted, the peripatetic John Lauder of Fountainhall gleefully recorded one such protest in Edinburgh. According to Lauder, 'finding that the dog which kept the yards of that hospital had a public charge and office',[74] the children of Edinburgh's Heriot's Hospital ordained that he should be required to take the test and:

> [t]o this end the children offered the dog a paper. But the dog, loving a bone better than the paper, absolutely refused it. The children then rubbed the paper with butter, which they called an Explication of the Test, an imitation of Argyle, and he licked off the butter, but did spit out the paper; for which they held a jury upon him, and in derision of the sentence against Argyle, they found the dog guilty of treason, and actually hanged him.[75]

Interesting as these events might be, however, neither the Edinburgh trial of 1671 nor the apparent trial, execution and burning of a dog in sixteenth-century Scotland can properly be said to amount to evidence of the operation of the formal legal process.[76] At most, they exemplify no more than the workings of informal popular justice.

The Trial of a Cock in Nineteenth-century Leeds

In respect of a cock alleged by *CPCPA* to have been prosecuted in nineteenth-century Leeds, Evans offered two references. The first, an essay of 1886 by Antonio Pertile does indeed refer briefly to a cock prosecuted in Leeds at that time.[77] But, in its turn, Pertile's Italian description is apparently taken verbatim from an 1861 German source (which I have been unable to find). Though they might simply be compounding one repetitive error or rhetorical flourish on top of another, another report—in 1887 translated into German by Sloet—of 'a [recent] case in Leeds' seems to derive simply from Pertile's Italian text of 1886.[78] This presumably indicates no more than that both Pertile and Sloet were working from the same questionable English-language description.

There appears to be nothing in local records to substantiate the existence of this case—neither in the *Leeds Mercury* nor in Leeds Crown Court nor in Leeds' local historical society (the Thorsby). However, a contemporary English report of the case does appear in *The Observer* newspaper. To summarize this report: On 4 October 1860, a coroner's inquest was held in Leeds on the body of Mary Tuckett, aged 19 months, who died from injuries inflicted on her by a ferocious game cock. The bird, kept by a youth, Joe Parkinson, had for some time been terrorizing the neighbourhood, flying at the inhabitants and attacking their heads. The court determined that the bird had attacked the deceased, knocked her down, and then flew at her head. Mary bled profusely for several days. One of the several wounds to her head led to an abscess near the right ear and so to the inflammation of her brain, from which she died. According to the newspaper report, the jury recommended that the bird should be killed at once, which Mrs Parkinson, to whose son the bird belonged, promised to see done in the presence of some of the members of the jury.[79]

While this seems a little closer to being an 'animal trial', it must be repeated that the raison d'être of a coroner's court proceedings is not the trial of an animal but, instead, determination of the cause of a human death. Perhaps the details of the coroner's inquest—if they ever existed—will never be known: all of the early records of the coroner's court in South Yorkshire (including those from Sheffield and also, perhaps, Leeds) were hit by a bomb and destroyed during the Blitz of December, 1940.

The Trial of Farmer Carter's Dog in Chichester, 1771

Other than the claim that it took place in Chichester in 1771, *CPCPA* adds nothing else to the 'Case of Farmer Carter's Dog'.[80] In trying to explore whatever the concrete facts of any real trial might have been, it is reasonable to expect that if the trial and execution by hanging of a dog was actually held in 1771 in or near Chichester, a town in western Sussex, then it would have been lodged in the Quarter Session records for the Western Division of the County of Sussex ('WDCS'). At that time, in 1771, the Quarter Sessions had four sittings, one each in Midhurst, Chichester, Horsham and Petworth. The 'Case of Farmer Carter's Dog', if it happened, should therefore have been tried at the Court of Quarter Sessions for Chichester City. However, this cannot be substantiated one way or another through the use of this method: no Quarter Sessions Rolls survive there for 1771. Moreover, a search of the index of the Minute Books for 1753–74 reveals no relevant entries. Additionally, none of the three other WDCS Quarter Sessions reveals any reference to the trial or hanging of a dog in 1771. A final search of the judicial records—this one of the Order Books, which summarize all sessional cases in both West Sussex and East Sussex—also met with no success.[81]

A somewhat minor provincial trial would almost certainly not have been reported in London in *The Times*—though if it had, it would have first been reported in local newspapers. Local newspapers offer no support for the existence of a real trial. In 1771 the only local newspaper in the Chichester vicinity was the *Sussex Weekly Advertiser or Lewes Journal*, published in Lewes, East Sussex. A non-digitalized, non-indexed search of this newspaper produced no reportage of a trial of Farmer Carter's dog either by a named court reporter or by an Anonymous. As such, *CPCPA*'s reference to this particular animal trial might at best betray a misleading error in Evans' chronological list or, at worst, a creative fiction.

However, whatever their basis in fact, there are at least two contemporary parodies of a trial of a dog who was tried, convicted and hanged in Chichester in 1771. How did these originate and what were their respective authors' intentions?

It is possible that Evans'—and also, therefore, von Amira's—knowledge of the 'Case of Farmer Carter's Dog' derived from a paragraph written by William Jones in his catalogue of oddities *Credulities Past and Present*. Thus:

> There is … a curious case of a dog, in 1771, near Chichester, [that] gave Rise to a facetious parody, a "Report of the Case of Farmer Carter's Dog

'Porter,'" by Mr. Long, a lawyer who died in 1813. Hone, in his *Every Day Book* (vol. ii), gives an account of this mock trial, somewhat abridged from the original pamphlet, then in his possession, but without other alteration, together with a portrait of the dog "Porter" in the dock. The names of the parties engaged in the *real* trial are given, with those of their nicknames in the parody, by which they were called after its publication. The squires were Butler, Aldridge, Challen, and Bridger. These were understood by J. Bottle, A. Noodle, Mat o' the Mill, and Osmyn Ponser.[82]

Jones' statement claims, then, that there exists *both* a 'real trial' of a dog and also a facetious parody of it. According to Jones, the real trial occurred in Chichester in 1771; in the parody, apparently penned by a lawyer named Long, the defendant was the dog Porter and, in some as-yet-undetermined capacity, the four human participants were Butler ('J. Bottle'), Aldridge ('A. Noodle'), Challen (Mat o' the Mill,') and Bridger ('Osmyn Ponser').

Despite the complete absence of confirming evidence in judicial records and newspaper reportage, it must be said that Jones' account above of the trial of Farmer Carter's Dog has some ring of credence because the last names of the parties alleged to have participated in the alleged trial do actually imply a local connection.[83] The surnames Butler, Bridger, Challen and Aldridge were quite common in the area around Chichester in the eighteenth century and people with these surnames are listed as landowners in several West Sussex parishes in the land tax records for 1785 (published by the Sussex Record Society). Perhaps there are other records of various sorts—newspapers, letters, diaries and so on—still waiting to be uncovered.

Moreover, in what now appears as a dizzying backwards spiral, Jones also claims that the authorship of the case of Farmer Carter's dog Porter can be traced to William Hone's *Every-day Book and Table-book; or Everlasting Calendar of Popular Amusements*, Hone does indeed state that '[t]his humorous "Trial" … was written … [in consequence of] a real event which actually took place, in 1771, near Chichester' and which was tried at a High Court of Oyer and Terminer and Gaol Delivery.[84] According to Hone's nomenclature in 'The Trial', he referred to the case as *Game Act* (Plaintiff) *versus Porter* (Defendant).[85] Its human participants ('Just-asses and Associates'), he recorded, included J. Bottle and others. In Hone's account, Porter pleaded not guilty to a charge of killing a hare. Despite his lawyer's submission that no witness had seen the hare or seen Porter murder the animal, the dog was nevertheless sentenced to be hanged from a beam in the corner of the courthouse (*ibid.*) (Fig. 4.5).

Hone claims that he had a copy of 'The Trial of Farmer Carter's Dog Porter for Murder' in his possession and that it had been written and published as a one-shilling pamphlet by Edward Long (1734–1813), a sometime Judge of the Vice-Admiralty Court of Jamaica.[86] Further, Hone further alleges that Justice Long had published 'The Trial' in 1771, two years after he had returned from a colonial judicial appointment in Jamaica. The two commentators who support Long's authorship do so in

Fig. 4.5 *Farmer Carter's Dog Porter on Trial for Murder*, charcoal drawing, William Hone 1827 (Source: Hone 1827, 2: 100)

an unconvincing way, however. Neither offers any independent confirmation.[87] In one respect—the question of authorship—the mystery deepens because there was indeed a real Justice Edward Long, resident of Jamaica from 1757 to 1769, and author of the three-volume *History of Jamaica* (1774). But on the face of it, it is quite implausible that Edward Long was the author of such a radical satire of British justice as 'The Trial'. Justice Long was a colonial administrator, a slave owner and a member of the Jamaican plantocracy (and a fierce critic of interracial marriage).

The strongest claim for the origin of the poem 'The Trial of Farmer Carter's Dog Porter for Murder', according to Thomas Clio Rickman,[88] is that it had been composed in 1771 by a certain Mr. Thomas Paine while he was serving as a minor customs and revenue officer in Lewes, Sussex, where he lived from 1768 to 1774. Written by Paine as a political satire and initially intended for distribution and discussion with fellow members of Lewes' Headstrong Club, 'The Trial' was published in London with its author the pseudonymous 'Edward Long'. As a piece of social criticism, Paine's 'Trial' comes from the same reforming tradition as the pamphlets of Henry Fielding and several of William Hogarth's irreverent prints and engravings of London life, such as his caricature of lawyers in the second of the 1751 series *The Four Stages of Cruelty*.

Furthermore, three of Paine's biographers each identify him as author of 'The Trial of Farmer Carter's Dog Porter'. One comments that Paine's output included 'unexpectedly a drama, *The Trial of Farmer Carter's Dog Porter* ... an antecedent of *Animal Farm* without Orwell's penetrating pity'.[89] Another writes of a poem by Paine that 'emerged out of a news item about three justices of the peace who revenged themselves upon a local dignitary they disliked by hanging his dog for starting a hare from a barrow'.[90] Still another adds, slightly differently, that Paine's 'Trial' ('a true story') '[d]ealt with the story of a Sussex farmer, a Mr. Short', whose dog Porter 'was ordered to be hanged by local judges who took offence at the farmer's decision to vote for a Member of Parliament whom they disliked'.[91] Eventually, though published without a title and attributing its authorship to 'Atlanticus', the fictitious New Shoreham trial of Farmer Short's dog Porter appeared in July 1775, in the *Pennsylvania Magazine*, whose editor at that very time was Tom Paine and 'Atlanticus' his pseudonym. (A comparison of the text of Paine's 'Long' version of 1771 reveals no substantive difference with Paine's 1775 version.) The untitled piece by Paine was introduced with the following editorial note:

> The following story, ridiculous as it is, is a fact. A farmer at New Shoreham, near Brighthelmstone, in England, having voted at an election for a member of parliament, contrary to the pleasure of three neighbouring justices, they took revenge upon his dog, which they caused to be hung, for starting a hare upon the road. The piece have been very little seen, never published, nor any copies taken.[92]

What should be made of Paine's 'Trial'? One can appreciate the exquisite humour of the soon-to-be-celebrated author of the 1791 *Rights of Man* and read backwards into its lines Paine's campaign against England for its feudal traditions, its lack of liberty and its unquenchable thirst for empire. One can sympathize, too, with Paine's barbs against the self-interested sophistry of the judges in the case against Porter.

> This logic, rhetoric, and wit,
> So nicely did the matter hit.
> That *Porter* – tho' unheard, was cast.
> And in a halter breathe' his last.
> The Justice, adjourned to dine
> And whet their logic up with wine.[93]

Presumably Tom Paine's depiction of the persecuted dog Porter is a poetic artifact designed to oppose the illegalities and social inequalities of the British state. Is the unfortunate Porter's fictive fate a reflection of Paine's willingness to extend moral consideration to an animal other? Possibly. But whatever he might be, Paine's Porter offers no evidence for the existence of a dog's formal prosecution for murder anywhere in England in 1771 or thereabouts.

***

To return for a moment to where this chapter began (the hanging of a cat in London in 1554). It is true that the image in *A Cat Hung Up in Cheapside* has all the spectacular accessories that tend to go with the animal executions recorded in Evans' *CPCPA*: an animal dressed in human garb; a gibbet; onlookers looking; clerics officiating; an execution; and a public showing of the body of the animal, overseen by the Bishop of London.[94]

But what was the symbolic significance of this hanged cat? This question quickly spawns others. Why was *this* particular cat hanged, for example? Why was a *cat* hanged rather than a member of another species? From details in John Foxe's illustration (Fig. 4.1 above) and from the placement of this image in his virulently anti-Catholic *Acts and Monuments of the Christian Martyrs*, the hanging appears to have been overseen by Protestant clerics who, in orchestrating the hanging of a tonsured cat robed as a priest, were bent on displaying both their ardent hatred of Catholicism—with its fetishism for elaborate priestly garb and its belief that the communion host was the body of Christ—and their willingness to torture and kill an animal often thought to be in league with the Devil. *Cave felem!* It could have been no accident that the 'gallowes [were] in Cheape, neere to the crosse': The 'crosse' was an imposing public monument erected c.1292 in West Cheapside in memory of Queen Eleanor of Castile—the wife of King Edward I—and to Protestant reformers symbolized her Roman Catholicism that they so hated.

To engage in some speculation and perhaps a little unfairness towards E.P. Evans: one has to wonder whether, had he seen a reference to 'A Cat Hung Up in Cheapside', he would have accepted it on face value as an animal trial and itemized it in *CPCPA* as such. One must wonder, as well, how Evans might have chronicled the conflict over the hunting and trapping of game on eighteenth-century Cannock Chase, Staffordshire. In his famous essay on the topic Douglas Hay has recorded how keen the hated gamekeepers were to catch and kill the poachers' 'lurchers' (cross-bred greyhounds, typically used for poaching rabbits). 'The destruction of their prized dogs caused almost as much pain and outrage to the poachers', Hay comments, and '[u]sually the keepers shot lurchers on the spot, but sometimes they took them before JPs who ordered them hanged as a parody of the rites of Tyburn'.[95]

The conclusion thus far is inescapable: neither Evans nor his evidentiary sources adequately scrutinized the authenticity of the three British animal trials lodged in *CPCPA*. In each case empirical evidence contradicts their facticity. In none of these cases was an animal herself a defendant.[96] The presence of doubtful or non-existent cases of uncertain number in *CPCPA* indicates, therefore, that its chronology of animal trials is less significant than its architect projected.

In whatever way such questions might eventually be answered, there is no factual evidence that the Cheapside cat was hanged as the result of a formal criminal prosecution. This finding tends also to confirm the complete absence in Britain of criminal trials with animal defendants. The absence of these trials in Britain was not because British and continental legal systems differed in their allegiance to the Great Chain of Being. European societies with animal trials tended mostly to be those that had received Roman law between approximately the eleventh and thirteenth centuries. With the exception of England, northern France and Scandinavia, according to Max Weber, Roman law triumphed wherever there did not exist a legal profession with a nationwide organization.[97] In this respect Britain was a deviant case.

Though Britain had no formal animal trials, from the perspective and interests of animal themselves: so what? It is true that on conviction by medieval and early modern secular courts, perhaps several hundred animals were executed in continental Europe, while in Britain no animal prosecutions or executions were demanded by the law of deodands. But it is also equally true that in both geographical regions theriocides without number were committed routinely and every day. In husbandry manuals, for example, advice was offered not only on fishing, livestock production and the rearing of game animals but also on how best to trap, mutilate, poison and dispose of undesirable animals. In rural areas catchers trapped and killed foxes, moles, hedgehogs, polecats, weasels and birds.[98] Metal and wooden traps for the killing of undesirable crows, blackbirds, magpies, rooks, cadows, buzzards and pigeons are illustrated in Mascall's 1590 *Booke of Engines and Traps to Take Polecats*.[99] In the City of London and Westminster the Lord Mayor, the Chamberlain and other officials episodically appointed 'dog killers' and 'dog whippers' to exterminate dogs who were roaming masterless and free in civilized spaces, or who were deemed aggressive or 'mad with fury'.[100] Stray dogs were snared

Fig. 4.6 *The Dog Killers of London & Westminster Or Licenc'd Cruelty*, engraved etching, Anon., 1760

with 'dog tongs' and then hanged or knocked on their heads (i.e. 'braynd': see the satirical Fig. 4.6). Often a panicked response to the publication of official mortality rates after bouts of plague and pestilence, large numbers of dogs were killed in this way: 3,720 stray dogs in the summer of 1636, for example, and at least 4,380 in 1665.[101] Mad and masterless dogs, in particular, were interpreted as scientific evidence of a rude rupture in the Great Chain of Being by animals whose transcorporeality knew no bounds. For such offences other species suffered similarly fatal consequences, among them cats, rats, spiders, coneys and fleas and not only in London but also in the provinces and in Scotland and Ireland.

Animal Trials and Other Tribulations: Against Speciesist Justice

The memory of animal prosecutions and executions—long ago eradicated in conformity with judicial and ecclesiastical doctrine—was resurrected by historians, anthropologists and moral philosophers, in particular, within the broader context of their thinking about the evolutionary development and eventual decay of various irrational practices, including animism among supposedly primitive peoples and witchcraft accusations in seventeenth-century Europe. E.P. Evans himself implicitly suggested that the decline of animal prosecutions was due to the emergence of a generalized scientific *Weltanschauung* and the creation of rational legal thought. Similarly, Finkelstein has argued that, because the execution of homicidal animals in Europe represented the literal implementation of ancient biblical dictates, the trials inevitably declined with the rise of science and reason during the Enlightenment.[102]

But such explanations smack of modernist smugness. If the pivotal fact in explaining the disappearance of animal trials was the rise of science and the secularization of religion, then why did the trials peak between 1600 and 1700, at the very moment when the movement in science was at its height, and why did they apparently continue, albeit sporadically, well into the nineteenth century? Why did other similarly irrational legal practices—such as judicial torture—disappear far earlier than animal trials? Plausible alternative explanations for the decline of animal trials and animal executions include a persistent reduction in the size of the agricultural sector—with an accompanying decline in everyday contact between humans and animals; the growth of urbanism and with it the rise of pet keeping practices; and the development of a moral sensibility towards animals cultivated by the civilizing process.[103]

This is not to say that animals have never appeared in the criminal process in Britain. Though not appearing as criminal defendants in a legalistic sense, animals have on occasion been drawn into witchcraft or bestiality prosecutions, for instance, at the conclusion of which both the convicted human and the animal were executed, sometimes together. A case at the Old Bailey provides a rare glimpse of a woman and her dog both condemned for bestiality. On 18 July 1677, Mary Hicks, a married woman aged between 30 and 40, was hanged at Tyburn. According to the original text 'she having not the fear of God before her eyes, nor regarding the order of Nature … did commit Buggery with a certain Mungril Dog'.[104] Mary Hicks' canine companion was not put on trial with her (however, the dog, 'being carried along with her in the Cart', '[was] hang'd upon a Tree near the Gallows before her face'). Similarly, in sixteenth- and seventeenth-century Essex women charged with witchcraft were sometimes prosecuted for bewitching cattle, destroying horses and drying up milking cows; but in the several hundred prosecutions animals themselves were never named in indictments.[105]

Moreover, how we understand the existence and practice of animal trials in part hinges on what geographical and temporal terrain is denoted in our concepts of 'animal trial', 'prosecution', 'punishment' and so on. In respect of the first of these—what is meant by an animal trial?—consider, for a moment, a legend in the old fishing town of Hartlepool, in England's County Durham. At the heart of this legend is a monkey who had been hanged by local fishermen.[106] During the Napoleonic Wars (1799–1815), at a time when many coastal dwellers feared a naval-led invasion from across the Channel, a French ship was apparently wrecked off Hartlepool by a violent storm. The ship sank and Hartlepool fishermen, looking through the wreckage, came across the ship's sole and very wet survivor. This was a pet monkey dressed in a military-style uniform. At a special trial held on the beach the fishermen questioned and perhaps tortured the monkey, mindful that the animal might be a French spy. The monkey was duly found guilty of espionage and sentenced to death by hanging. To that end a makeshift gallows was summarily erected from a ship's mainmast.

Should the notion of an animal trial or prosecution be extended to include those cases where animals have been tried, condemned and executed according to determinations by informal popular justice? If so, then other spectacular candidates for inclusion are the cats hanged in 1730s France by hungry printer's apprentices; a dog tried and hanged in New Zealand by seamen in the British navy in 1777; and an elephant, Mary, who through municipal consensus was shot and then hanged from a large railway crane in Erwin, Tennessee, in 1916.[107] From the perspective of these and numerous other condemned animals, of course, it probably matters not one whit which of the variety of humans' judicial and institutional procedures accompanied their shortened lives and violent deaths.

Whether or not animal trials have really declined is moot. No one today seriously believes that animals are capable of having the intent necessary to commit crime, and it is true that animals are not *formally* prosecuted for crime. Nor are they subject to the penalties of criminal law. Nevertheless, far from declining, there has been a dramatic rise in the number of animals lawfully and routinely prosecuted and executed. In effect, late medieval and early modern courtrooms have been displaced by the euthanizing practices of twenty-first-century animal shelters and animal control officers.[108] The awesome power of bygone criminal law to punish animals has been usurped by the bureaucratic regulations attached to the circumstances in which animal shelters and animal control officers routinely put animals to death. (According to one estimate, about 2.4 million healthy, adoptable cats and dogs are nowadays killed in shelters each year in the United States alone.)[109] The rack and the gibbet have been displaced by the clinically painless euthanasia dispensed by lethal injections and vacuum chambers. Nowadays, animals are far more likely to be executed silently, invisibly and without advocates for offences such as homelessness, overpopulation, aggression and the lack of a fashionable pedigree. Speciesism rules.

Appendix 1: Animals and Crime in Lombrosian Criminal Anthropology

The idea that animals can engage in crime was energetically espoused by late nineteenth-century criminal anthropologists, who sought support from Darwin's claim in *Descent of Man* that those with the worst moral dispositions revert to a savagery from which we are not far removed.[110] This idea was pursued by the Italian prison doctor Cesare Lombroso, whose demarcation in 1876 of *Homo criminalis* from *Homo sapiens* was based on his notion of the born criminal. In a self-described Archimedes moment, the source of criminality was revealed to Lombroso during his postmortem analysis of the skull of a notorious brigand: 'I instantly perceived that the criminal must be a survival of the primitive man and the carnivorous animals.'[111]

Lombroso employed anthropometry to claim that born criminals exhibit a constellation of atavistic, ape-like features. After this discovery, he and his disciples next explored the range of species that might be characterized as criminal. Most agreed on the need to start with intelligent animals, common criminal examples of whom were said to be murdering hawks, rogue elephants, lazy beavers, thieving monkeys, wild goats, robber bees and sparrows. In associating criminality with animality, Lombroso himself held that in the search for the origins of crime one might need to go as far back as the lives of various insectivorous plants.[112]

The English eugenicist Havelock Ellis disagreed, reasoning that one could scarcely hope to find genuine vegetable criminals because to be criminal 'the deed must be exceptional in the species, and must provoke a social reaction among the other members of that species'.[113] In seeking the atavistic origins of crime, some even suggested that, like *Homo criminalis*, animals could be born criminals; others argued that the laws of criminal heredity applied equally to humans and animals. William Ferrero divined that almost every form and variety of human crime is found among animals, though he distinguished between animals who harm other animals in the course of the struggle for existence, which is not crime, and those who harm or even murder members of their own species, which is.[114] Some Lombrosians insisted animals can and do commit crimes against other animals.[115]

If animals can commit crime, then it is only a short step to claiming either that human criminals are animals or, more weakly, that human criminals have animal characteristics. In *Crime: Its Causes and Remedies*, Lombroso reasoned that the atavism of born criminals may go back 'far beyond the savage, even to the brutes themselves'—facts which prove 'the most horrible crimes have their origin in those animal instincts of which childhood gives us a pale reflection'.[116] At times, he and his followers posited that violent men always had animal instincts, at others that they erupted only with the presence of further inhibition-loosening anomalies such as epilepsy. Some even claimed that criminals were zoophiles (perhaps a Victorian circumlocution for bestiality). Lombroso himself suggested that animals commit crime in the same factual, albeit unconscious, way as members of a mob.[117] On this point, at least, the Lombrosians stood on the same ground as theorists of crowd psychology, including committed anti-Lombrosians such as the French sociologist Gabriel Tarde, who referred to crowds and mobs as feminine, fickle and beastly.

Lombrosian criminal anthropology wielded intellectual and social power in Europe from the mid-1870s until roughly the beginning of the 1914–18 war. Its rise and fall have been much studied.[118] In the United States Lombrosianism exerted considerable influence well into the 1930s; its ideology contributed to the passage of sexual sterilization laws and their accompanying tragedies.[119]

Notes

1. *The Diary of Henry Machyn Citizen and Merchant-Taylor of London, from A.D.1550 to A.D.1563* (1828, London: printed for the Camden Society by J.B. Nichols, 59). On the killing of the cat-priest see also Crawford (2005: 34–37).
2. John Foxe (1563: 1054). The hanging of the cat-priest is said to have enraged Queen Mary, who demanded that the human perpetrators be found and fined. This does not necessarily imply that Mary's attitude to cats differed much from that of her younger half-sister Queen Elizabeth, who is reputed to have been delighted at their screeching as they were thrown onto bonfires celebrating her coronation. On this see further Thomas (1983: 146–47).
3. Baraz (2003: 165).
4. As for any 'Whydunnit?', I tend to agree with Gary Francione (1995: 93–94; see also Spencer and Fitzgerald 2015: 5–8), who throws up his hands in despair, describing the animal trials as a legal anomaly whose true justifications we will never know.
5. Besides Evans (1906: 28, 277, 285), among others who have claimed that animal trials occurred in Britain are Hyde (1916: 709), Ives (1914: 256), Ritvo (1987: 1–12) and Tester (1991: 72–77). Trial naysayers include Finkelstein (1981: 74), Thomas (1983: 97–98), Salisbury (1994: 108), Dinzelbacher (2002), Fudge (2002: 121–25) and Shannon (2013: 240). The leading historian of human–animal relationships, Keith Thomas, seems to favour the latter view, though he also somewhat hedges his bets when he observes that 'England has no real counterpart to that curiosity of continental legal history, the trial and execution of homicidal animals' (1983: 97).
6. The nineteenth-century transcription of the executioner's receipt is itemized in Evans (1906: 335; my translation). For some of the transcription's errors, see Friedland (2012: 2–11, 285, n.3).

7. On how not to understand the concept of *auctor criminis* see Westermarck (1906, 1: 257).
8. For example, see Evans (1906), Westermarck (1906, 1: 249–60), Hyde (1916), Frazer (1923: 397–417), Kelsen (1923: 3–8), Finkelstein (1981), Cohen (1986), Tester (1991: 73–75), Berman (1994), Ewald (1995), Wise (2000: Chap. 4), Dinzelbacher (2002), Girgen (2003), Leeson (2013), Oldridge (2005: 40–55), Friedland (2012: 110–16, 280–84), Leeson (2013), Phillips (2013: 30–41), and Spencer and Fitzgerald (2015: 5–8). For descriptions of the belief that inanimate objects such as falling rocks and collapsing beams can commit crime and that they should be punished for harming humans, see Westermarck (1906, 1: 260–65), Hyde (1916: 700, n.17) and Finkelstein (1981: 60). Friedland (2012: 91, 110–12) discusses the burning and 'execution' of animal effigies in late medieval and early modern France.
9. On the details of this exaggeration see Friedland (2012: 5–8). Moreover, repeating embellished nineteenth-century descriptions of the hanging of the homicidal sow in Falaise in 1386—of which the only confirmed record is the brief executioner's quittance (see the document above)—E.P. Evans complained with perhaps unwitting dramatic effect that 'for having torn the face and arms of a child … the tribunal … sentenced a sow to be mangled and maimed in the head and forelegs, and then to be hanged … the sow was dressed in man's clothes … a pair of gloves [was given] to the hangman' (1906: 140). Ian O'Donnell has generously pointed out to me that this sow 'was dressed in man's clothes' when female attire would surely have been more appropriate. Note also that the cat hanged in London in 1554 (see pp. 71–73 above) was dressed as a priest (male again). Does this mean that in popular and/or juridical consciousness it would have been more shocking to hang an animal whose body and garb resembled that of a female criminal?
10. Friedland (2012: 111).
11. About the burning of condemned animals and of the trial records, Cohen documents that '[t]his was done, in the words of one French jurist, in order to eradicate all memory of the act' (Cohen 1986: 18, n.39). Similarly, Finkelstein has speculated that

> the death of a human being of which … [the homicidal ox] … was the unwitting instrument precipitated a condition in the social environment that was held to be dangerous—like that caused by a virulent disease—and its traces had to be completely eradicated (1981: 77).

12. The judge's admonition (my italics) in this Senlis case is provided in Evans (1906: 356–57).
13. This assessment is also expressed in Langbein (1976: 39, n.21). An appendix to the *Enchiridion rerum criminalium* was published in 1601. Organized alphabetically, it lists crimes, terms, definitions, categories of harm and many of its major legal and religious antecedents. On civil law see Damhoudere's (1567) *Praxis rerum civilium*.
14. It is sometimes claimed that Damhoudere's *Enchiridion rerum criminalium* merely translated and reproduced *Practijke criminele* by the Bruges lawyer Philip Wielant (c.1508–10). It is indeed true that Damhoudere's text was published under his name and without mention of Wielant's, though this was not an uncommon practice for medieval legal texts. On this issue see further van Caenegem (1988: 43–44).
15. Damhoudere (1570: 435–38). My translation of Damhoudere's unfamiliar and very difficult (Latin) medieval legalese is greatly indebted to the good advice of Maurice Herson.
16. Damhoudere (1570: 437).
17. Damhoudere (1570: 437). In this respect *Enchiridion rerum criminalium* follows Ulpian, 'If a Four-Footed Animal is Alleged to have Committed *Pauperies*' (9.1.1. in Watson 1985: 276).
18. Damhoudere:

> [I]f someone in his own home is feeding a dog, boar, goat, fox, bear, lion, wolf or other wild beast which was a nuisance to someone else, or bit him, or injured him, then this house-owner would be condemned to make reparations for the damages at the discretion of a judge. Because no one has the right to feed or look after this kind of beast to the detriment of another [person] (1570: 437).

19. Damhoudere (1570: 436). On the notion of *pauperie* in Roman law see Watson (2006). See also Ashton-Cross (1953). On the intermingling of Roman, Greek and Hebraic law on owners' or custodians' non-criminal liability for harm caused by their animals in classical Rome, see Jackson (1978).
20. Damhoudere (1570: 436).
21. Damhoudere (1570: 436).
22. Damhoudere (1570: 63).

23. Damhoudere (1570: 63). Damhoudere sensibly adds that executioners—who were often despised by their fellow citizens, especially when they botched their work—should not be gamblers, whoremongers, scandalmongers, impious blasphemers, assassins, thieves, murderers or robbers. Thus, in 1576 an executioner who lacked the proper authorization was banished from the interestingly named town of Schweinfurt, Bavaria, never to return, after he had outraged the citizenry by hanging a sow who had been convicted of killing a carpenter's child by biting off his ear and tearing his hand. This case led to the proverbial phrase '*Schweinfurter Sauhenker* (Schweinfurt sow-hangman)'. It was used, according to E.P. Evans (1906: 147):

> to characterize a low and lawless ruffian ... It was not the mere killing of the sow, but the execution without a judicial decision, the insult and contempt of the magistracy and the judicatory by arrogating their functions, that excited the public wrath and official indignation.

24. Ulpian in Watson (1985: 276). Presumably soon thereafter most of those domesticated animals who had physically injured or killed humans would have been 'put down'. These animal deaths would have been swelled by the similar fates of those animals forced to participate in the ancient Roman practice of the public execution of condemned humans by putting them in an enclosure with hungry lions and leopards ('*Damnatio ad bestias*'), also indulged in as entertainment or sport. On how this might have been done, see Aldrete (2014).
25. Damhoudere (1570: 436–37). A handful of early French jurists struggled with the issue of animal intentionality somewhat more than did Doumhedere. For example, see the critical comments of Philippe de Beaumanoir in 1285 and Pierre Ayrault in 1591, and the excellent discussion of their scepticism in Friedland (2012: 112–13, 115–16).
26. According to Cohen (1993: 114–15), customals seldom referred to animal justiciability because to have done so would have flouted the superior status of and respect due to Roman law.
27. Friedland (2012: 45). See also Cohen (1993: 110).
28. Aquinas in *Summa Theologica* (1266–74, vol. ii, part lxxxvi, article 2, 5143). Thus, a Swiss ecclesiastical court ruled in 1666 that 'an ox is created for man's sake, and can therefore be killed for his sake; and in doing this there is no question of right or wrong as regards the ox' (quoted in Finkelstein 1981: 70).

29. These three questions appear in *Malleus maleficarum*, at Sprenger and Kramer (1486: 201–10, 330–33 and 375–80, respectively). With the continuing saga of the Autun case of 1510–1530, the prosecution of animals for the felony of crop destruction coincided with that of humans for heresy. On the details of this aspect of the Autun case see Pignot (1880: 225–26) and Ewald (1995: 1901).
30. Dubois-Desaulle (1933: 58). Damhoudere's *Praxis rerum criminalium* claimed that Christians who cohabited with Jewish or Turkish women were in fact copulating with animals and should be tried and executed for bestiality (1570: 308–09); and see Aquinas (c.1260, 20: 25).
31. Evans (1906: 162).
32. Evans (1906: 186).
33. Evans praises Bentham's utilitarian strictures against animal cruelty, for example, and he refers to Henry Salt's (1892) pioneering book *Animal Rights*. This is Evans, in his later book *Evolutionary Ethics and Animal Psychology*, on Salt's foundational text: 'if animals may be rendered liable to judicial punishment for injuries done to man, one would naturally infer that they should also enjoy legal protection against human cruelty' (1898: 13). On his praise for Bentham's objection to animal suffering—'Why should the law refuse its protection to any sensitive being? The time will come … when humanity will extend its mantle over everything which breathes' (1789: 282)—see Evans (1898: 14).
34. Evans (1884b: 302; see also Frazer 1923: 416–17). *CPCPA* contains a second, if less ostentatious concern, namely, a rejection of the biological reductionism in Lombrosian criminal anthropology (see further Appendix 1 at the end of this chapter). This is evident from the manner of *CPCPA*'s presentation, which consists of just two chapters which are 'Bugs and Beasts Before the Law' (Chap. 1) and 'Mediæval and Modern Penology' (Chap. 2). These two chapters are expanded but discursively identical versions of essays with similar titles that Evans (1884a, b) had published twenty-two years before *CPCPA*. The first chapter, by Evans the animal rights activist, must thus be seen as a quizzical attack on the mistreatment of animals. The second chapter Evans composed as an essay prior to the stormy 1885 Rome International Congress of Criminal Anthropology as a contribution to the mounting campaign against Lombrosianism. Evans' aim here was to attack criminal anthropology largely on the grounds that its biologism denied the responsibility and hence the accountability of humans for their crimes. To this end his chosen strategy was iconoclasm, that is, the hurling of ridicule at the penal implications of criminal anthropology.

35. Evans (1906: 18–19). See further Ewald (1995: 1898–901), who is especially helpful on providing details of Chassenée's career as a lawyer.
36. Evans (1906: 135).
37. Evans (1906: 153–54). See also Westermarck (1906–08, 1: 25).
38. Evans (1906: 150). From Evans' comment that the ass 'had not participated in her master's crime of her own *free-will*' (my emphasis) it is unclear if he thought some animals were convicted precisely because they had freely chosen to engage in crime. Perhaps his reference to free will here was just a loose use of language on his part, though he adds that '[a]s a piece of exculpatory evidence it may be regarded as unique in the annals of criminal prosecutions' (1906: 151). Even here, he fails to clarify whether the unique 'it' refers to the juridical acceptance of free will or to the good *curé*'s testimony.
39. On early modern notions of vermin, see Cole (2016).
40. Evans notes that in Ansbach in 1685 a ravenous werewolf, supposedly the incarnation of a deceased burgomaster, was tried and hanged by order of the court for having 'prey[ed] upon the herds and even devouring women and children' (1906: 195). On the mythology and prosecution of werewolves in early modern Europe see further Otten (1986).
41. On the alleged trial of a dog in Delémont, see Evans (1906: 334).
42. In 1713 Franciscan friars in Brazilian Piedade no Maranhão prosecuted a colony of ants because '[they] did feloniously burrow beneath the foundation of the monastery and undermine the cellars of the said Bretheren, thereby weakening the walls of the said monastery and threatening its total ruin' (Evans 1906: 123–24; and see Frazer 1923: 410–11). Counsel were named for both plaintiffs and defence and, after learned legal argument, the conciliatory judge ruled that the Brethren should appoint a neighbourhood field suitable for habitation by the ants and that the latter should shift their quarters to the new abode or suffer excommunication.
43. About the lone Canadian case Evans states only that it involved turtle-doves in the late seventeenth century (1906: 331).
44. On the Connecticut case of 1662 reported by Cotton Mather, see further note 96.
45. On historians' successive distortions of the Falaise case, see pp. 74–75 above.
46. Finkelstein (1981: 62).
47. Hyde (1916: 700).

48. With regard to Hyde's controversial discovery of animal trials in classical Athens, Finkelstein's response is that there are no surviving records of actual animal trials in the city. The surviving accounts of trial procedures, he continues, reveal that they were ceremonial or magical in nature rather than legal (Finkelstein 1981: 58–64).
49. Cohen (1986: 18).
50. *Calendar of Letter-Books of the City of London 1275–1298 and 1291–1309*. In 1419 the *Liber Albus* of the City of London relaxed the status of those who could lawfully kill wandering pigs when it stated '[a]ny swine found in City streets or lanes may be killed by those who found them. Those who kill them should have them to keep freely' (1419: 235–36).
51. Humphrey (1987: xxix, n.1).
52. By way of addition, for example, Vagn Greve (1999) describes a case of 1806 in southern Denmark in which citizens had complained that their houses were being overrun by millions of black rats. A householder from Ebberup offered to get rid of the rats. He ordered that they be summoned and that a procurator should be appointed to defend them. A judge then authorized a subpoena for the rats to appear in court, which was issued to them in front of the affected houses. The case was adjourned, however, and the supposed rat exterminator was declared a fraud. (My thanks to my colleague Ragnhild Sollund for generously pointing out this Danish text and also translating it.) See also the five Dutch cases identified in this book (Chap. 3, n.14), none of which is reported in *CPCPA*.
53. Humphrey (1987: xxiv, n.1).
54. On these diverse and rich sources see further Seetah (2007). For the London area between 1700 and 1900 the zooarchaeologist Yeomans (2007) has charted the geographical relocation of sites for labouring on animal carcasses—the hornworking and the light and heavy leather industries—after the decline of the guilds and the rise of techniques of capitalist production.
55. A major source of irritation was animals' sludge and stench, which heavy rains aggravated. Blackstone (1765–9, book 3, Chap. 13), for example, recorded in his *Commentaries on the Laws of England* that animals' stench could be cause for actionable nuisance:

> [I]f a person keeps his hogs, or other noisome animals, so near the house of another, that the stench of them incommodes him and makes

the air unwholsome, this is an injurious nusance, as it tends to deprive him of the use and benefit of his house. A like injury is, if one's neighbour sets up and exercises any offensive trade; as a tanner's a tallow chandler's or the like: for though these are lawful and necessary trades, yet they should be exercised in remote places.

56. Coke (1648, Chap. 9: 57). See further Bracton (c.1260, 2: 328).
57. *Coroners Rolls of the City of London A.D. 1300–1378* (1913: Roll B (29): 56–57). See also a case of 14 February 1268, when a little boy, John, was lying in a cradle when, 'through the carelessness of his nurse, a ravenous sow bit off his ear' (*Calendar of the Rolls*, 1266–1272: 193). And see the Litton case of 30 May 1590 (documented in Forbes 1973: 379–86):

> a London coroner's inquest recorded that Christopher Litton, a brewer, was riding his master's blind horse near Puddle Wharf. Litton rode the horse into the river Thames so that he could water and bathe the animal. The horse reared his head, however, and threw Litton into the river. As a result, Litton was swept away by the current and drowned. The horse, which was valued at five shillings, was left in the custody of the brewer 'for the work and use of the said Sovereign Queen' according to the law of deodand.

58. Roll A (30): 30–31.
59. Roll F (10): 57–58.
60. Roll G (28): 219–20.
61. Roll H (37): 264–65.
62. Train (1845, 2: appendix to Chap. 13: 3, n.1), who also reproduces the documents that formulated the Manx laws of deodand.
63. 'Deodands Abolition', 1846, *Parliamentary Debates*, House of Commons, 11 August: 1624–26. On the Scottish practice of escheats, see further Forte (1990).
64. Kelly (2000: 100). See further MacCormack (1984).
65. Evans (1906: 186–90) himself, who thought the deodand 'an accursed thing', complained about cases where animals had caused human deaths (1769, book 1, part 2, Chap. 8: 302):

> [b]ut juries have of late very frequently taken upon themselves to mitigate these forfeitures, by finding only some trifling thing, or part of an entire thing, to have been the occasion of the death. And in such cases, although the finding of the jury be hardly warrantable by law, the

court of king's bench hath generally refused to interfere on behalf of the lord of the franchise, to assist so odious a claim.

On deodands and their abeyance and abolition in 1846, see Jamieson (1988) and Pietz (1997).

66. Evans (1906: 129).
67. Todd and Curry (1850–53). See also Scot (1665).
68. Evans (1906: 192).
69. Evans (1906: 277).
70. Louandre (1854: 334).
71. Shakespeare, *The Merchant of Venice*, Act 4, scene 1, ll. 128–38; and see Evans (1906: 157).
72. Holden (1990: 143). In arguing that Shakespeare's wolf is perhaps a direct reference to the Lopez case, Holden adds that 'if a punning translation of his name were not enough, the word "Wolf" is capitalized (significantly, unless it was a compositor's error) in the quarto' (1990: 143; and see Enders 2002).
73. Jackson (2003).
74. Lauder (1671: xxxii).
75. Jackson (2003: 151, n.86) has recorded that in 1682 the Heriot's hospital anecdote prompted an anonymous pamphleteer ('M.D.') to depict Argyll:

> as a dog who apparently swallowed the *Test Act* whole, but [who] subsequently retched up certain parts, upon which all the assembled child-advocates decreed that 'all his irksome champing and chowing of it, was only … to separate the concomitant nutrient, and that was mikel worse than a flat refusal of it, and if it were rightly examined, would upon Tryal, be found no less than Leising-making.

76. For a more detailed and fanciful account in which the dog, a mastiff Tyke named 'Watch', was said to have escaped and was never recaptured, see Hone (1827, 2: 380–82) and Crockett (1895).
77. Pertile (1886: 147).
78. With some slight embellishment, the latter reported (Sloet 1887: 248):

> Some 25 years ago a cock was punished as a murderer. The *Allgemeine Deutsche Strafrechtszeitung*, 1861 No. 2 wrote:
>
> Recently, in Leeds, a fighting cock attacked and wounded a child of one year and seven months. This resulted in the death of both the child

and ultimately of the cock as well because the jury examining the death decided that the cock should die. The jury personally attended the execution.

In this case, the Cock was punished for an act that only a human can commit and it was thus treated as equal to a human. However, a cock (i.e. the male hen) is able to commit crimes that are impossible for us humans.

79. This newspaper reportage appears in *The Observer* ('Death Caused by a Game Cock'), 8 October 1860, p. 7. On the very same page another story was reported in which 'a married woman named Bellier, at Corville, in France, died of hydrophobia a few days since (having been bitten in the arm by a cat' ('Death From the Bite of a Cat').
80. Even in providing these meagre details, Evans was merely reproducing an earlier uninformative reference to it by von Amira (1891: 559).
81. For his generosity in helping me gather much of this information, I am indebted to Richard Childs, County Archivist of the West Sussex Record Office.
82. Jones (1880: 302–03). An epitaph is appended to Hone's (1827, 2: 105) 'The Trial', as follows:

EPITAPH FOR HONEST PORTER
Composed by Sam. Snivel, the parish clerk,
proposed to be put, at Farmer Carter's expense, on
the unfortunate malefactor's tombstone:

    Here lie the remains
      of
    honest PORTER;
      who,
  after an innocent and well-spent life,
    was dragged hither, and
      tried,
  for a *crime* he never committed,
  upon *laws*, to which he was unamenable,
    before *men* who were no judges
    found *guilty* without *evidence*,
    and *hanged* without *mercy*:
  to give to future ages an example,

> that the spirit,
> of Turkish despotism, tyranny, and
> oppression,
> after glutting itself with the conquest of
> *liberty*
> in British *men*,
> has stooped at length to wreak its bloody
> vengeance
> on *British dogs*!
> Anno. Dom. 1771, Requiescat in pace! S.S.

83. Jones (1880: 302–03).
84. Hone (1827, 2: 105).
85. Hone (1827, 2: 99–105). See E.P. Thompson on the Game Law requirement that dogs who were not 'law-abiding and truly loyal and who hunted game illegally, should be destroyed' (1975: 30–33). See also Douglas Hay's personal communications to me at note 95 below.
86. Hone (1827, 2: 105).
87. Conway (1896, 4: 478, n.1), and Hone (1827: 99).
88. Rickman (1819: 40).
89. Williamson (1973: 41).
90. Hawke (1974: 15).
91. Keane (1995: 70).
92. Paine (1775: 331).
93. Paine (1775: 332).
94. In his book *The Great Cat Massacre*, Robert Darnton describes the informal justice meted out to offending cats—some of whom were owned and adored by their master's wife—by a group of hungry male printer's apprentices in Paris during the late 1730s. One night the boys, who felt themselves wronged by the well-fed cats 'gathered round and staged a mock trial, complete with guards, confessor, and a public executioner. After pronouncing the animals guilty and administering the last rites, they strung them up on an improvised gallows' (Darnton 1985: 77). But why *cats*? According to Darnton, sensible folk greatly feared cats' reputed occult powers—and because they had long represented female genitalia and were associated with the cuckolding of men, by killing her cats the apprentices thereby took exquisite revenge on Madame and on her as her husband's property.

95. Hay (1975: 196). In a personal email (20 June 2016) Douglas Hay informed me that:

'[t]he comment at p.196 … re the comparison to Tyburn … is mine. It was based on information in a letter (cited in note 5) from Ridgway, Uxbridge's steward, telling him that a keeper had caught a man on Cannock Wood with some crawfish; the local magistrate, Sir Edward Littleton, who sentenced many of the poachers of Uxbridge's game, took the opportunity to order that the man's bulldog be hanged.' Hay also confided that he had 'never heard of a lurcher or any other dog being tried. The crime was that of the owner' (Hay to PB, 23 June 2016).

96. Similarly, Evans (1906: 148–49) claimed, wrongly, that an 'animal trial' had occurred in 1662 in the New Haven Colony. In this case 'a pious wretch' named Potter, aged about 60, was indeed executed for 'damnable Bestialities' with a cow, two heifers, three sheep and two sows, who were killed at the gallows before his eyes. The basic facts of Potter's case are reported in Mather (1662, 2: 348–49).

97. One of the difficulties with Weber's (for example, 1978: 855–56) finding is that 'Roman law' was an evolving body of rules that varied considerably over time and in the purity with which it was received in different European societies. On the geographic penetration of Roman law, see Friedland (2012: 25–67). Bruce Jackson, a leading scholar of Roman law, has argued that by the sixth century the structure of Roman law remedies was not dissimilar to that in modern Britain, including 'a strict liability remedy based on ownership or custody; traces of strict liability for trespassing cattle; a special form of strict liability for dogs … and all dangerous animals; and general fault-based liability' (1978: 142–43).

98. This is not to say that the cultural fixedness regarding which particular species were considered vermin and pests was ever steadfast. About moles, for example, Karen Raber (2013: 151–56) shows in her *Animal Bodies, Renaissance Culture* how, in small numbers, their digging could be useful for loosening the soil prior to cultivation. See also the excellent discussions in Lucinda Cole's (2016: 111–42) *Imperfect Creatures* on humans' perceptual fluidity around dogs as both dangerous and familial in seventeenth- and eighteenth-century Britain, and in Laurie Shannon's *Accommodated Animal* (2013: Chap. 5) on 'hang-dog looks.'

99. See also Edward Topsell's (1658) *History of Four-Footed Beasts and Serpents*, which can be regarded as an early attempt at zoological taxonomy; and Thomas Tusser's (1593) *Five Hundredth Points of Good*

Husbandrie, which may have provided Shakespeare with his knowledge of husbandry and agriculture. The discursive intent of such manuals was nothing short of the transformation of local communities into pre-capitalist, profit-seeking individuals who worked the land with proper knowledge, ambition, hard work and thrift. Their intended audience, as stated by the influential husbandry author Gervase Markham, was anyone connected to the land but especially 'every man of discretion and judgement who was desirous of self-improvement' (1636: 20).

100. For example, see the advice in *Read's Weekly Journal*, 1733 (6 January, issue 407). See also the satiric print *The Dog Killers of Westminster & London or Licenc'd Cruelty* 1760 (Anon. 1760: see Fig. 4.6 above). The *Gentleman's Magazine*, the *St. James Evening Post* and other newspapers also regularly advertised the utility of various other measures to alleviate the problem of encounters with biting dogs. One was the use of a walking stick; another was the much-touted measure of introducing a dog tax, which was intended to prevent dogs from roaming the streets and fields at will.
101. Jenner (1997: 49).
102. Finkelstein (1981: 81).
103. Of the many explanations attaching primacy to the cultivation and internalization of humans' moral sensibilities towards other animals, see especially Thomas (1983) and Elias (1986).
104. *Proceedings of the Old Bailey*, ref. 16770711-1, accessed 8 June 2015 at http://www.hrionline.ac.uk/luceneweb/bailey.
105. Macfarlane (1970). However, as recently as the early decades of the 19th-century, in cases of murder and manslaughter involving poison, English coroners were sometimes aided in their diagnoses by feeding animals the suspect food or vomit Watson (2006: 381). How frequently coroners' courts have ordered animals' deaths in this way or for other reasons is not known, since very few Coroners' Rolls survive.
106. This legend I have pieced together from contemporary Hartlepool-based local history websites. One website informs visitors that the mascot of the local football club, Hartlepool United, is a monkey named H'Angus, and that in 2002 a candidate for mayor successfully campaigned for election wearing a monkey suit and promising free bananas for school children (see BBC News, 3 May 2002; and 'Monkey Mascot Elected Mayor' at www.thisishartlepool.co.uk/history, accessed 29 May 2015). The Hartlepool legend must be given some credence because, according to

the *Act Concerning Wrecks of the Sea* (1275), all ships and goods forced on shore were not to be considered wreckage if 'a Man a Dog or a Cat escape quick out of the Ship'—in such cases the contents of the ship were to pass into the possession of members of the town where the goods were found. On the *Act Concerning Wrecks of the Sea*, see further Rule (1975). In the absence of further evidence, however, it remains unclear whether the legendary Hartlepool theriocide speaks more to salvage rights than it does to issues of xenophobia and speciesism.
107. See, respectively, Darnton (1985), Salmond (2003: 4–9) and Burton (1971).
108. Several arguments in favour of extending due process to animals and against 'backyard executions' are made in Girgen (2003: 131–33). See also Sykes (2011: 308–11).
109. The Humane Society of the United States, 'Pet Overpopulation', accessed 3 July 2016, at www.humanesociety.org/issues/pet overpopulation.
110. Darwin (1871, 1: 173).
111. Lombroso (1895a: 35).
112. Lombroso (1895b: 31, 1918: 365–68).
113. Ellis (1890: 248).
114. Ferrero (1895: 492).
115. Examples include Ellis (1890: 249–50) and Lombroso (1895, 1: 28–34).
116. Lombroso (1918: 365, 368).
117. Lombroso (1895b: 31).
118. On its scientific aspirations and its changing fortunes see especially Gibson and Rafter (2006: 1–36); see also Rafter, 'Psychopathy and the Evolution of Criminological Knowledge,' *Theoretical Criminology*, 1997, 1(2): 235–59. On its demise after its partial methodological unmasking, see Beirne (1993), *Inventing Criminology* (Albany, NY: SUNY Press, Chap. 6); see also L.A. Farrall (1969), *The Origins and Growth of the English Eugenics Movement, 1865–1925* (New York: Garland); and Daniel Pick (1989), *Faces of Degeneration: A European Disorder, c.1848–1918* (Cambridge: Cambridge University Press).
119. On this history see Mark A. Largent (2011), *Breeding Contempt: The History of Coerced Sterilization in the United States* (NJ: Rutgers University Press).

Bibliography

Aldrete, Gregory S. (2014). 'Hammers, Axes, Bulls, and Blood: Some Practical Aspects of Roman Animal Sacrifice,' *Journal of Roman Studies*, 104: 28–50.

Amira, K. (1891). 'Thierstrafen und Thierprocesse,' *Mittheilungen Instituts für Öestterreichische Geschichtsforschung*, 12: 545–605.

Anon. (1760). *The Dog Killers of London & Westminster Or Licenc'd Cruelt*. Engraved etching.

Aquinas, Thomas. (c.1260). (1964). *Summa Theologica*. 61 vols. London: Blackfriars.

Ashton-Cross, D.I.C. (1953). 'Liability in Roman Law for Damage Caused by Animals,' *The Cambridge Law Journal*, 11(3): 395–403.

Baraz, Daniel. (2003). *Medieval Cruelty: Changing Perceptions, Late Antiquity to the Early Modern Period*. Ithaca, NY: Cornell University Press.

Beirne, Piers. (1994). 'The Law Is an Ass: Reading E.P. Evans' The Medieval Prosecution and Capital Punishment of Animals,' *Society & Animals*, 21(1): 27–46.

Beirne, Piers. (2011). 'On the Facticity of Animal Trials in Early Modern Britain, Or A Note onthe Curious Prosecution of Farmer Carter's Dog for Murder,' *Crime, Law and Social Change*, 55(5): 359–74.

Bentham, Jeremy. (1789). *An Introduction to the Principles of Morals and Legislation*. Edited by J.H. Burns and H.L.A. Hart. London: Athlone Press.

Berman, P.S. (1994). 'Rats, Pigs, and Statues on Trial: The Creation of Cultural Narratives in the Prosecution of Animals and Inanimate Objects,' *New York University Law Review*, 69(2): 288–326.

Blackstone, William. (1765–1769). (1778). *Commentaries on the Laws of England*. 4 volumes. Oxford: Clarendon Press.

Bracton. (c.1260). (1968). *On the Laws and Customs of England*. Edited by G.E. Woodbine. Translated by Samuel E. Thorne. Cambridge: Harvard University Press.

Burton, Thomas G. (1971). 'The Hanging of Mary, a Circus Elephant,' *Tennessee Folklore Society*, 37(1): 1–8.

Caenegem, R.C. van. (1988). *An Historical Introduction to Private Law*. Translated by D.E.L Johnston. Cambridge: Cambridge University Press.

Calendar of the Rolls, 1266–1272, p. 193, London: HMSO.

Cohen, Esther. (1986). 'Law, Folklore and Animal Lore,' *Past and Present*, 110: 6–37.

Cohen, Esther. (1993). *The Crossroads of Justice: Law and Culture in Late Medieval France*. Leiden: E.J. Brill.

Coke, Edward. (1648). (1817). *The Third Part of the Institutes of the Laws of England*. London: W. Clarke & Sons.
Cole, Lucinda. (2016). *Imperfect Creatures: Vermin, Literature, and the Sciences of Life, 1600–1740*. Ann Arbor, MI: University of Michigan Press.
Conway, Daniel Moncure. (1896). 'General Introduction.' In: Conway (ed.), *The Life of Thomas Paine*. New York: G.P. Putnam's Sons, 1–15.
Coroners Rolls of the City of London A.D. 1300–1378. (1913). Edited and Introduced by Reginald R. Sharpe. London: Richard Clay and Sons.
Crawford, Julie. (2005). *Marvelous Protestantism: Monstrous Births in Post-Reformation England*. Baltimore, MD: The Johns Hopkins University Press.
Crockett, Samuel Rutherford. (1895). *The Men of the Moss-Hags: Being a History of Adventure*. London: Macmillan.
Damhoudere, Joost de. (1567). *Praxis Rerum Civilium*. Antwerp: Joannes Beller.
Damhoudere, Joost de. (1554). (1570). *Enchiridion Rerum Criminalium, Praetoribus, Consulibus, Proconsulibus, Magistratibus*. Antwerp: Ioannem Bellerum.
Darnton, Robert. (1985). *The Great Cat Massacre and Other Episodes in French Cultural History*. New York: Vintage.
Darwin, Charles. (1871). *The Descent of Man and Selection in Relation to Sex*. 2 vols. London: John Murray.
Dinzelbacher, Peter. (2002). 'Animal Trials: A Multidisciplinary Approach,' *Journal of Interdisciplinary History*, 32(3): 405–21.
Dubois-Desaulle, Gaston. (1933). *Bestiality: An Historical, Medical, Legal and Literary Study*.
Elias, Norbert. (1986). 'An Essay on Sport and Violence.' In: Norbert Elias and Eric Dunning (eds.), *Quest for Excitement: Sport and Leisure in the Civilising Process*. Oxford: Basil Blackwell, 150–74.
Ellis, Havelock. (1890). *The Criminal*. New York: Scribner and Welford.
Enders, Jody. (2002). 'Homicidal Pigs and the Antisemitic Imagination,' *Exemplaria*, 14(1): 201–38.
Evans, E.P. (1884a). 'Bugs and Beasts Before the Law,' *Atlantic Monthly*, 54: 235–46.
Evans, E.P. (1884b). 'Medieval and Modern Punishment,' *Atlantic Monthly*, 54: 302–08.
Evans, E.P. (1898). *Evolutionary Ethics and Animal Psychology*. New York: D. Appleton.
Evans, Edward Payson. (1906). *The Criminal Prosecution and Capital Punishment of Animals*. New York: E.P. Dutton. (Reprinted in 1987, London: Faber and Faber).

Ewald, William. (1995). 'Comparative Jurisprudence (I): What Was It Like to Try a Rat?' *University of Pennsylvania Law Review*, 143(6): 1889–2149.

Finkelstein, J.J. (1981). 'The Ox that Gored,' *Transactions of the American Philosophical Society*, 71(part 2): 3–89.

Forbes, T.R. (1973). 'London-Coroner's Inquests for 1590,' *Journal of the History of Medicine and Allied Sciences*, 28(4): 376–86.

Forte, A.D.M. (1990). 'The Horse that Kills: Some Thoughts on Deodands, Escheats and Crime in Fifteenth Century Scots Law,' *The Legal History Review*, 58(1): 95–110.

Foxe, John. (1563). (1776). *Acts and Monuments of the Christian Martyrs*. London: H. Trapp.

Francione, Gary. (1995). *Animals, Property, and the Law*. Philadelphia, PA: Temple University Press.

Frazer, Sir James George. (1923). *Folk-Lore in the Old Testament: Studies in Comparative Religion, Legend and Law*. New York: Tudor.

Friedland, Paul. (2012). *Seeing Justice Done: The Age of Spectacular Capital Punishment in France*. Oxford: Oxford University Press.

Fudge, Erica. (2002). *Perceiving Animals: Humans and Beasts in Early Modern English Culture*. Urbana, IL: University of Illinois Press.

Gibson, Mary and Nicole Hahn Rafter. (eds.). (2006). *Cesare Lombroso. Criminal Man*. Durham, NC: Duke University Press.

Girgen, Jen. (2003). 'The Historical and Contemporary Prosecution of Animals,' *Animal Law*, 9: 97–133.

Greve, Vagn. (1999). 'Om kålorm og andre voldsmænd, tyve og røvere' ['On Caterpillars and Other Violent Men, Thieves and Robbers'], *Materialisten : Tidsskrift for forskning, fagkritikk og teoretisk debatt*, 27(3): 81–89.

Hawke, David Freeman. (1974). *Paine*. New York: Harper & Row.

Hay, Douglas. (1975). 'Poaching and the Game Laws on Cannock Chase.' In: Douglas Hay, Peter Linebaugh, John G. Rule, E.P. Thompson and Cal Winslow (eds.), *Albion's Fatal Tree: Crime and Society in Eighteenth-Century England*. New York: Pantheon Books, 189–253.

Holden, Anthony. (1990). *William Shakespeare: The Man Behind the Genius*. Boston: Little, Brown.

Hone, William. (1827). *Every-day Book and Table-book; or, Everlasting Calendar of Popular Amusements*. 2 vols. London: Hunt and Clarke.

Humphrey, Nicholas. (1987). 'Foreword.' In: E.P. Evans, (1906), *The Criminal Prosecution and Capital Punishment of Animals*. London: Faber and Faber.

Hyde, Walter Woodburn. (1916). 'The Prosecution and Punishment of Animals and Lifeless Things in the Middle Ages and Modern Times,' *University of Pennsylvania Law Review*, 64(7): 696–730.
Ives, George. (1914). (1970). *A History of Penal Methods: Criminals, Witches, Lunatics*. Montclair, NJ: Patterson Smith.
Jackson, Bernard S. (1978). 'Liability for Animals in Roman Law: An Historical Sketch,' *The Cambridge Law Journal*, 37(1): 122–43.
Jackson, Clare. (2003). *Restoration Scotland, 1660–1690: Royalist Politics, Religion and Ideas*. Woodbridge, Suffolk: Boydell Press.
Jamieson, Philip. (1988). 'Animal Liability in Early Law,' *Cambrian Law Review*, xix: 45–68.
Jenner, Mark S.R. (1997). 'The Great Dog Massacre.' In: William G. Naphy and Penny Roberts (eds.), *Fear in Early Modern Society*. Manchester: Manchester University Press, 44–61.
Jones, William. (1880). *Credulities Past and Present*. London: Chatto and Windus.
Keane, John. (1995). *Tom Paine: a Political Life*. Boston: Little, Brown.
Kelly, Fergus. (2000). *Early Irish Farming*. Dundalk: Dundalgan Press.
Kelsen, Hans. (1923). (1945). *General Theory of Law and State*. Translated by Anders Wedberg. Cambridge: Harvard University Press.
Langbein, John. (1976). 'The Historical Origins of the Sanction of Imprisonment for Serious Crime,' *Journal of Legal History*, 5: 35–60.
Lauder, Sir John. (1671). (1900). 'Journals of Sir John Lauder Lord Fountainhall, 1665–1676,' *Publications of the Scottish History Society*, 36 vols.
Leeson, Peter T. (2013). 'Vermin Trials,' *Journal of Law and Economics*, 56(3): 811–36.
Liber Albus: The White Book [of the City of London]. (1419). (1861). Translated from Latin by Henry Thomas Riley. London: Richard Griffin.
Lombroso, Cesare. (1895a). 'Criminal Anthropology: Its Origin and Application,' *Forum*, 20: 33–49.
Lombroso, Cesare. (1895b). *L'Homme criminal*. Paris: F. Alcan.
Lombroso, Cesare. (1918). *Crime: Its Causes and Remedies*. Translated by Henry Pomeroy. Boston: Little, Brown.
Louandre, Charles. (1854). 'L'Épopée des Animaux,' *Revue des Deux Mondes*, 25: 331–36.
MacCormack, G. (1984). 'On Thing Liability (*Sachhaftung*) in Early Law,' *The Irish Jurist*, xix: 322–49.

Macfarlane, Alan. (1970). *Witchcraft in Tudor and Stuart England*. New York: Harper & Row.

Markham, Gervase. (1636). *The Inrichment of the Weald of Kent*. London: Anne Griffin.

Mascall, Leonard. (1590). *Booke of engines and traps to take polcats, buzardes, rattes, mice and all other kindes of vermine and beasts whatsoeuer, most profitable for all warriners, and such as delight in this kinde of sport and pastime*. London: John Wolfe.

Mather, Cotton. (1662). (1820). *Magnalia Christi Americana: Cotton Mather*. 2 vols. New Haven: Silas Andrus.

Nichols, John. (1828). *Literary Anecdotes of the Eighteenth Century*. London: J.B. Nichols.

Oldridge, Darren. (2005). *Strange Histories: the Trial of the Pig, the Walking Dead, and Other Matters of Fact from the Medieval and Renaissance Worlds*. London: Routledge.

Otten, Charlotte. (ed.). (1986). *A Lycanthropy Reader: Werewolves in Western culture*. Syracuse, NY: Syracuse University Press.

Paine, Tom. [anon.]. (1775). (1896). 'Farmer Short's Dog Porter.' In: Daniel Moncure Conway (ed.), *The Writings of Thomas Paine*. New York: G.P. Putnam's Sons, 478–81.

Pertile, Antonio. (1886). 'Gli animali in Giudizio.' In: *Atti del Reale Istituto Veneto*, book 4, series 6. Venice: Press of the Institute of Science, Letters and Arts, 135–53.

Phillips, Patrick J.J. (2013). *Medieval Animal Trials: Justice for All*. New York: Edwin Mellen Press.

Pietz, W. (1997). 'Death of the Deodand: Accursed Objects and the Money Value of Human Life,' *Res*, xxxi: 97–108.

Pignot, J.-Henri. (1880). *Barthélemy de Chasseneuz*. Paris: L. Larose.

Raber, Karen. (2013). *Animal Bodies, Renaissance Culture*. Philadelphia, PA: University of Pennsylvania Press.

Rickman, Thomas Clio. (1819). *Life of Thomas Paine*. London: T.C. Rickman.

Ritvo, Harriet. (1987). *The Animal Estate: The English and Other Creatures in Victorian England*. Cambridge: Harvard University Press.

Rule, John G. (1975). 'Wrecking and Coastal Plunder.' In: Douglas Hay, Peter Linebaugh, John G. Rule, E.P. Thompson and Cal Winslow (eds.), *Albion's Fatal Tree: Crime and Society in Eighteenth-Century England*. New York: Pantheon Books, 167–88.

Salisbury, Joyce E. (1994). *The Beast Within: Animals in the Middle Ages*. New York: Routledge.

Salmond, Anne. (2003). *The Trial of the Cannibal Dog. The Remarkable Story of Captain Cook's Encounters in the South Seas*. New Haven: Yale University Press.

Scot, Reginald. (1665). *The Discoverie of Witchcraft, Wherein the Lewde Dealing of Witches and Witchmongers is Notablie Detected*. London: R.C.

Seetah, Krish. (2007). 'The Middle Ages on the Block: Animals, Guilds and Meat in the Medieval Period.' In: Aleksander Pluskowski (ed.), *Breaking and Shaping Beastly Bodies: Animals as Material Culture in the Medieval Ages*. Oxford: Oxbow Books, 18–31.

Shannon, Laurie. (2013). *The Accommodated Animal: Cosmopolity in Shakespearean Locales*. Chicago: University of Chicago Press.

Sloet, Ludolf A.J.W. (1887). *De dieren in het Germaansche volksgeloof en volksgebruik*. Amsterdam: Martinus Nijhof.

Spencer, Dale C. and Amy Fitzgerald. (2015). 'Criminology and Animality: Stupidity and the Anthropological Machine,' *Contemporary Justice Review*, 1–14.

Sprenger, James and Henry Kramer. (1486). (2009). *The Hammer of Witches: A Complete Translation of the Malleus Maleficarum*. Edited and translated by Christopher S. Mackay. Cambridge: Cambridge University Press.

Sykes, Katie. (2011). 'Human Drama, Animal Trials: What the Medieval Animal Trials Can Teach Us about Justice for Animals,' *Animal Law*, 17: 273–311.

Tester, Keith. (1991). *Animals & Society: The Humanity of Animal Rights*. London: Routledge.

Thomas, Keith. (1983). *Man and the Natural World: Changing Attitudes in England 1500–1800*. New York: Oxford University Press.

Thompson, E.P. (1975). *Whigs and Hunters: The Origin of the Black Act*. London: Penguin.

Topsell, Edward. (1658). *History of Four-Footed Beasts and Serpents*. London: E. Cotes.

Train, Joseph. (1845). *Historical and Statistical Account of the Isle of Man*. 2 vols. London: Simpkin, Marshall.

Tusser, Thomas. (1593). *Five Hundredth Points of Good Husbandrie* London: R. Tottel.

Watson, Alan. (ed.). (1985). *The Digest of Justinian*. 1 vol. Translated Edited by Alan Watson. Philadelphia, PA: University of Pennsylvania Press.

Watson, Katherine D. (2006). 'Medical and Chemical Expertise in English Trials for Criminal Poisoning, 1750–1914,' *Medical History*, 50: 373–90.

Weber, Max. (1978). *Economy and Society: An Outline of Interpretive Sociology.* Edited by Gunther Roth and Claus Wittich. Berkeley: University of California Press.

Westermarck, Edward. (1906–1908). *The Origin and Development of the Moral Ideas.* 2 vols. London: Macmillan.

Williamson, Audrey. (1973). *Thomas Paine: His Life, Work and Times.* London: Allen and Unwin.

Wise, Steven M. (2000). *Rattling the Cage: Toward Legal Rights for Animals.* Cambridge, MA: Perseus.

Yeomans, Lisa. (2007). 'The Shifting Use of Animal Carcasses in Medieval and Post-Medieval London.' In: Aleksander Pluskowski (ed.), *Breaking and Shaping Beastly Bodies: Animals as Material Culture in the Middle Ages.* Oxford: Oxbow, 98–115.

5

Hogarth's Patriotic Animals: Bulldogs, Beef, Britannia!

Charges of adherence to a bewildering variety of -isms and -ologies have frequently been hurled at the English artist and social critic William Hogarth (1696–1764). Plaguing him for much of his very public career and continuing long after his death, even until today, the major charges against him include his alleged plagiarism of classical continental paintings; monarchism and anti-monarchism; misogyny; radical, counter-cultural populism bordering on anarchism; ultra-individualism; critical deism; anti-Semitism; bourgeois social reformism; and patriotism.

Whether extended as accusatory barb or as high praise, none of these charges has likely been more common than that of Hogarth's patriotism.[1] Certainly, none has been more deserved. From the early 1740s to the mid-1750s Hogarth's embrace of British and especially English patriotism lies at the very centre of his art. During this tumultuous decade of ongoing military conflict between Britain and France, and amid widespread fear of a French invasion, Hogarth attempted to craft and then to propagandize the nature of what it was to be British. This he did with a panoply of images in *Calais Gate, Or O the Roast Beef of Old England* (1748–49), *March to Finchley* (1749), *Gin Lane* (1751), *Beer Street* (1751) and the invasion series *France* (1756) and *England* (1756).

© The Author(s) 2018
P. Beirne, *Murdering Animals*, Palgrave Studies in Green Criminology, https://doi.org/10.1057/978-1-137-57468-8_5

Among the patriotic artifacts on display in Hogarth's (1751) iconic *Beer Street*, for example, are the Union Jack attached to the steeple of St Martin's church, raised annually on George II's birthday; a copy of the King's pro-bourgeois speech to parliament advocating 'the advancement of our commerce'—in particular, that of the British herring fishery, which was hurting from French competition; and francophobic verse: 'Beer, happy Produce of our Isle … We quaff the balmy Juice with Glee, and Water leave to France.' When set against *Gin Lane*'s (1751) shockingly dismal scenes of poverty and despair, *Beer Street*'s patriotic stench is strong indeed.

Hogarth sometimes expressed his patriotism through animal imagery, the exposure of which is this chapter's main focus. I should say beforehand that I have tried to throw some critical light on Hogarth's animal images on two other occasions. In the first—an essay, 'Hogarth's Animals'—I began with Hogarth's own overnumerous intentions and then uncovered how and why, in his paintings, drawings and printed engravings, he represented animals as hybrids, as edibles, as signs of satire, as companions ('pets') and as objects of cruelty. In the second—a short book, *Hogarth's Art of Animal Cruelty*—my target was the artist's depiction of the public and private forms of animal cruelty in mid-eighteenth-century London. My particular focus there was Hogarth's frenzied activity in six weeks of January and February 1751, during which he executed, produced and marketed *Gin Lane*, *Beer Street* and the four prints in the *Four Stages of Cruelty* series.

The identity and configuration of animals in Hogarth's pictures varied over the course of his career and according to whether the artist was working as an engraver of book plates and heraldic coats of arms, as a painter of religious or comic histories, as a portraitist, as a social critic and satirist or as a prophet of general doom and decay. But his interest in British dogs and British cattle was lifelong. In this chapter I try to show how Hogarth fashioned images of dogs (very much alive) and cattle (slaughtered and transformed into edibles) in order to cultivate an ideology of Britishness based on masculinity and carnism operating in tandem.

The chapter unfolds in two stages. In the first I uncover how Hogarth used images of dogs to point the way to a rekindling of the virtues of the

Elizabethan Golden Age. Mastiffs, pugs and bulldogs, in particular, for him embodied the bravery and strength of character which he believed had to be cultivated in England were the country ever to overcome the military and political challenges posed from across the channel and from north of the border. The second part of the chapter delves into various aspects of Hogarth's advocacy of the consumption of the edible flesh of cows, bulls and oxen (British 'beef'). Taken together, in other words, the true English Patriot kept manly dogs and ate the roast beef of old England. In this way would the warriors of Britannia rule.

Let Slip the Dogs of War!

[Bulldogs are c]reatures superior to all for obstinate bravery, and peculiar the Growth of England; nor is their Courage, like that of most other Creatures, excited only by Hunger and Lust. I hope I don't flatter myself and Countrymen in advancing that Bravery is the true Characteristick of an Englishman.[2]

By the middle of the eighteenth century, in the evolving litany of petting practices, dogs had become the repository of all manner of sentiments related to gender, class and patriotism. Numerous dogs are among the canids in Hogarth's pictures—dogs, small, medium and large, dogs coddled as pets and posed in portraiture, and dogs who growl, bark, whine, whimper, eat and sleep. Mostly the occupants of some point within the matrix of status symbol, objet d'art, companion and servant,[3] dogs are frequently to be seen in Hogarth's portraits of eminent persons and of family life in townhouses and country mansions, inside and out.

Hogarth's *Portrait of Mary Edwards* (1742) is a good example of his patriotism hard at work. Commissioned by his wealthy patron and close friend of the same name, it is among his most famous portraits, second only to the iconic *Shrimp Girl* of (c.1740–45). It is one of the only Georgian portraits by a well-known artist that portrays a woman outside the context of marriage and family (Fig. 5.1).

The painting's warm and tender atmosphere reflects the close personal relationship between sitter and painter. Moreover, Mary Edwards

Fig. 5.1 *Portrait of Mary Edwards*, oil on canvas, William Hogarth, 1742 (Source: https://commons.wikimedia.org/wiki/File:Miss_Mary_Edwards_-_Hogarth_1742.jpg)

(1705–43) and William Hogarth suited each other's purposes quite well. Reputedly the wealthiest woman in England, she was desirous of conveying her intelligence, her resolute determination and her patriotic politics to a public sphere of connoisseurship almost entirely closed to women. For his part, Hogarth himself was always in need of patronage and, at least until the success of his modern moral subjects in the late 1730s, was very much dependent on income from portraiture (a genre which he generally despised). The portrait was therefore mutually beneficial to sitter and painter. She confronts the viewer's gaze directly.

Now look at the dog in *Portrait of Mary Edwards*. Hogarth had probably been instructed by his patron to allot him an unusually large space near the centre of the canvas, a placement that likely reflects both Mary's devotion to her pet hound and also William's affection for him.[4] The hound is alert. He is at her knee, loyal. He adores his mistress.[5] His eyes are sharply focused on a scroll, which is to her right and which she appears to have just been reading. The scroll is intended to indicate Mary Edwards' strong political convictions, which were decidedly against appeasement with the Spanish and in favour of the new pro-Elizabethan 'Patriot King' politics championed by Lord Bolingbroke and kindred members of the Walpole Opposition.

Indeed, the composition of *Portrait of Mary Edwards* emulates *Portrait of Elizabeth*, an anonymous painting of 1588. In *Portrait of Elizabeth* Good Queen Bess sits with her right hand on a globe, her eyes looking directly at the viewer. She exudes power and wisdom. Behind her hang two paintings of the defeated Spanish armada. The scroll at Mary's side in *Portrait of Mary Edwards* is apparently a record of Queen Elizabeth's address to English troops on the eve of the crushing defeat of the Spanish Armada in 1588 ('I know I have the body of a weak and feeble woman, but I have the heart and stomach of a king, and of a king of England too'). The scroll contains the stirring advice[6]:

> Remember, Englishmen, the Laws the Rights
> The generous plan of Power deliver'd down
> From age to age by your renown'd Forefathers
> So dearly bought the Price of so much Contest
> Transmit it careful to Posterity
> Do thou great Liberty inspire their Souls
> And make their Lives in thy possession happy
> Or their Deaths glorious in thy Just defence.

Like all patriotic and nationalist projects, Hogarth's imaginary community of England was based mostly on myth and deceit. He and presumably it both yearned for the glorious English past, which was said to stretch from the liberty, the commercial successes and the genius of Shakespeare in the Elizabethan Golden Age all the way back to the first monarch of the Anglo-Saxons, King Alfred the Great. Indeed, busts of King Alfred and Queen Elizabeth can be seen in the background of Hogarth's portrait of Mary Edwards.

Some of this very patriotism is also on display in Hogarth's depictions of his own aggressive-looking pugs and bulldogs (Shakespeare's mastiffs of 'unmatchable courage').[7] These dogs, his inseparable companions, Hogarth placed in both commissioned portraits and self-portraits, sometimes to juxtapose them with the spoiled and puny lapdogs associated with the French court.[8] Nowhere is Hogarth's affection for dogs and his symbolic uses of them more on show than in his self-portrait *Hogarth: The Painter and His Pug* (1745; Fig. 5.2). Here, with great sympathy and

Fig. 5.2 *Hogarth: The Painter and his Pug,* oil on canvas, William Hogarth, 1742

not a little comedy, Hogarth portrays the self-detected resemblance between himself and his dog Trump—especially in the similarity of their eyes, their snub noses and their short squat torsos; he 5 feet or less in height, Trump perhaps 15 inches at the shoulder, both with much-in-little and packing-a-punch personalities. Note, too, how brazenly Hogarth depicts himself as the enlightened artist of Englishness that he rightly knew he was—he with the wisdom imparted by a copy of his own *Analysis of Beauty* next to folio volumes by English luminaries Shakespeare, Milton and Swift.

Some of the dogs in Hogarth's pictures do not enjoy the good health and well-being as those in *Mary Edwards* and *Hogarth: The Painter and His Pug*. These less fortunate creatures Hogarth tended to portray as masterless, starving and aggressive.[9] These are the dogs he depicts in the first and the second of the *Four Stages of Cruelty* (1751). These two prints—cheaply produced for a mass audience and thereby intended by Hogarth to oppose the animal cruelties practised by London's working-class and gin-besotted poor—depicted the burning of a songbird's eyes, cat killing, bear baiting, cock-fighting, cock-throwing, dog killings and horse maiming. Among these animals is a hungry dog whom a gloating boy tantalizes by tying a bone to her tail and another who, having been forced to savage a cat, is about to devour her entrails ('*various Scenes of sportive Woe, The Infant Race employ*'). The focus of the action in the *First Stage*, moreover, is on a dog who is being held off the ground by arch villain Tom Nero and by another youth who elevates the canine's head, pulling him up by a rope attached to his neck. Nero holds the dog's rear legs off the ground while he sodomizes him with the tip of a barbed metal arrow ('*And torture'd Victims bleeding shew, The Tyrant in the Boy*'). In the fourth of the *Four Stages of Cruelty* (*Cruelty's Reward*) a hungry dog is seen devouring the boiled intestines of Tom Nero, whose hanged body had been snatched from the Tyburn gallows and sold for an anatomical demonstration at the College of Surgeons at Cripplegate.[10]

Almost needless to say, the *Four Stages of Cruelty* has multiple meanings and an array of coded clues. But the one most relevant to this chapter is how Hogarth links his opposition to animal cruelty to his patriotism, a coupling which he was far from alone in formulating. Animal cruelty was widely condemned as an evil, a national disgrace and a source of great shame and embarrassment. When animal abuse was witnessed by foreigners, it caused English nationalism no end of anguish—even more so if the foreigners happened to be from France.[11] One French national who visited Hogarth's London declared that the cruelties inflicted on animals at Smithfield market were far worse than the bear baitings of the Elizabethan era.[12] Commenting on the animal cruelty depicted in London in *The First Stage of Cruelty*, an early admirer of Hogarth wrote[13]:

> The delineation of such scenes must shock every feeling heart, and their enumeration disgust every humane mind. I hope, for the honour of our nature and our nation, that they are not so frequently practised as when these prints were published.

It must be said that among the potential links between British dogs and British beef that Hogarth chose not to develop was the long-standing practice of bull-baiting. There is no explicit evidence that he opposed the carnist practice of setting bulldogs on a chained-up but not altogether defenceless bull in the belief that their biting and gnawing and scratching would significantly soften the animal's flesh for subsequent roasting and eating. But he does include, in the far-off background in the *Second Stage of Cruelty*, the image of gawkers encouraging dogs to bait a bull—either as sport or to soften his flesh for eating or both. The bull has managed to heave one of his human tormentors into the air. While not banned nationwide for another seventy years, bull-baiting was gradually disappearing with the rise of the civilizing process.

Beef and Liberty! Hogarth's Consuming Passions

> [In the French encampment …] *Lord Rambures*: That island of England breeds very valiant creatures. Their mastiffs are of unmatchable courage.
> […]
> *Constable of France*: […] and the men do sympathize with the mastiffs in robustious and rough coming on, leaving their wits with their wives: and then give them great meals of beef and iron and steel, they will eat like

wolves and fight like devils. (Shakespeare, *Henry V*, Act 3, scene 7, ll. 155–68)

Though Shakespeare's French warrior Lord Rambures was not the first to extol the beneficial effects of beef consumption for Englishmen—for their bodily health and for their bravery in battle especially—an explicit link between a wished-for national identity and beef consumption was perhaps first articulated by Joseph Addison, the editor of *The Tatler*, in a popular diatribe of 1710. Addison stressed that military victories at Crecy and Agincourt had been ensured by the thrice-daily consumption of roast beef by the English soldiers. Addison implored his readers to eat plenty of beef—'[t]his excellent food … a noble sirloin [and] what work our countrymen would have made at Blenheim and Ramillies if they had been fed with fricasees and ragouts.'[14]

Soon thereafter and enduring throughout the eighteenth century, there was a huge increase in the demand for the edible flesh of cattle and their milk. Other parts of their bodies were used for leather, glue, oil, soap, candles, buttons, bone, combs, pipes and hair-clips. Describing agriculture in the London area around 1760, the land surveyor John Middleton documented that in the area of 'Hackney, Islington, Paddington, and several miles thereabouts, the cow-keepers engross every inch of land they can procure. Some of these men have remarkable large stocks of cows. One of them … has very near one thousand.'

By mid-century the large-scale consumption and ostentatious display of beef had become an important cultural and symbolic item in an emerging national identity. The patriotic link between beef consumption and national identity was promoted at carnivals and on feast days, and in literature, theatre, music and the graphic arts. Evidence for the innate Englishness of beef was especially manifest, it was thought, in success in military adventures.[15] Francophobia and anti-popery were coupled with and then merged into this ideology of carnism. As Hogarth historian Jenny Uglow writes: '[t]he oozing red meat, the feasts and freedoms—like the wearing of leather shoes instead of wooden clogs—set the English against the feeble, starving peasants of the Continent'.[16]

Hogarth's antipathy to the French had been apparent in his art at least since his *Four Times of the Day* (1738) series. In this series there are two bodies of moving water. One appears in *Noon*. It is the dirty Fleet-ditch separating the area's poor English from the well-to-do French Huguenot refugees. Hogarth sets this scene on Hog Lane in grim St. Giles-in-the-Fields. The other flows the length of the romanticized English countryside and bucolic river in *Evening*. This scene is replete with a woman milking a cow and a healthy dog admiring the river's gentle flow (Figs. 5.3 and 5.4). Items on the dinner menu in *Taste in High Life, or Taste à la Mode* (1742; Fig. 5.5) include cocks' combs, ducks' tongues, rabbits' ears, *fricassée* of snails and *grande d'oeufs beurre*—all of which Hogarth would have despised because they were French and (therefore) insubstantial tidbits or kickshaws.

On closer inspection *Noon* and *Evening* reveal Hogarth as the master showman with a knack for presenting conflicting, even contradictory, values for his audience to ponder. An anti-classical Diana is the central figure in *Evening* (1738), where the pregnant matriarch waves a fan sporting a scene from the Diana and Actaeon myth.[17] In *Evening*, in the course of a walk along a tranquil riverbank after a performance at Sadler's Wells theatre, she dominates her hen-pecked husband, who walks timidly in front of her, his eyes transfixed. Hogarth identifies him as Actaeon with the clever visual pun of a cow's horns, which resemble a stag's antlers, seemingly attached to the crown of his head. His future will not be pleasant. Their tired-looking canine companion walks with them. The husband must hope that the dog does not recognize him as Actaeon.

On the English side of the Fleet-ditch, to the left of the picture, the humorous *Noon* is chiefly about food and drink. The latter is announced by two tavern signboards: on one is the figure of a maid, though her head is missing; on the other, on a plate, is the head of John the Baptist with the accompanying mutton-festooned inscription 'Good Eating'. In this neighbourhood the dining is likely to be a raucous affair—indeed, in an upstairs window a man and a woman argue; she drops her leg of mutton to the street below. An amorous couple, likely tavern servants, engrossed in each other, spill their pies and gravy onto the ground. A destitute young girl picks up the scraps. This slice of England is far removed from the promised land of good roast beef. It is a gastronomic disaster.[18]

Hogarth's Patriotic Animals: Bulldogs, Beef, Britannia! 145

Fig. 5.3 *Noon* (*Four Times of the Day 2*), printed engraving, William Hogarth, 1738

Fig. 5.4 *Evening (Four Times of the Day 3)*, printed engraving, William Hogarth, 1738

Fig. 5.5 Detail: Monkey with scrolled French menu in *Taste in High Life, or Taste à la Mode*, oil on canvas, William Hogarth, 1742 (Reproduced with permission of *La Clé des langues* (Clifford Armion, dir.) and ENS Média (Vincent Brault, photo))

One needs to remember how difficult it often is to decipher Hogarth's intentions. Sometimes his emblems and symbols lead nowhere, having been playfully inserted by the artist as red herrings. So it is with the object suspended from the wall of a Hog Lane church in *Noon*. Ben Rogers has suggested that in this picture 'the kite' hanging limply from the French Protestant church 'looks suspiciously like a flatfish, and is mirrored by a leg of lamb being hurled out of a window on the English side of the picture'. It is true, as Rogers also points out, that 'just as meat was associated with England, fish, eaten by Catholics on Fridays and during Lent, was associated with France—poor, bony flatfish especially so'.[19] But the 'kite' or 'flatfish' might well have been intended by Hogarth to resemble the sort of inflated and sewn-up cow's bladder notoriously used by young males in experiments to see if cats are capable of assisted flight—which is exactly what is depicted as an Icarus-like failure in Hogarth's *First Stage of Cruelty* (1751).

In Hogarth's art a bounty of edible animals signifies prosperity and embourgeoisement—the fruits of hard work in *Beer Street* (1751), for example, which he contrasts with the starvation and emaciation of humans and animals in *Gin Lane* (1751). Neither animals nor those who transform them into edibles are ever far away from Hogarth's scenes of daily life in the metropolis. English butchers, for example, Hogarth tended to endow with a pugnacious and no-nonsense character. Two cudgel-bearing butchers are involved in a mêlée in *Hudibras' First Adventure* (1727); in his *Industrious 'Prentice Married to his Master's Daughter* (1747) a company of butchers adds rhythm to a musical celebration by banging their meat cleavers with bones, as they do again in *The Industrious' Prentice Lord Mayor of London* (1747); in *Beer Street* (1751, first state), a prosperous pint-quaffing butcher laughs as he sees a blacksmith tossing an effete Frenchman into the air with one hand; and in *An Election Entertainment* (1755) a butcher, 'Pro Patriae' inscribed on his cap, pours wine onto the head of a street fighter.

Hogarth's worship of beef of course reflected something even more passionate than personal gustatory preference. Indeed, he and the theatrical scene painter George Lambert were two of the original twenty-four members of the eccentric gentlemen's club known as the Sublime Society of Beef Steaks (founded in 1735 by John Rich, the celebrated harlequin and machinist of Covent Garden Theatre). Among the Society's early luminaries, along with Hogarth himself and his father-in-law the celebrated artist Sir James Thornhill, were the Earl of Sandwich, the Prince of Wales (the future George IV), the great Shakespearean actor David Garrick, the politician John Wilkes and the satirist Charles Churchill.[20] The 'SSBS', as it was popularly known, met once a week, usually on Saturdays, in order to devour, with shallots and onions, vast quantities of beef: beef boiled, fried, stewed, toasted or roasted.[21] Its members ('Brothers') sported uniforms—blue coats with red capes and cuffs, and buff waistcoats, each of whose brass buttons was embossed with a gridiron and the motto 'Beef and Liberty'.[22]

Little is known with certainty about what antics actually transpired when Hogarth was present at the SSBS dinners, though presumably these meetings concluded in drunken revelry.[23] The Society's chronicler, Brother Arnold, recorded that '[t]oasted cheese ended the repast; and so appetising was the dinner, that with many who foreswore suppers, supper was the inevitable result. Porter (in pewter), port wine, punch and whisky toddy were the accompaniments of this simple dinner.'[24] Indeed, as Roy Porter has indicated, '[b]eefsteak was a natural emblem for Englishmen whose manhood seemingly hinged upon being three bottle fellows'.[25]

Fig. 5.6 *A Song in Praise of Old English Roast Beef*, words and music by Richard Leveridge, c.1745 Several versions of Fielding's and Leveridge's *Song in Praise of Old English Roast Beef* are currently in circulation (for one with a ring of authenticity about it see: https://www.youtube.com/watch?v=MTH5gnluOVg) (Source: an unidentified London publisher, n.d. [c.1750])

Each SSBS meeting had a Song of the Day, the most requested of which originated in a patriotic ballad composed by Henry Fielding on the virtues of roast beef.[26] Fielding had been led to this composition after he had witnessed the wildly enthusiastic reaction of ticket-buying London audiences to ballads in John Gay's *Beggar's Opera*. This convinced Fielding

Fig. 5.7 *Calais Gate*, printed engraving, William Hogarth, 1748–49 (Reproduced with permission of *La Clé des langues* (Clifford Armion, dir.) and ENS Média (Vincent Brault, photo))

to embrace the comical and iconoclastic aspects of the lowly ballad because he saw it as a musical form whose advance might successfully oppose the dominance of Italian opera and other foreign music in Britain. In 1731 he set about reproducing an anonymous seventeenth-century ballad—'The King's Old Courtier'—and then inserted it as the forty-fifth air of his *Grub-Street* (or Welch) *Opera*. Not long afterwards, one of Hogarth's friends, the playwright and balladeer Richard Leveridge, added more stanzas and set it to what was to become the very popular three-verse melody *A Song in Praise of Old English Roast Beef* (Fig. 5.6 above).[27]

Hogarth's Patriotic Animals: Bulldogs, Beef, Britannia! 151

Fig. 5.8 *Transubstantiation Satirized*, aquatint etching, William Hogarth, n.d. (Source: Samuel Ireland (1794, 1: opposite 122))

Fig. 5.9 *France* (*The Invasion* 1), engraved etching, William Hogarth, 1756 (Reproduced with permission of *La Clé des langues* (Clifford Armion, dir.) and ENS Média (Vincent Brault, photo))

Hogarth's most explicit lectures on the subject of food and national identity appear in *Calais Gate* (1748), *Transubstantiation Satirized* (n.d.), *France* (1756) and *England* (1756) (Figs. 5.7, 5.8, 5.9 and 5.10).

* *Calais Gate* (1748–49). This is the most famous of all francophobic and anti-Catholic pictures by a British artist.[28] Its message: epistemologically, we and the body politic are what we feed them. Hogarth has placed himself at centre left and is about to be arrested on suspicion of having sketched military fortifications. The focus of the painting is a side of beef—*English* beef—about to be delivered to the English inn. Everyone

Hogarth's Patriotic Animals: Bulldogs, Beef, Britannia! 153

Fig. 5.10 *England* (*The Invasion* 2), engraved etching, William Hogarth, 1756 (Reproduced with permission of *La Clé des langues* (Clifford Armion, dir.) and ENS Média (Vincent Brault, photo))

except the Franciscan friar is starving. Among them are shabby French soldiers, fisherwomen and two exiled members of the Jacobite cause.

In order to reinforce his visual puns about food and national identity, Hogarth—a member of the Academy of Ancient Music—nudges viewers of *Calais Gate* into seeing that its message also has an auditory component. Actively encouraging the juxtaposition of patriotic images with patriotic words and patriotic melodies, Hogarth beckons his audience to recall and to sing the popular ballad *In Praise of Old English Roast Beef* (Fig. 5.6). Like many of Hogarth's earlier pictures, *Calais Gate* is a noisy shew.[29]

Transubstantiation Satirized (n.d.). Hogarth had much earlier placed on a wall in his oil sketch *The Marriage Contract* (c.1732) the jaw-dropping etching *Transubstantiation Satirized*. In it he scoffs at the Roman Catholic doctrine of transubstantiation by depicting the Virgin Mary dropping her plump baby into a wind-powered thresher. The desacralized baby Jesus emerges, minced and flattened, at the other end. His body has been transformed into edible communion hosts, which a French priest administers to his flock.[30] Hogarth's point, almost needless to say, is to contrast the satisfying British roast beef with the insubstantial spiritual fare administered by the Catholic priesthood.

* *France* (1756). In March 1756 the looming Seven Years' War prompted Hogarth to renew the major themes of *Calais Gate*. Just as the nation was rife with rumours about the threat of invasion by millions of French soldiers from across the Channel, Hogarth executed *France* (1756) and *England* (1756). Their author clearly intended that with *Calais Gate* these two *Invasion* paintings should form a visual lecture series in support of English nationalism. In *France* a battalion of armed soldiers prepares to board a frigate moored off a coastal port. Emaciated French soldiers subsist on soup maigre, frogs and bare bones. An officer points to a military banner decorated with the hopeful words *Vengence et le Bon Bier et Bon Beuf de Angletere*. However weak and puny the French military, Catholic clergy are once again depicted as living off whatever fat the impoverished land can yield; in the far distance two women plough a sterile promontory. A corpulent friar sharpens an axe, clearly lusting after English blood. He has readied a horse-drawn cart containing instruments of torture and execution, and a copy of a plan for a *Monastère dans Black Friars à Londre* after the invasion. Below Hogarth's images is David Garrick's warning verse:

> With lanthern jaws, and croaking Gut,
> See how the half-starv'd Frenchmen Strut;
> And call us English Dogs!

But soon we'll teach these braging Foes,
That *Beef* & *Beer* give heavier Blows,
Than Soup & Roasted Frogs

The Priests inflam'd with righteous hopes,
Prepare their Axes, Wheels & Ropes,
To Bend the Stiff neck't Sinner.

But should they sink in coming over:
Old Nick may fish twixt *France* and *Dover*
And catch a Glorious dinner*!*

* *England* (1756). In *England*, by contrast with *France*, the British Nation appears prosperous. The scene is set in the tavern courtyard of the Duke of Cumberland (the victorious hero/butcher of the battle at Culloden that ended the '45, the last serious Jacobite threat). At the centre of the picture are good beer and an ample round of English beef ('Roast & Boil'd every Day'). Life is good for Britannia. Brave grenadiers defend her government and the English way of life. The beef itself is protected by a regimental sword and supported by Thomas Arne's nationalist ditty of 1740: *Rule Britannia/Britannia Rules the Waves/Britons never will be Slaves*!

After Hogarth

How successful was Hogarth in harnessing beef consumption to nationalism and the ideology of state formation? In advertisements and posters for military recruiting his puppet-like representations of starving French soldiers (in *Calais Gate* and *France*) were juxtaposed with images of the well-fed British military (in *England*) all the way through to the end of the Napoleonic Wars in 1815. A cantata *O the Roast Beef of Old England*, probably composed by Theodosius Forrest, the son of Hogarth's old friend Ebenezer Forrest, was sung at public performances in English gardens and taverns and at the weekly meetings of the Sublime Society of Beefsteaks. Its lyrics are interwoven with characters from *Calais Gate*: 'Renowned Sir-Loin, oft-times decreed/The theme of English ballad.'

The last verse of Forrest's cantata has Hogarth's Highlander singing 'O! the beef the bonny, bonny beef/when roasted nice and brown;/I wish I had a slice of thee,/how sweet it would gang down!'[31] In 1757 Hogarth accepted a sought-after position at the royal court—Serjeant Painter to the King, no less.

Do such accolades indicate a job well done on Hogarth's part? Not necessarily. Though the literary entrepreneur John Trusler allowed that Hogarth's patriotic prints 'at the time of publication must have had great effect',[32] little or no actual evidence is offered in support of such a claim. Looking forward, moreover, Hogarth's influence on the formation of national identity and on the war effort cannot confidently be disentangled from the effects of the exertions of other Georgian artists who were just as inflammatory. In this regard, to Hogarth's labours must at least be added those of Bunbury, Collet, Cruikshank, Gillray, Richardson, Rowlandson and Adam Smith.

But Hogarth's painterly linking of roast beef with English patriotism and nationalism merged into and actually did encourage the growth of two other movements. One was the massive increase in beef consumption, the other a greater sensitivity towards animal suffering. Though both movements quickly became robust hallmarks of modernity, their coincidence was not a happy one. The increase in beef consumption during the second half of the eighteenth century was accompanied by a parallel decline in public hygiene in densely populated urban areas. Between metropolitan Lambeth and Greenwich, for example, the torrents of slaughtered animals' blood, offal, fat and unwanted body parts were routinely flushed into porous underground cellars, eventually working their way into the Thames estuary, upriver and down. The royal river Thames was widely condemned as a cesspool of disease, the daily confirmation of which was expressed in irate letters to the press and in poetry, literature and moral philosophy. In addition to anger at the contamination of its waterways by London's numerous slaughterhouses, fish markets and tanneries, there was a mounting visceral reaction towards the sight, the sound and the smell of animals as reputedly hard-hearted butchers transformed them into edible objects.[33]

That these tender sensibilities did not undermine the meteoric increase in beef consumption was made possible by the ingenious solution of altogether removing animal slaughter from the public gaze. Yet it was not in Hogarth's England that the modern regime of invisibilized slaughterhouses was invented and first put into practice. It was in Napoleonic France.

Iconography: Hogarth

Beer Street, 1751, engraved etching
Beggar's Opera, The, 1728, oil on canvas
Bruiser, The, 1763, printed etching
Columbus Breaking the Egg, 1752, printed etching
Cruelty's Reward (*The Four Stages of Cruelty* 4), 1751
Election Entertainment, An (*Humours of an Election* 1), 1754, oil on canvas
England (*Invasion Series* 2), 1756, engraved etching
Enraged Musician, The, 1741, engraved etching
Evening (*Four Times of the Day* 3), 1738, printed engraving
First Stage of Cruelty, The, 1751, printed engraving
France (*Invasion Series* 1), 1756, engraved etching
Calais Gate, Or O the Roast Beef of Old England, 1748–49, printed engraving
Gin Lane, 1751, engraved etching
Hogarth: The Painter and his Pug, 1747, oil on canvas
Hudibras' First Adventure (*Hudibras* 3), 1727, engraved etching
Idle 'Prentice Executed at Tyburn, The (*Industry and Idleness* 11), 1747, engraved etching
Industrious 'Prentice Married to his Master's Daughter (*Industry and Idleness* 6), 1747, engraved etching
Jane Hogarth, c.1740, retouched printed engraving
Lady's Death, The (*Marriage à la Mode* 6), 1745, oil on canvas
March to Finchley, The, 1749, oil on canvas
Mr. Wood's Dog Vulcan, c.1735, oil on canvas
Noon (*Four Times of the Day* 2), 1738, printed engraving
Portrait of Mary Edwards, 1742, oil on canvas
Sancho Panzo's Feast, c.1725–34, printed engraving

Second Stage of Cruelty, The, 1751, printed engraving
Shrimp Girl, c.1740–45, oil on canvas
Southwark Fair, 1731, engraved etching
South Sea Scheme, The, 1721, printed engraving
Taste in High Life, or Taste à la Mode, 1742, oil on canvas
Transubstantiation Satirized, n.d., aquatint etching

Notes

1. The self-signed 'Brito-phil' of British art, Hogarth declared himself the great champion of aesthetic nationalism. In a widely circulated letter he attacked '[p]icture-Jobbers from abroad who continually import shiploads of Dead Christs, Holy Families, Madonnas, and other dismal, dark subjects, neither entertaining nor ornamental … and fix on us poor Englishmen the character of universal dupes' (1737: 385).
2. Anon., *The Craftsman*, June 1738.
3. On the complex development of human–animal relationships and canine petting practices in eighteenth-century Britain see Paulson (1979: Chap. 5); Thomas (1983: 101–08); and MacInnes (2003).
4. On Hogarth's *Portrait of Mary Edwards* see especially Bindman (1997: 47–48), Uglow (1997: 363–65). Paulson (1971: i, 335–36) identifies Mary Edwards' dog as a spaniel, though Einberg identifies him as a 'large adoring hound' (2016: 246). If a hound is his breed, then perhaps he is a pointer.
5. There are other pets who entered Hogarth's life and for whom he obviously felt great personal affection. In *Jane Hogarth* (c.1740), for example, he portrayed his wife with a lamb on her lap—a masculinist, if sweet, declaration that she was his pet lamb and in need of his protection and care. See also Hogarth's *Mr. Wood's Dog Vulcan* (c.1735).
6. Below 'they Just Defence' the writing on the scroll is indecipherable. The visible eight lines are usually identified as from a portion of Elizabeth I's Tilbury address, though Elizabeth Einberg (2016: 246) supports the view that it is a 'close adaptation' of Addison's tragedy *Cato*, 1713, Act III. However, we may never know its precise provenance, in part because there are at least three extant versions of Elizabeth's speech.
7. For example, aboard the sixty-gun *HMS Nottingham* in the patriotic *Captain Lord George Graham in his Cabin* (1745), painted not long after

Graham had captured several French privateers, Trump can be seen intruding on the space of the captain's pet dog.

8. For more on the cultivation of peculiarly English bulldogs see Rogers (2003: 123–45) and Paulson (1979: Chap. 5; and 2018, forthcoming). Paulson (2018, forthcoming) is of the strong view that Hogarth deliberately chose 'attack dogs' as his canine companions, and that his dogs in his 1747 *Self-Portrait* and *The Bruiser* (1763) are bulldogs:

   > Hogarth's dog in the painting [the *Self Portrait*] … was not a pug … but a pit bull, or what then would have been called an English bulldog or early type of bull terrier. In retrospect, would Hogarth have associated himself with a lapdog? His own face in the self-portrait shows a prominent scar on his forehead, suggesting his affinity with attack dogs. (Paulson 2018: 25)

9. For example, see the dogs depicted in Hogarth's *South Sea Scheme* (1721), *Sancho Panzo's Feast* (c.1725–34), *Gin Lane* (1751) and *Columbus Breaking the Egg* (1752). In *The Lady's Death* (1745), a skeletal dog frantically snatches a decapitated pigs's head adorning a festive dinner table (and see Chap. 1, p. 2).

10. On the visual context of Hogarth's execution images see Carrabine (2011).

11. Hogarth was also the social reformer whose outraged depiction of throwing at cocks in *The First Stage of Cruelty* (1751) is, in all likelihood, an allegory of his enmity to France. On this opinion see also Ireland (1793, 2: 55). This self-same Hogarth also gave voice to the French aristocrat who reacted to his viewing of the horrors of his *Cockpit* (1759) with an outraged 'Sauvage! Sauvage! Sauvage!'

12. Anon. (1851: 21–22).

13. Ireland (1791, 1: 53–54). Again: 'From what they [i.e. foreigners] have witnessed in the streets, they have been heard to designate us the most cruel people on earth' (Curling 1851: 13).

14. *The Tatler*, 29 April 1710. See also the comments by the puritan William Vaughan (1630: 3), for example, that beef made the English courageous and undaunted in the face of danger.

15. In times of war and blockade, the eighteenth-century British navy's demand for salted beef was insatiable. See also Ritvo, who argues that when Britain was vulnerable to blockade, 'meat was a particularly valuable commodity in international competition, because the ability of especially urban industrial workers to buy it was an index of British com-

mercial prowess, and because, according to popular belief, it was the consumption of red meat that distinguished brave and brawny soldiers from puny, sniveling Frenchmen' (1987: 47).
16. Uglow (1997: 274).
17. For more discussion of the Diana and Actaeon myth see Chap. 3 above (at pp. 51–52).
18. Rogers (2003: 94).
19. Rogers (2003: 94).
20. A report has it that Hogarth and Thornhill had joined the Society because they were 'stimulated by their love of the painter's art, and the equally potent charm of conviviality' (Timbs 1872: 113).
21. The following poem—recited at one of the Society's weekly meetings—shows how thoroughly committed was its pained author to the ideology and practice of beef consumption (quoted in Timbs 1872: 109):

> ON AN OX
> Most noble creature of the horned race,
> Who labours at the plough to earn thy grass,
> And yielding to the yoke, shows man the way
> To bear his servile chains, and to obey
> More haughty tyrants, who usurp the sway,
> Thy sturdy sinews till the farmer's grounds,
> To thee the grazier owes his hoarded pounds:
> 'Tis by thy labour, we abound in malt,
> Whose powerful juice the meaner slaves exalt;
> And when grown fat, and fit to be devour'd,
> The pole-ax frees thee from the teasing goard:
> Thus cruel man, to recompense thy pains,
> First works thee hard, and then beats out thy brains.

22. Arnold (1871: 4, 9–10). Alongside mention of the Society of Scare-Crows and Skeletons, the Confederacy of the Kings, the Kit-Kat Club (reputedly named for mutton pies after Christopher Cat) and the Club of Fat-Men, the first reference to a 'Beef-Steak Club' was likely made in *The Spectator* (1710–11, March, no. 9), though this also suggests that it had been founded in Queen Anne's time. On the Beefsteak Society see also Timbs (1872: 105–35).

23. Nevertheless, a good hint of the frolicks at SSBS dinners is contained in an anecdote about Hogarth and some of his rambunctious friends. In mid-1746 Hogarth, John Hoadly and David Garrick staged an irreverent play. This amateurish afternoon's carnivorous caper was a bawdy parody of Shakespeare's *Julius Caesar*. In it Hogarth acted as Caesar's ghost Grilliardo—the Devil's Cook—and Garrick played Cassiarse. When Grilliardo, the butcher/cook, enters the scene, Brutarse (Hoadly) asks him 'Zounds, who are you?' To this Grillardo (Hogarth) replies:

> I am Old Nick's Cook – & hither am I come
> To slice some Steaks from off thy Brawny Bum,
> Make Sausage of thy guts, & Candles of thy Fat,
> And cut thy Cock off, to regale his Cat.

(Cited in Paulson [1979: 259], who suggests 'given what we know of Hogarth's piety, the casting was appropriate'.)

24. Arnold (1871: 13).
25. Porter (1993: 59).
26. Fielding introduces 'The King's Old Courtier' with an animated conversation between Lady Apshinken (i.e. Queen Caroline) and Susan (the Queen's cook), in the course of which the latter laments (Fielding 1731: 54; see further, Train 1845: 108–09):

> So, as the smell of the old English sentimentality used to invite people in, that of the present is to keep them away … Would I had lived in those days! I wish I had been born a cook in an age when there was some business for one, before we had learnt this French politeness and been taught to dress our meat by nations that have no meat to dress.

27. Fielding (1731: 54). See further Roberts (1964), who provides an excellent account of Fielding's *Grub-Street Opera* and of Leveridge's role in the creation of the extended melody.
28. For a reading of *Calais Gate* see Beirne (2018, forthcoming).
29. For example, see and hear the awful cacophonies in Hogarth's *Hudibras Encounters the Skimmington* (1726), *The Enraged Musician* (1741)—in which a songbird mouths 'Vivat Rex'—*Southwark Fair* (1731), *The Idle 'Prentice Executed at Tyburn* (1747) and *March to Finchley* (1750). On the importance of music to Hogarth and on the precise depiction of old instruments and music scores in his art, see Simon (2007: 243–56).

30. Although *Transubstantiation Satirized* is marked 'Hogarth pinxit' (i.e. painted by Hogarth), Elizabeth Einberg (2016: 133) comments that it might have been executed by Richard Livesay after Hogarth. But the British Museum (Image AN548331001) has a printed engraving of Hogarth's *Enthusiasm Delineated* (c.1760) with marginal notations by the artist himself, including a rough sketch of some of the key elements in *Transubstantiation Satirized*.
31. Forrest (1752). See further Rice (2013) and Roberts (1964).
32. Trusler (1833: 114; similarly, see Nichols 1781: 111; and Bindman 1997: 23, 45). Robin Simon has commented that 'Hogarth is one of the few artists of whatever kind who have formed the imaginative consciousness of a nation. Indeed, he shares that distinction only with Shakespeare and Dickens. Together, they remain the three British artists who have made a comparable impact world wide' (2007: 275).
33. See Chap. 2 above (pp. 20, 39n10) for discussion of the legislative banning of slaughterhouses from cities and their relocation to invisibilized sites in rural areas.

Bibliography

Anon. (1851). *A Frenchman's Visit to England*. London: W.N. Wright.

Arnold, Walter. (1871). *The Life and Death of the Sublime Society of Beef Steaks*. London: Bradbury, Evans, & Co.

Beirne, Piers. (2018, forthcoming). 'Raw, Roast or Half-Baked? Hogarth's Beef in *Calais Gate*.'

Bindman, David. (1997). *Hogarth and His Times*. Berkeley, CA: University of California Press.

Carrabine, Eamonn. (2011). 'The Iconography of Punishment: Execution Prints and the Death Penalty,' *Howard Journal of Criminal Justice*, 50(5): 452–64.

Curling, Henry. (1851). *A Lashing for the Lashers: Being an Exposition of the Cruelties Practised Upon the Cab and Omnibus Horses of London*. London: W.N. Wright.

Einberg, Elizabeth. (2016). *William Hogarth: A Complete Catalogue of the Paintings*. New Haven, CT: Yale University Press, for the Paul Mellon Centre for Studies in British Art.

Fielding, H. (c.1731). (1968). 'The King's Old Courtier.' In: Edgar V. Roberts (ed.), Fielding, *The Grub-Street Opera*. Lincoln, NE: University of Nebraska Press, 54.

Forrest, Theodosius. (c.1752). (1781). 'The Roast Beef of Old England. A Cantata,' *The Vocal Magazine, or, Compleat British Songster*, 1: 6.
Hogarth. (1737). 'Weekly essay, from Britophil,' *The London Magazine*, July: 385–86.
Ireland, John. (1791). *Hogarth Illustrated*. London: J. & J. Boydell.
Ireland, John. (1793). *Hogarth Illustrated*. 2 vols. London: J. and J. Boydell.
Ireland, Samuel. (1794). *Graphic Illustrations of Hogarth*. 2 vols. London: R. Faulder and J. Egerton.
MacInnes, Ian. (2003). 'Mastiffs and Spaniels: Gender and Nation in the English Dog,' *Textual Practice*, 17(1): 21–40.
Nichols, John. (1781). (1833). *Anecdotes of William Hogarth Written by Himself*. London: J.B. Nichols and Son.
Paulson, Ronald. (1971). *Hogarth: His Life, Art, and Times*. New Haven, CT: Yale University Press.
Paulson, Ronald. (1979). *Popular and Polite Art in the Age of Hogarth and Fielding*. Notre Dame, IN: University of Notre Dame Press.
Paulson, Ronald. (2018, forthcoming). 'Hogarth's Ghost, His Pug, and the Pit Bull: A Memoir.' In: Bernd W. Krysmanski (ed.), *250 Years On: New Light on William Hogarth*. Krysman Press.
Porter, Roy. (1993). 'Consumption: Disease of the Consumer Society?' In: John Brewer and Roy Porter (eds.), *Consumption and the World of Goods*. London: Routledge, 58–81.
Rice, Paul F. (2013). 'Eighteenth-Century British Patriotic and Political Cantatas.' In: *Sharing the Voices: The Phenomenon of Singing*. St. John's: Memorial University of Newfoundland, 185–94.
Ritvo, Harriet. (1987). *The Animal Estate: The English and Other Creatures in Victorian England*. Cambridge: Harvard University Press.
Roberts, Edgar V. (1964). 'Henry Fielding and Richard Leveridge: Authorship of the "Roast Beef of Old England",' *Huntington Library Quarterly*, 27(2): 175–81.
Rogers, Ben. (2003). *Beef and Liberty*. London: Chatto & Windus.
Simon, Robin. (2007). *Hogarth, France & British Art: The Rise of the Arts in 18th-Century Britain*. Cornwall: Hogarth Arts and TJ International.
Thomas, Keith. (1983). *Man and the Natural World: Changing Attitudes in England 1500–1800*. New York: Oxford University Press.
Timbs, John. (1872). *Clubs and Club Life in London. With anecdotes of Its Famous Coffee Houses, Hostelries, and Taverns, from the Seventeenth Century to the Present Time*. London: John Camden Hotten.

Train, Joseph. (1845). *Historical and Statistical Account of the Isle of Man*. 2 vols. London: Simpkin, Marshall.

Trusler, John. (1833). *The Works of William Hogarth; In a Series of Engravings with Descriptions, and a Comment on their Moral Tendency*. London: Jones.

Uglow, Jenny. (1997). *Hogarth: A Life and a World*. New York: Farrar, Straus and Giroux.

Vaughan, William. (1630). *The Newlanders Cure*. London: N[icholas] O[kes].

6

Gallous Stories or Dirty Deeds? Representing Parricide in J.M. Synge's *Playboy of the Western World*

Piers Beirne and Ian O'Donnell

Gallous, 1. n., alt. gallows; 2. adj., deserving to be hanged; 3. daring, wicked, mischievous; 4. type of humour.

Preamble

I'll say a strange man is a marvel with his mighty talk; but what's a squabble in your back-yard and the blow of a loy have taught me that there's a great gap between a gallous story and a dirty deed. (*The Playboy of the Western World* (Act 3, ll. 570–73))

John Millington Synge's *Playboy of the Western World* (henceforth, *Playboy*) was in the vanguard of the Irish literary renaissance at the beginning of the twentieth century. Its narrative was never quite finished to the satisfaction of its author, John Millington Synge (1871–1909). *Playboy*'s first public performance was on 26 January 1907 at the Abbey Theatre in

---

This chapter adds a few details to Piers Beirne and Ian O'Donnell, 'Gallous Stories or Dirty Deeds? Representing Parricide in J.M. Synge's *Playboy of the Western World,*' 2010, *Crime Media Culture*, 6(1): 27–48. © Piers Beirne and Ian O'Donnell.

© The Author(s) 2018
P. Beirne, *Murdering Animals*, Palgrave Studies in Green Criminology, https://doi.org/10.1057/978-1-137-57468-8_6

Dublin. Staged by the Irish National Theatre Society, the performance was jointly directed by Synge himself and by his friends, the poet W.B. Yeats and the English playwright and theatre patron Lady Augusta Gregory. *Playboy*'s first run was short lived. Following noisy protests by the audience and the subsequent deployment of the Dublin Metropolitan Police in the auditorium, future performances were abruptly cancelled less than a week after opening night. Four years later—in Philadelphia and afterwards in New York City—similar disturbances accompanied the Abbey Theatre's inaugural touring production of *Playboy* in the United States.[1]

The culture wars and associated frenzy around the play partly reflect the transition of a particular colonial society lurching towards national self-determination. Our primary focus here, however, is more the problem of how well the story of the parricide in *Playboy* represented, to put it crudely, the situation of intergenerational violence at the time when the play was first being imagined and performed.[2]

In short, while Synge's authorial intentions are not open to complete reclamation, was the violent parricide around which *Playboy*'s plot swirls a gallous story or a dirty deed? In addressing this question about fin-de-siècle Ireland we attach to literary criticism's preoccupation with authorial intentions and textual meanings a sociological analysis of interpersonal violence. To cultural criminology's concerns with the representation of crime and harm in the media, we add the cultural productions of playwrights and the social contexts and effects of their play(s). While *Playboy*'s parricidal Christy Mahon is not as well known in criminology as Foucault's murderous French peasant Pierre Rivière, to a certain extent the same issues are involved in the unravelling of their respective identities. Who was he and how was he so identified? Why did he do what he did? Within what power structures was he entrapped?

Murder and Mayhem in Three Acts: Synopsis

Playboy is a story in three acts. It is set in a shebeen (a small pub), in remote County Mayo on Ireland's western coast. At the beginning of Act 1 the shebeen's dramatis personae include Michael James Flaherty (the publican), his daughter Margaret Flaherty (known as Pegeen Mike), her second cousin Shawn Keogh, the Widow Quin and several small farmers. Simmering away in the background, though offstage for the entire play, are the authoritarian threats posed respectively by the parish priest Father Reilly, by the police (the 'peelers') and by other elements of English rule in Ireland (Fig. 6.1).

Act 1 begins on a dark autumn night when a young, landless peasant, Christy Mahon, stumbles frightened, tired and dirty into the shebeen. There is considerable speculation among the assembled customers that this young man might be on the run from the law. All are stunned when Christy claims, at first with reticence but soon thereafter with increasing boldness, that eleven days earlier he killed his father. Among the reactions to Christy's Oedipal claim are 'There's a daring fellow', 'Oh, glory be to God!' and '[*with great respect*] that was a hanging crime, mister honey. You should have had a good reason for doing the like of that' (1: 262–65). Additionally, Pegeen asks 'Did you shoot him dead?' 'Did you do it with a hilted knife, perhaps?' inquires Michael. Christy, adamant that he is a law-fearing man, blurts out by way of an explanation:

> I just riz the loy [a long shovel] and let fall the edge of it on the ridge of his skull, and he went down at my feet like an empty sack, and never let a grunt or groan from him at all. (1: 279–81)

Christy implies that he committed this deed because his father had treated him very roughly. He rues, moreover, that his father was 'a dirty man, God forgive him, and he getting old and crusty, the way I couldn't put up with him at all' (1: 266–68). Later in the play, Christy embellishes his motive by stating that just before the murder, while they were digging potatoes together, his father was demanding that Christy marry the Widow Casey (so that the father would 'have her hut to live in and her gold to drink' [2: 126–27]). But Christy bluntly refused his father's request, complaining that Widow Casey was much older than he and, moreover, that she was mean and unattractive and that, anyway, for six weeks had been his wet nurse. Then, said Christy, somewhat redescribing the murder:

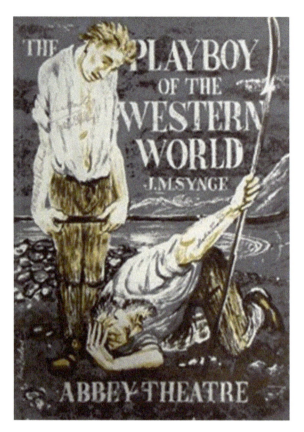

Fig. 6.1 Representing parricide (Source: Abbey Theatre Poster, 1968. Reproduced with permission of Abbey Theatre)

'She's too good for the like of you,' says he, 'and go on now or I'll flatten you out like a crawling beast has passed under a dray.' 'You will not if I can help it,' says I. 'Go on,' says he, 'or I'll have the divil making garters of your limbs tonight.' 'You will not if I can help it,' says I … 'God have mercy on your soul,' says he, lifting a scythe; 'or on your own,' says I, raising the loy … He gave a drive with the scythe, and I gave a lep to the east. Then I turned around with my back to the north, and I hit a blow on the ridge of his skull, laid him stretched out, and he split to the knob of his gullet. (2: 137–54)

After his announcement of the murderous deed, Christy at once commands the fear and the grudging admiration of the local men for his bravery and also the amorous attentions of young and middle-aged women alike. Pegeen, who is informally betrothed to the fawning Shawn Keogh, quickly falls in love with Christy, eagerly offering him a job as a pot boy and a bed for the night with board. After some tussling and squabbling for Christy's affection between Pegeen and the Widow Quin, Act 1 ends with:

> CHRISTY ([…] *settles his bed slowly, feeling the quilt with immense satisfaction*) […] it's great luck and company I've won me in the end of time – two fine women fighting for the likes of me – till I'm thinking this night wasn't I a foolish fellow not to kill my father in the years gone by. (1: 593–97)

Act 2 begins with three village girls entering the shebeen in search of the celebrated man who has killed his father. Anxious that Christy might already have gone, one of the girls, Susan Brady, worries to another 'you'd have a right so to follow after him, Sara Tansey, and you the one yoked the ass cart and drove ten miles to set your eyes on the man bit the yellow lady's nostril on the northern shore' (2: 44–47). On seeing Christy, the girls, Magi-like, present him with ducks' eggs, cake and a chicken, and then make him breakfast. Christy and the Widow Quin, who buried her children and killed her husband, are referred to by Sara as 'heroes' (2: 163).[3]

The love-match between Christy and Pegeen developing rapidly, she compliments him as 'you a fine lad with the great savagery to destroy your da' (2: 277). However, later in the same day—after the local sports competitions (at which Christy wins prizes in the horse race and at jumping) and after Pegeen agrees to marry Christy—a man with bloodied head bandages bursts through the door of the shebeen.

Like an old-fashioned patriarch full of fire and brimstone, he announces that he is Old Mahon and that eleven days ago his lazy son Christy ('a dirty stuttering lout' [2: 434]) tried to kill him with a shovel. The son had then set off on foot from Kerry, where the blow was struck, and traipsed across several counties and over many miles to arrive in Mayo, with his battered father, unbeknownst to him, in dogged pursuit. Protective of

Christy, the Widow Quin informs Old Mahon that his son has already left for the coast to catch a steamer and escape capture. Off goes Old Mahon and, for a few hours at least, Christy is spared his father's wrath.

But Old Mahon suddenly reappears: '[*Hubbub outside. Old Mahon rushes in, followed by all the Crowd and Widow Quin. He makes a rush at Christy, knocks him down and begins to beat him*]' (3: 428). The fickle crowd now turns against Christy, believing that with his gallous story he had lied and fooled them into thinking that he had committed the brave act of killing his father. Christy then delivers his father a savage blow on the head with a shovel. In the ensuing quiet it seems that, this time, Christy has finally done the deed; now, doubtless, a double murder for him to be telling the girls. However, with plot and counterplot changing at a bewildering rate, circumstances once again take an unexpected turn. Instead of adulating his murderous act, and wishing not to be seen as accomplices to murder, members of the crowd, including his new love, Pegeen, try to truss Christy up with a rope in order to deliver him to the police to answer for his dirty deed.

In the final scene, the still un-murdered Old Mahon reappears in order to rescue his son from the mob. Christy and Old Mahon manage to exit together, the arm of one firmly around the other. Off they go into the sunset, the son now the master of future fights and the father willingly subservient. All the villagers are now left to the solace and to the peace and quiet of their solitary porter, while a distraught Pegeen wails:

> [*Putting her shawl over her head and breaking out into wild lamentations.*]
> Oh my grief, I've lost him surely. I've lost the only playboy of the western world. (3: 652–54)

Riot Revisited

At the time, by the media, by Irish nationalists and by Unionists, then afterwards chiefly by literary scholars, numerous explanations have been given as to why the first production of *Playboy* was greeted with such hostility in Dublin. Foremost among these is that the production was a great insult to Irish nationalists: to them Synge's characters, in his depiction of their way of life and their language, seemed so backward and fickle. *The Freeman's Journal*, for example, objected that:

> [*Playboy* is an] unmitigated, protracted libel upon Irish peasant men and, worse still, upon Irish peasant girlhood. The blood boils with indignation as one recalls the incidents, expressions, ideas of this squalid, offensive production, incongruously styled a comedy in three acts … No adequate idea can be given of the barbarous jargon, the elaborate and incessant cursings of these repulsive creatures.[4]

Intergenerational conflict and parricide were not the exemplars of a pure Irish way of life that progressive and independent-minded nationalists wished to see projected in, of all places, Ireland's new national theatre, with its founding manifesto determined to portray Ireland as 'the home of an ancient idealism'. Moreover, to that great majority of nationalists who were also Catholics, it was unforgivable that Synge, a member of the Protestant Ascendancy, dared to vaunt his anti-familism, his anti-clericalism and his anti-papism on the national stage. To the protesters, moreover, the image of Irish womanhood conjured up by Synge in *Playboy*—symbolized by the loose morals and the flagrant flaunting of the females, both adult and juvenile, all of whom fussed and fawned over the young stranger Christy Mahon, and he portrayed somewhat as a Christ-like figure—was an untruthful affront to the natural modesty and chaste manners of the gentler sex. George Bretherton writes of Christy's characterization: 'there can be little doubt that he is meant to represent and remind us of some aspects of Christ, that his entry into a community, apotheoses, and rejection by that community followed by his own leave taking, an ascendancy of sorts, echoes the progress of Christ on earth'.[5] Perhaps, too, for most patriarchal tastes *Playboy*'s female leads were portrayed as too strong in character, too independent of men and not committed enough to familism. For its critics, the blatant reference to female undergarments in the use of the term 'shift' encapsulated all that was wrong with the play. (We return soon enough to the relationships among Synge's dialogue, cultural sensibilities and the background circumstances of lethal violence)

Such contemporary interpretations of *Playboy* no doubt stemmed largely from Irish nationalism's tendency to identify every nook and cranny of all social practices and institutions, including the scripts and props of playwrights, as sites of warfare for Irish independence, for national identity and against English imperialism. This all-consuming Us/Them tendency might have had its political advantages, of course, though it belied the difficulty that, like all the best stories, *Playboy* was and is open to multiple and competing interpretations. Over the years, productions of *Playboy* sometimes emphasized its imagination and its poetic language, sometimes its numerous comic moments and sometimes its violence, especially the fight between Old Mahon and Christy in Act 3.[6]

Synge's characters in *Playboy* are neither the drunken Irish sloths so lampooned on the English stage nor the embodiment of Irish pre-conquest virtues. They instead include assertive and independent women, flirting girls, heavy drinkers, a murderous widow and a wimpish, priest-terrified coward. Catholicism is repeatedly mocked and vilified, as are other authoritarian tendencies like patriarchy and English colonialism. During the tumult about the play, in an interview of 1907 with 'A.F.' in *The Mail*, Synge was asked:

> [T]he main idea of your play is not a pretty one. You take the worst form of murderer, a parricide, and set him up on a pedestal to be worshipped by the simple, honest people of the West. Is this probable?

To which he responded, 'No, it is not; and it does not matter. Was Don Quixote probable? And still it is art'. Synge was then asked by A.F., 'What was it that at all suggested the main idea of the play?' To this he replied:

> 'Tis a thing that really happened. I knew a young fellow in the Arran [sic] Islands who had killed his father, and the people befriended him and sent him off to America.

The exchange continued:

> But did the girls make love to him because he had killed his father, and for that only, the sorry-looking, bedraggled, and altogether repelling figure though he was personally?

No, those girls did not, but mine do … It is to bring out the humour of the situation. It is a comedy, an extravaganza, made to amuse … I don't care a rap how the people take it. I never bother whether my plots are typical Irish or not, but my methods are typical.

Two days later, in a letter published in *The Irish Times*, Synge (1907a), complained that his views 'had been rather misunderstood in an interview which appeared in one of the evening papers' and, moreover:

> The Playboy of the Western World is not a play with 'a purpose' in the modern sense of the word, but although parts of it are, or are meant to be, extravagant comedy, still a great deal that is in it, and a great deal more that is behind it, is perfectly serious, when looked at in a certain light […] There are, it may be hinted, several sides to *The Playboy*.[7]

A few months after the Abbey riots, in a letter about various interpretations of *Playboy*, including whether its events and characters were possible or not, Synge harrumphed that:

> It isn't quite accurate to say, I think, that the thing is a generalization from a single case. *If* the idea had occurred to me I could and would just as readily [have] written the thing, as it stands, without the Lynchehaun case or the Aran case. The story – in its ESSENCE – is probable, given the psychic state of the locality. I used the cases afterwards to controvert critics who said it was *impossible*. Amen.[8]

Playboys and Parricides

The notion of 'playboy' at work in *Playboy* is not only that of a man of gaiety and pleasure. Most of all, it has a distinctively Janus-faced character of past and present. In the past it represents firmly embedded heroic qualities. Thus, as Christy's autobiography is dragged out from him, he takes on a new lease of life, gains more confidence and begins to speak in rhythms not altogether unlike the warrior-poet heroes of ancient Gaelic myth. Indeed, Christy's language and tenor variously reflect rival Irish poetic traditions. For example, when voicing his love for Pegeen, especially in tender passages, he embodies the rejected lover ubiquitous in Irish poetry; and his vicious speeches against his father reflect Gaelic cursing rituals.[9]

The central action in *Playboy*—Christy's violent blow to his father's head—in part displays Synge's deployment of the elemental myths associated with the ancient Gaelic beheading game in 'The Championship of Ulster'.[10] (Foremost among these myths are the feats of the heroic Cúchullain, a champion game player who was especially skilled at hurling.) Christy's actions, therefore, hint at continuity with legends past. At the same time, Christy's self-proclaimed brutal slaying of his father suggests a violent rupture with the past. Old Mahon is an 'Old Testament God',[11] all fire and brimstone and recrimination, a spoiled child grown into a savage patriarch. Christy, the youth, dares to slay this dragon, not once but twice, and in so doing liberates himself from the yoke of childhood, captures his own manhood, and is able spontaneously to enter a love-match. As Kiberd described it, 'By recreating some of the traits of the ancient hero in a puny peasant playboy, Synge offered his own caustic comment on the similarities and dissimilarities between the Irish past and present.'[12]

It is now worth returning to Synge's comment that he could just as easily have written *Playboy* 'as it stands, without the Lynchehaun case or the Aran case'. What does his comment imply about these cases' respective contributions to Synge's dramatic efforts? (For convenience we reverse their order of presentation.)

The 'Aran Case': William Maley's Parricide

In the 1880s and the 1890s the Aran Islands became the site of a provocative Darwinian-driven discourse about race. Struggles over the question of whether the racial and cultural purity of the islanders was similar to that of pre-conquest Aran appeared in anthropology and ethnography and were manifest in investigative visits by Gaelic

Leaguers and by J.M. Synge. Crucial questions concerned the degree to which the islanders had intermarried with the somewhat less pure stock on the mainland and how much their bloodlines had been diluted by Oliver Cromwell's installation on Inis Mór in 1652 of an English garrison (many of whose members chose to stay on after the cessation of hostilities).[13] The linguistic and cultural purity of the Aran Islands would be part of the cultural resurrection of an independent, Gaelic and Catholic Ireland.

At the suggestion of his friend W.B. Yeats, Synge visited the islands each summer from 1898 to 1902. In his book *The Aran Islands*, Synge recounted that on Inishmaan an old man, the oldest on the island, who was 'fond of telling me anecdotes – not folk tales' often spoke of:

> a Connaught man who in a fit of passion had killed his father with the blow of a spade and who then fled to the Aran Islands, where he placed himself at the mercy of some of the islanders with whom it was said he was related. They hid him in a hole – which the old man has shown me – and kept him safe for weeks, though the police came and searched for him, and he could hear their boots grinding on the stones over his head. In spite of a reward which was offered, the island was incorruptible, and after much trouble the man was safely shipped to America.[14]

On the old man's story Synge commented that '[t]his impulse to protect the criminal is universal in the west [of Ireland]' and, he said, it is partly due to the association between justice and the hated English jurisdiction, but even more directly:

> to the primitive feeling of these people, who are never criminals yet always capable of crime, that a man will not do wrong unless he is under the influence of a passion which is as irresponsible as a storm on the sea. If a man has killed his father, and is already sick and broken with remorse, they can see no reason why he should be dragged away and killed by the law. Such a man, they say, will be quiet [i.e. depressed] all the rest of his life, and if you suggest that punishment is needed as an example, they ask, "Would anyone kill his father if he was able to help it?"[15]

In Kiberd's words: 'The ethic here is existential: one is punished less *for* one's sins than *by* one's sins.'[16]

We believe that Synge's development of the character and actions of Christy Mahon was inspired by a 'real-life' parricide, namely, the slaying of Patrick Maley by his son William on 28 January 1873, at Calla, a remote part of County Galway. With suitable methodological and other sorts of care and caveats, several layers of detail about Maley's death can be uncovered from contemporaneous police records and newspaper reportage. While these are brief, amounting in total to little more than a few paragraphs, they contain many of the ingredients essential to making sense of this particular parricide and some of its consequences. They at least give us a sense of who William might have been and why he cracked a spade over his father's head after years of supporting him with wages earned in the US Navy. While there was for a time an ocean between them, and even if relations between the two men were less than harmonious, it seems perfectly natural that when William returned to *terra firma* he would think nothing of wanting to scratch a living from the soil beside his father.

The case was categorized as manslaughter in the *Outrage* report filed by the Royal Irish Constabulary (RIC), as follows:

> Patrick Maley, farmer and provision dealer, at about 9 o'clock, A.M., went to work in a potato garden next his house. His married son, William Maley, who lives next door, went into the garden and asked his father what he was doing; on receiving answer that he was sowing the ground, as it was his, the son denied it was his father's, and a struggle ensued, and William Maley struck his father on the head with a spade, from the effects of which he died about three hours after. The assailant absconded, and was arrested in Arran [sic] Island, but escaped. William Maley had been some years at sea, and had sent some money to his father, with which the latter traded. Having married on his return home, a division of the property was made, and dissatisfaction on the part of the son at the portion allotted to him, led to this outrage.

More details can be gleaned from a report published in the *Galway Express: Mayo, Roscommon, Clare and Limerick Advertiser* under the headline 'Awful Murder of a Father by His Own Son', though no reference is made in the newspaper report to an arrest.

> On Tuesday morning, the 28th ult., a quiet and elderly farmer, named Pat Maley, residing in Calla, seven miles from Clifden, was informed that his married son, William, was preparing a little paddock (not larger than an ordinary room in size) for early potatoes; he went out to prevent him, when a scuffle ensued; the son lifted his spade and struck the father with it; he fell insensible. The son rushed into the house, returned soon again to behold the prostrate parent. He seized him, helped him up, carried him insensible to his bed, and laid him on it, bleeding, but still living, though unable to speak. The son then changed his clothes, provided himself with what money he could find, and when informed the police were coming to arrest him, he walked slowly lest he police should notice him, and for the last two days no trace can be found. Some believe he drowned himself, as the sea was quite near his father's house, and he was seen last going in that direction; another report is, that he lay concealed in a relative's house until nightfall, and was seen leaving it when it was dark.[17]

Perhaps we can surmise from this that William, who carried his father indoors while he drew his final breaths, was not a remorseless killer who exulted in the destruction of a foe. This contrasts sharply with the braggart Christy Mahon who hit the father and ran, not waiting to see whether he was alive or dead.[18] One wonders what words, if any, were exchanged between father and son? Did the former advise the latter to flee? The newspaper reports that the father did not speak. But what escaped his lips as he lay on the small patch of land where he had scrabbled a living, or as he met his end indoors? Perhaps, having drawn his father's blood, William left with his blessing. He was informed the police were coming to arrest him, yet managed to walk slowly and surreptitiously away. Does this suggest other persons present felt no compunction to hold him until the authorities arrived or to alert the police to his direction of travel? That the possibility of suicide by drowning was raised further supports the notion of a killer whose actions were not universally condemned and whose grief and regret may have been all too evident.

Whatever the nature of community sentiment, the RIC put its members on alert and spared no effort trying to track down the fugitive. After the killing the very next issue of the biweekly *Police Gazette, or Hue-and-Cry* to appear carried this 'Wanted' notice:

> Description of William Malley, a seafaring man, who stands charged with having, on the 28th instant, at Calla, in Clifden district, murdered his father, – Malley: – Fresh cut on nose; gray eyes, medium make, 5 feet high, about 40 years of age, dark hair, red shirt; will endeavour to emigrate; may be dressed in Connemara frieze. The Constabulary at seaports are directed to use endeavours to arrest him.[19]

The subsequent issue of the *Gazette* carried a slightly different version with what was presumably a more accurate description.[20] Here, the culprit was described as being seven inches taller, he had lost one 'l' from his surname and had acquired whiskers, a more complicated nose and a strange accent.

> Description of William Maley, native of Calla, near Errismore, district of Clifden, stands charged with having, on the 28th January, 1873 … killed his father, Patrick Maley, by striking him on the head with a spade: – Fresh cut on nose, large feet, sailor-like appearance; gray eyes, hooked and drooped nose, pale fair complexion, long face, medium make, 5 feet 7 inches high, about 38 or 40 years of age, brown hair, red beard and whiskers, no hair on lip; wore an old black hat, gray Connemara frieze coat, old pilot trousers, gray Connemara frieze vest, red shirt; was 9 years a sailor, and will endeavour to reach a seaport and re-engage as a sailor; mixture of Scotch and English accent grafted on Irish accent.

The 'fresh cut' on the suspect's nose is curious. Does it imply an exchange of blows with his father and a more reciprocal engagement than has previously been thought? (In Synge's version blows are not exchanged, the father being dispatched with a single, sudden, swipe.) Or did Patrick strike first with William reacting in self-defence? Or did a keening mother claw at the face of her son, the killer? Or had William somehow injured himself immediately prior to the encounter with his father, thereby worsening his mood and increasing his irascibility?

William lived as a fugitive for some time and was reported to be hiding in the mountains or in fishing boats or on islands off the Connemara coast. To no avail, a reward of £20 was offered for his arrest. Before he swung his loy in the paddock, the sea had been a source of employment and a way of keeping the homestead intact through remittances. Now it became a route of escape from domestic circumstances that William had obliterated through his own actions; he is forced to take to the water again, however reluctantly. A record in the National Archives of Ireland, offers a clue about extradition proceedings begun in 1877, but there is nothing to indicate that they were executed; an application to increase the reward was refused, perhaps suggesting the level of priority associated with the case after the trail went cold.[21] We know that Maley was recently married when he took his father's life. But what happened to his wife? If he ever had a son of his own, what happened to him and did they come to blows?

The Case of James Lynchehaun

Besides the 'Aran case', Synge also referred to the 'Lynchehaun case.' What is the latter's bearing on *Playboy*?

Not a great deal is known about James Lynchehaun, though some basic details can be pieced together from the records of his trial, from newspaper accounts and from James Carney's biography *The Playboy & the Yellow Lady*.[22] James Lynchehaun (c.1860–c.1937) was born in Pulrannay, one mile from Achill Sound, County Mayo. After work as a school teacher and in England as a member of Manchester's Metropolitan Police, he was employed in 1888 as a bailiff or land agent at her Valley estate on Achill Island by Mrs Agnes MacDonnell, a wealthy English landowner. After six years and he and she having developed, for whichever of several reasons, a bitter hatred for each other, MacDonnell dismissed Lynchehaun from his position. In addition, she served him with notices of eviction from the small house that came with his job. On 6 October 1894, Lynchehaun, probably acting alone, set fire to her stables, a shed and her mansion and, with the use of horrific violence, savaged her to within an inch of her life. The next morning Lynchehaun was arrested for attempted murder.

On 20 October, while being transported for a deposition from Castlebar jail to Pulranny and onwards to the remains of Mrs MacDonnell's residence, Lynchehaun slipped away from police custody and into the night. A £300 reward was offered for his capture. (Compared with the

£20 bounty for William Maley, this shows that, as always, the bodily integrity of the rich is valued most highly.) *The Times* (of London) reported:

> Lyncheham [sic], the Achill islander who is charged with the murderous attack upon Mrs. Agnes M'Donnell … was rearrested at 2 o'clock this morning in the house of a man named Gallagher. It will be remembered that after he was arrested on the charge immediately after the outrage he effected his escape from the police, who have since been untiring in their efforts to recapture him. They watched the island so closely that it seemed all but impossible for him to get clear away, but it was generally believed that he was concealed in a cave waiting for the chance of a hooker taking him off at night. Gallagher's house was frequently searched in vain, but the police recently got information that he was concealed in a hole under Gallagher's bedroom, and he was there found. The police arrested Gallagher and a girl named Mary Masterson, a cousin of Lyncheham, on the charge of harbouring a criminal and assisting him in his efforts to escape from justice.[23]

Clearly, the 'impulse to protect the criminal' about which Synge had written (see p. 175), could be trumped by hard cash, the prospect of a large reward loosening an informant's tongue. Several months later, Lynchehaun was tried for attempted murder at the Castlebar Assizes. The jury found him guilty and he was sentenced to penal servitude for life. During the three-day trial evidence was presented by Mrs MacDonnell and others about what *The Times* described as 'an amount of barbarity on the part of the prisoner which was almost incredible'.[24] The same newspaper report continued:

> On the night of October 6 she [Mrs MacDonnell] was alone and in bed in the house, when she was aroused, and looking out, saw that her stables were on fire. The prisoner came to the house and asked for the keys to let out the horses. She gave them to him and was returning to the house when he caught her and dragged her into the burning building and made a determined effort to throw her into the flames. In her struggle she fell and he tried to strangle her, and struck her a tremendous blow on the head. She became insensible and remained unconscious for several days. The frontal

bone of her head was fractured. Her nose was bitten off, and also a portion of her lip by human teeth. One of her eyes was destroyed and the other permanently injured.

Having served seven years of his life sentence, Lynchehaun once again escaped, this time finding sanctuary in the US. After the failure of the British government's arduous attempts to have him extradited (the US Supreme Court even ruling in his favour), Lynchehaun apparently returned to Achill in disguise around 1917. He likely died in 1937 in Girvan, Scotland, aged about 77.[25]

In trying to uncover the influence of the Lynchehaun case on Synge's orchestration of characters and events in *Playboy*, one can begin by noting that Synge first visited County Mayo in 1904, the year before he began to write *Playboy*. (According to Bourgeois, *Playboy* was 'laboriously written in 1905–6'.)[26] The stage Synge sets is actually near a village on a wild coast of Mayo, far enough away from his treasured Aran Islands so as to do them neither a cultural nor literary disservice, nor to create an influx of gawkers there. It is otherwise hard to fathom, textually, why Synge relocated the parricide that he had heard about in Galway to Kerry (it would undoubtedly have made more sense to think of a Galway killer escaping to Mayo, than a Kerryman trekking halfway across the country). Indeed, Synge provides several textual clues about where in coastal Mayo the action of *Playboy* takes place and what events might have nurtured aspects of his play. These references, singly and collectively, lead us directly to James Lynchehaun, to his gruesome violence, and to his flight from British justice.

Thus, first, Christy refers to 'the heaths of Keel' (3: 480–1) and, curiously, to 'the madmen of Keel, eating muck and green weeds on the faces of the cliffs' (3: 580–1), implying that the action of *Playboy* occurs near the village of Keel on Achill Island. Moreover, there is a two-mile sandy beach nearby on which Christy Mahon became the playboy, with his triumphs in the carnival races and athletic competitions. Second, there is Susan Brady's comment to Sara Tansey about 'the man [who] bit the yellow lady's nostril on the northern shore' (2: 46–47). This is a direct description of Lynchehaun's facial mutilation of Agnes MacDonnell and, in addition, at that time 'yellow lady' was a derogatory Irish term for

English females, especially those women who were members of the hated forces of occupation or allied with them. Third, consider Widow Quin's promise, while trying to help Christy flee the crowd's murderous intent, 'I'll take him in the ferry to the Achill boat' (3: 537–38). The Achill boat was doubtless a ferry which plied the western coast and by which Christy and Lynchehaun might eventually have found safe passage from northern Mayo to escape justice on a transatlantic steamer.

Did Synge model Christy Mahon's situation on that of James Lynchehaun? The similarities noted above between the Lynchehaun case and Christy's situation in *Playboy* notwithstanding, there are crucial differences between them. For example, Lynchechaun tried to kill a propertied Englishwoman—an oppressor—and afterwards sought shelter with relatives and friends. But Christy was on the run for the self-proclaimed killing of his father and sought shelter in a community of strangers (we will have more to say on this later). The level of viciousness associated with Lynchehaun's assault on MacDonnell was widely condemned, though he himself—his willingness to poke his thumb in the eye of British justice, to escape from the police and from prison and to find sanctuary in the US—was doubtless viewed by the Irish, if not altogether with rapture, then with a degree of sympathy. However unusual and shocking, perhaps it was simply a form of agrarian outrage committed against the Anglo-Irish landlord class. Yet, for his self-proclaimed parricide, Christy was received, initially at least, with great respect and hero worship.

From the possible influence of two sensational case studies, we now ascend to a somewhat broader plateau.

Lethal Violence in *Fin-de-siècle* Ireland

Playboy was imagined and written at a time when life in post-famine Ireland continued to entail the virtual elimination of young rural men with few attachments and fewer prospects, who often found diversion in fighting. The abrupt decline in the country's population through starvation, disease, emigration and celibacy made society safer for those who remained. However, this was also a time when there was little respect for those who were enfeebled by age; infanticide occurred with troubling regularity and when it came to lethal brawling the elderly were not spared.[27] In this sense, the killing of an older man would not have been such a remote prospect so as to cause widespread shock and consternation. Indeed, it could be argued that that the response to *Playboy* reflected a metropolitan view of a rural idyll held by people who were trying to reinterpret an agricultural past from which they would hardly have been more than one generation removed.

It is amusing to think of farmers' sons and daughters standing outside the Abbey Theatre, or interrupting the performance within, to vent their displeasure at the offence caused to their sensibilities, given what they must have known about the quotidian hardships and brutality of rural life! That the protests took place a short walk from such a notorious red-light area as 'the Monto', where prostitution and all of the associated vices were rampant, adds a delicious twist to this irony. (The area features as 'Nighttown' in James Joyce's *Ulysses*; Leopold Bloom and Stephen Dedalus visit a brothel in the Monto during their perambulation on 16 June 1904).

Pimps, prostitutes and their clients must have wondered what all the fuss was about as they strolled past the Abbey Theatre in January 1907, en route to the brothels of Tyrone Street and the adjoining thoroughfares. While theatregoers expressed horror at the utterance of the word 'shift' and what they believed to be a scurrilous depiction of country life, all around them was evidence of carnality and its consequences. The appetite for criminal sex and violence was well established and clearly evident at the time that some Dubliners raised their voices against *Playboy*. The sexual hypocrisy of some of the protesters is captured in Synge's observation to Yeats that a young doctor had declared 'I wish medical etiquette permitted me to … point out among the protesters in the name of Irish virtue the patients I am treating for venereal disease.'[28]

By examining the *Outrage* reports held in the National Archives of Ireland for the period 1905 to 1907 we get a sense of the sort of homicide problem reported by the public to the police and documented in newspapers when Synge was finalizing the text of *Playboy* and during its ill-fated first performances.[29] During the triennium in question, RIC narratives were available for 106 incidents.[30] This yields an incomplete perspective on Irish homicide; the capital city is omitted as it was not policed by the RIC. However, the level of detail is better than from other sources and allows an examination of the characteristics of offenders and victims, the relationships between them, the causes of death and the sentences imposed.

So, what do we learn about the social circumstances of homicide at this time? Turning first to the key demographic variables of gender and age, we find that male victims predominated, accounting for three-quarters of incidents (75.5 per cent; 80/106). The average age of victims was 45.8, ranging from 3 years to 90 years. The offenders were considerably younger, averaging 35.6, with a narrower range from 16 years to 78 years. Looking at the geographical pattern, lethal violence was widely spread. Most counties experienced at least one killing over the period in question but a few were the location for as many as half a dozen. The Connaught counties of Galway and Mayo—where the Maley and Lynchehaun attacks took place—averaged two killings each year. There were noticeable clusters around the major cities of Belfast and Cork and, of course, Dublin where, according to the judicial statistics for Ireland, the Dublin Metropolitan Police dealt with fifty-four incidents of lethal violence between 1905 and 1907.

Around two-thirds of deaths resulted from beatings. These involved bare fists and booted feet, sticks and stones, household items that happened to be at hand during the encounter such as a poker, sweeping brush or porter bottle, and tools such as a spade, fork, hammer or flail. About one in four victims was stabbed or shot and the remainder died under a variety of circumstances, some being criminally injured by drunk drivers, one being strangled and one drowned. Christy Mahon's use of a spade to resolve a squabble with his father had the hallmark of a typical dispute where the harm caused was heavily dependent on whatever happened to be seized upon as a potential weapon. During spontaneous outbursts of violence the outcome was unpredictable and the opportunities afforded by the immediate physical environment were sometimes more important than the offender's intent. James Lynchehaun's *modus operandi* was quite different and statistically unusual; only 1 per cent of victims were strangled. So too was his persistence unusual; when throttling failed, he struck, bit and tried to burn Agnes MacDonnell. Her survival seems to have resulted from a peculiar resilience rather than a lack of intent on the part of her assailant. This was a woman of remarkable fortitude. In Carney's account she defied expectation to 'live on vigorously for another twenty-eight years, wearing a false nose, an eye-patch and a veil, constantly guarded by the police'.[31]

Almost one in four killings was followed by the perpetrator's suicide or committal to an asylum. In another one in five cases the prosecution failed. Where sentences were imposed they tended to be relatively short, with the great majority under five years. In five cases a sentence of death was passed but each was commuted to penal servitude for life. If the courts tended to be lenient, why should we be surprised that the citizenry sometimes took a similar view? Carolyn Conley has shown in her work on 'melancholy accidents' that where a man felled another in the heat of the moment, and there was no evidence of planning or the use of a knife or gun, Irish courts were often merciful.[32] Given the embedded nature of this perspective, the population of Dublin who found *Playboy*'s plot so at odds with their preferred portrayal of Irish life should not have been all that surprised that there was a certain measure of ambiguity when it came to judging those who had killed in temper (or in their cups). However, on occasion, as when confronted with an expression of violence as grotesque as James Lychehaun's, the courts were prepared to award severe sentences, in his case penal servitude for life.

Christy was well aware of the qualitative differences between killings. When asked if he had shot his father, he replied, shaking his head: 'I never used weapons. I've no licence and I'm a law-fearing man' (1: 270–71). When then asked if the murder weapon was perhaps a knife, he was scandalized, exclaiming: 'Do you take me for a slaughter boy?' (1: 274). His account of the circumstances was that he was digging potatoes when he 'just' raised the spade—almost as if it was a natural extension of his arm—and brought it down on his father's head. In his view, and one that was commonly shared at the time, this was a world away from a cold-blooded killing. Often fights took place to establish who was the 'better man'. By tackling his father, who by all accounts was made of stern stuff (given his double resurrection), it is not surprising that Christy won bragging rights to some extent.[33] Had the age difference been greater, or the father more obviously weak, his 'achievement' in this regard would have earned him fewer plaudits. Also the reason for his assault—namely the desire to avoid a forced marriage—would probably also have evoked some sympathy in the public at large.

Lethal disputes between intimates (whether parents and children, other relatives or lovers) accounted for more than a quarter of deaths in the sample. The single greatest category was where the parties came together in a haze of alcohol, with intoxication being assigned the status of a causal factor by police investigators; inebriation, it seems, made the search for a motive somewhat redundant. Workplace disputes were sometimes lethal (the Lynchehaun case is an extreme example of this), as too were arguments over rights of way and access to land for grazing and planting. In a small number of cases, death resulted from the commission of a crime such as robbery or rape.

The Particulars of Parricide

How rare was parricide? Did it imply such an aberrant state of family affairs that Synge would have had to resort to a case that had taken place three decades earlier to justify *Playboy*'s plot? Could he have credibly written his play without reference to the violence of William Maley and James Lynchehaun? Did he capture what he described in his own words as 'the psychic state of the locality'? The RIC records show that lethal squabbles between parents and children were regular enough occurrences during the years when Synge was writing *Playboy* and at the time that elements of the Dublin public were reacting so strongly against it. Of the 106 homicides studied, 9 were intrafamilial and intergenerational. Four of these involved children who were killed by their parents. In another, a father died of heart failure in the course of forcibly ejecting his son from the house in the aftermath of the latter using 'some offensive words towards his mother'. The remaining deaths comprised three matricides and one patricide, whose details are briefly set out next.

On 17 June 1905, Patrick Hasson beat his mother (aged 70) with a stick and smashed in her head with a large stone. He was found guilty but insane. The report of the case in *The Irish Times* noted that Patrick was 'a man of violent temper' who had been known to drink ether; at the inquest into his mother's death the coroner condemned the use of ether in the area and called for 'legislative repression'.[34] On 20 January 1907, Lavinia Forsythe (aged 52) was found dead in her home. Her son Francis stated that she had fallen out of bed thereby bruising her face and head. But a neighbour testified hearing the deceased scream 'murder, murder' and the son reply that he 'would hang for the old cat'. This exchange was followed by the sound of a body falling to the floor. Another witness reported seeing Francis knock his mother down 'with his clenched fist' on the night she died and then threaten to take her life if she did not light the fire and make his supper. The first jury was unable to reach a verdict and the second, while convicting, made a strong recommendation to mercy.[35] Francis received three years' penal servitude. On 30 March 1907, William Bell (aged 62) was assaulted in bed by his son, David. David seems to have been somewhat indiscriminate in his violence, having originally been arrested on a warrant for an assault on his mother.[36] Finally, Rose Johnston (aged 65) was attacked by her son Edward on 8 September 1907. According to the *Outrage* report: 'Edward who was anxious to get married wanted to get his mother out of the house, and had been quarrelling with her and treating her badly for some time previously.' He was sentenced to five years' penal servitude.

Clearly, then, parricide was not unknown in Ireland during the early years of the twentieth century. Indeed, the week before the curtain was first raised on *Playboy*, Lavinia Forsythe died at the hands of her son, the first of three parricides to occur in 1907. Given the relative ease with which we have pieced together plausible narratives of these cases from police records and newspaper reports, it is reasonable to assume that they would have excited significant interest at the time.

Defending the Indefensible

Returning to the riotous reaction to *Playboy*'s 1907 performance in Dublin, Synge felt he had to justify the plot when he came under attack for traducing the character of rural Ireland. This criticism of the play seems to have assumed that the events described were unimaginable, or at least so highly improbable as to be unbelievable. While Christy's enthusiastic reception as a self-confessed murderer might have been an exaggeration, the likelihood is that there would have been sympathy for a man who raised his hand to his father to protest against an attempt to match him in marriage to a woman for whom he could feel no affection, and who then fled for fear of what he might have done.

In an insightful review of the play, 'Pat' complained that Synge's central message had been obscured by the language he chose to express it in, which had caused genuine shock to theatregoers.[37] The core of the drama, which Pat describes as the 'inner' play, shines 'a dreadful searchlight into our cherished accumulation of social skeletons … It is as if we looked in a mirror for the first time, and found ourselves hideous. We fear to face the thing. We shrink at the word for it. We scream.' It is Pat's contention that neither Pegeen's infatuation with a killer nor the expressions attributed to the peasantry are at odds with reality.

For Pegeen, a lively young woman facing the inevitability of married life with the spineless and insipid Shawn Keogh, Christy had obvious attractions. Here stood a man who had resisted his father's domination and who had struck a blow for his independence rather than marrying a woman he found repellent. A man capable of demonstrating his resolve in such a way might also be capable of wooing and loving sincerely. Furthermore, as Pat reminds us:

> The difference between a hero and a murderer is sometimes, in the comparative numbers they have killed, morally in favour of the murderer; and we all know how the "pale young curate" loses his drawing room popularity when the unmarried subaltern returns from his professional blood-spilling.[38]

Controversy has raged about whether Synge misunderstood, romanticized or mocked the Irish peasantry who blunder around the pages of *Playboy*. Nowhere are these rival interpretations so evident as in Synge's use of the word 'shifts' (3: 532). While the Gaelic Leaguers complained that such 'vulgar' words misrepresented the western Irish peasantry, in an interview with *The Freeman's Journal* Synge stressed that a shift was 'an everyday word in the West of Ireland, which would not be taken offence at there, and might be taken differently by people in Dublin. It was used without any objection in Douglas Hyde's "Songs of Connaught," in the Irish, but what could be published in Irish perhaps could not be published in English!'[39]

Pat's view that the language of the play was true to the region in which it was set is captured by his remark that:

> As to the discussions on feminine underclothing, I have often heard discussions more familiar among the peasantry themselves, without the remotest suggestion of immorality, and if Dublin is shocked in this connection, it is because its mind is less clean than that of the Connacht peasant woman.

However, this acknowledgement of the accuracy of the idiom is tempered by a feeling that the use of terms that could be considered objectionable is overdone to the extent that it becomes irritating and deflects attention from the 'dramatic essentials'. Pat was not alone in adopting this position. Another review published in *The Irish Times* elaborated on this theme:

> While there is not a word or a turn of expression in the play that is not in common use among peasants, it is quite another matter to reproduce some of the expressions on a public stage in a large city. People here will not publicly approve of the indiscriminate use of the Holy Name on every possible occasion, nor will they quietly submit to the reproduction of expressions which, to say the least, are offensive to good taste, however true they may be to actual life.[40]

The review went on to note that the audience resented these 'indiscretions' on the part of the author and as a result what could have been a 'brilliant success' was brought to an 'inglorious conclusion'. The sentiment here is quite clear, namely, that what might be acknowledged should not be named; that tacit acceptance and shared secrets should trump public avowals; that the avoidance of scandal is more important than the expression of truth. Even the audience's most puritanical and austere members must have been aware that women wore undergarments and that these were known as 'shifts'. But to identify such a garment by name—and by association to draw the public mind to the body that it covered and the temptations of the flesh that it barely concealed—was a step too far. Such brazenness was held to pose a threat to the purity of the emerging Irish nation. This was to confirm the worst fears of those who opposed the move to national self-determination by highlighting in three acts an appetite for sex, violence and community perfidy. As *The Irish Times* reluctantly concluded, 'Mr. Synge, we are afraid, must to some extent sacrifice the "remorseless truth" if his play is to be made acceptable to healthy public opinion.'[41]

In this regard, one wonders if the production would have excited the same level of scandal if it had retained its original title. This would have at least had the virtue of transparency and only the most obtuse could have felt misled by the play's content. That title: 'Murder Will Out'.

Finale

In focusing here on *Playboy*'s controversial provenance, we have tried to offer insight on intergenerational violence in Ireland to demonstrate that the play's parricide was quite plausible *in its essence*. On just this Synge himself insisted. However, given that violent killings, including parricides, were regularly reported to the police and publicized in the Irish press, we encourage some still-to-be-written history additionally to ask: why was the public response to *Playboy*'s first performance so intensely negative on the grounds of the purported flimsiness of its evidence base and of the impropriety of its language (when Synge's text seems properly to have reflected peasant idiom and the first staging in the Abbey took place in the vicinity of a busy red-light district)?[42]

Playboy contains other puzzles, too, that whet our appetite for the unsolved or unknowable. For example, why did the apparent parricide of Old Mahon happen in Kerry, with Christy walking for eleven days before his arrival in Mayo? By introducing the idea of a sustained pursuit, was Synge providing another faint echo of the past (e.g. harkening back to the famous tragic myth *An Toraíocht Dhiarmada agus Gráinne* [The Pursuit of Diarmuid and Gráinne]?) What image is Synge trying to conjure here? Is it another example of the eternal truth of his portrayal or, at least, of its distinguished literary lineage? Moreover, is it only a matter of convenience for Synge's orchestration of the play that Christy has neither a mother nor siblings further to complicate the generational conflict with his father? Does his father own any land or is he, more likely, a landless squatter?

Questions are also raised about the reception Christy received in other places that he must have passed by or rested in during his epic walk. It is not at all probable that his arrival at the shebeen was the first time that anyone had questioned him about his circumstances. Similarly, it is likely that his father must have been previously alerted to or somehow been made aware of his son's direction of travel because it was very soon after Christy entered the shebeen that Old Mahon arrived there too. What transpired in the interlude between quitting Kerry and finding safety and comfort in Mayo? What are we to make of this silent period? Where did Christy go for food and shelter? How could an old and injured man keep pace with a younger, healthier son? Are we led to conclude that nowhere along the way did anyone feel the need either to bring Christy to justice or to join his father in the chase (further emphasizing Synge's view about popular antipathy towards the justice system)?

Progress and failure, triumph and despair, tragedy and comedy—the swirling plot and counterplot in *Playboy* indeed offer fertile ground for criminology. Besides shedding fresh light on some of the shenanigans around *Playboy*, we hope this chapter shows the worth of paying attention not only to a medium upon which criminology seldom dwells, namely, the cultural productions of playwrights and their aesthetic properties and performance, but also to the social context of their patterns of production and consumption.

Notes

1. In Philadelphia, for example, most of the cast was arrested under the MacNichol anti-indecency law (Bourgeois 1913: 194; see also Dallett 1996 and Trotter 1998).
2. This is not to say that animal abuse and theriocide do not appear in *Playboy*. Far from it, and not only just below the surface. Pegeen, for example, refers to 'Marcus Quin, God rest him, got six months for

maiming ewes' (*PWW*, 1: 48–49). Again, Christy admits that he never had 'a sight of joy or sport saving only when I'd be abroad in the dark night poaching rabbits … and I near got six months for going with a dung-fork and stabbing a fish' (*PWW*, 1: 432–35). Moreover, Jimmy remarks that he knew someone once who 'was kicked in the head by a red mare, and he went killing horses a great while' (*PWW*, 3: 74–76).

3. Pegeen described the widow's crime as 'a sneaky kind of murder' (1: 520) which involved a cut with a rusty pick that caused blood poisoning and eventual death and won 'small glory' with the locals (1: 518–21). Widow Quin admits that she 'destroyed her man' and 'buried her children' (1: 524). This means that she killed her husband. Possibly, too, she also killed her children or, like so many others, they succumbed to one of the hazards or illnesses of infancy. One wonders whether, in keeping with the spirit of *Playboy*, a flagrant assault generating more blood and gore and split bones would have commanded greater respect from the widow's peers.
4. *The Freeman's Journal*, 28 January 1907: 10.
5. Bretherton (1991: 323).
6. See further Frazier (2004).
7. Synge (1907a).
8. Synge (1907b: 333).
9. Kiberd (1979: 20–21).
10. Bessai (1968).
11. Bretherton (1991: 332) and see Doggett (1997).
12. Kiberd (1995: 171).
13. About Irish anthropological investigations on Aran and on the influence of the opening of an anthropometric laboratory in Dublin in 1891, see Jones (1998) and Ashley (2001).
14. Synge (1907c: 62). Tomás O Máille has challenged Synge's brief recounting of these events in *The Aran Islands* as being 'for artistic reasons … factually inaccurate and also a misrepresentation of the kindness of the Inishmore people' (cited in Súilleabhain 1972: 21–22). He claims, moreover, that rather than romanticizing the would-be patricide, the islanders took pity on the downcast son wrongly deprived of land he had given to his father. In O Máille's version the father survived his son's attack and the latter found shelter on the Aran Islands, escaped to Cork, and later to the US. A few years later, he captained a ship to Galway, where he made his identity known to a few trusted friends.
15. Synge (1907c: 62).
16. Kiberd (2000: 426).

17. *Galway Express: Mayo, Roscommon, Clare and Limerick Advertiser*, 1 February 1873: 3.
18. Although Christy claimed to have buried his father after splitting his head, this is contradicted by his father's withering observation: 'Weren't you off racing the hills before I got my breath with the start I had seeing you turn on me at all?' (3: 444–45).
19. *Police Gazette, or Hue-and-Cry*, 31 January 1873: 1.
20. Issue of 4 February 1873: 1.
21. Allen (1997).
22. Carney's (1986) book is based largely on the accidental discovery of a hand-written manuscript by Franciscan Brother Paul Carney, who had lived in Achill. This narrative, entitled *A Short Sketch of the Life and Actions of the Far-Famed James Lynchehaun, the Achill Troglodyte*, we have been unable to find.
23. *The Times*, 7 January 1895: 10.
24. *The Times*, 18 July 1895: 9.
25. On these details see Carney (1986: 219–24).
26. Bourgeois (1913: 193).
27. O'Donnell (2005, 2010).
28. In Yeats (1907: 630).
29. National Archives of Ireland, *Return of Outrages Reported to the Constabulary Office in Ireland* (Chief Secretary's Office: Irish Crime Records).
30. The reports included details of 108 killings, 2 of which have been omitted because they relate to deaths inflicted in 1904 (one each in Fermanagh and Londonderry). In addition, there were thirty-four infanticides, for which no official narratives were available.
31. Carney (1986: 222).
32. Conley (1999).
33. We learn early on, when Christy has yet to learn the value of exaggeration and was more likely speaking with candour, that his father was in and out of custody 'for battering peelers or assaulting men' (1: 466–67).
34. *The Irish Times*, 19 June 1905: 9.
35. *The Irish Times*, 26 March 1907: 5 and 27 July 1907: 4.
36. *The Irish Times*, 18 April 1907: 5.
37. 'Pat' (1907).
38. 'Pat' (1907).
39. Synge, in *The Freeman's Journal*, 30 January 1907: 7.
40. *The Irish Times*, 28 January 1907: 8.

41. In a letter to Stephen MacKenna in Paris, Synge (1907d: 329) enquired:

> I wonder did you hear that Dublin and the Freeman were chiefly outraged because I used the word 'shift,' instead of 'chemise' for an article of fine linen, or perhaps named it at all. Lady G. asked our charwoman – the Theatre charwoman what she thought of it. The charwoman said she wouldn't mention the garment at all if it could be helped, but if she did she hoped she would always say 'chemise,' even if she was alone!

The woman's modesty and decorum were at once questioned when she was overheard remarking to the stage carpenter, 'Ah, isn't Mr Synge a bloody old snot to write such a play!'

42. *Playboy* continues to excite interest. In 2004, for example, director Garry Hynes and Galway's Druid Theatre Company staged it several times on the Irish mainland and three times on the Aran Islands. In 2006 it was performed in Mandarin in Beijing with an all-Chinese cast; the action was shifted (pun intended!—PB/IOD) to a hairdressers and foot massage parlour. In 2007—the centenary of the 'Playboy Riots'—the Abbey Theatre staged Bisi Adigun and Roddy Doyle's version of *Playboy*. This time the action was moved from the west of Ireland to a west Dublin pub; the playboy became Christopher Malomo, a well-educated refugee from Nigeria, on the run after 'killing' his father with a pestle for pounding yams. In 2009 Galway's Druid Theatre performed *Playboy* several times in Britain and for one week in Galway City. A second run of the Adigun and Doyle version resulted in a legal action being taken by Mr Adigun against the Abbey Theatre for copyright infringement. He argued, successfully, that his royalties had been underpaid and that the script had been altered without his authorization. The case was settled in 2013.

Bibliography

Allen, G. (1997). 'An Irishman's Diary,' *The Irish Times*, January 31, p. 13.
Ashley, S. (2001). 'The Poetics of Race in 1890s Ireland: An Ethnography of the Aran Islands,' *Patterns of Prejudice*, 35(2): 5–18.
Bessai, Diane E. (1968). 'Little Hound in Mayo: Synge's Playboy and The Comic Tradition in Irish Literature,' *Dalhousie Review*, 48(3): 372–83.
Bourgeois, Maurice. (1913). *John Millington Synge and the Irish Theatre*. London: Constable.
Bretherton, George. (1991). 'A Carnival Christy and a Playboy for All Ages,' *Twentieth-Century Literature*, 37(3): 322–34.

Carney, James. (1986). *The Playboy & the Yellow Lady*. Dublin: Poolbeg.
Conley, Carolyn. (1999). *Melancholy Accidents: The Meaning of Violence in Post-Famine Ireland*. Lanham, MD: Lexington Books.
Dallett, Athenaide. (1996). 'Protest in the Playhouse: Two Twentieth-Century Audience Riots,' *New Theatre Quarterly*, 12(48): 323–32.
Doggett, Rob. (1997). 'The Three Fathers of the Past: A Sociological Reading of *The Playboy of the Western World* and the Playboy Riots,' *Colby Quarterly*, xxxiii(4): 281–94.
Frazier, Adrian. (ed.). (2004). *Playboys of the Western World*. Dublin: Carysfort Press.
Jones, Greta. (1998). 'Contested Territories: Alfred Cort Haddon, Progressive Evolutionism and Ireland,' *History of European Ideas*, 24(3): 195–211.
Kiberd, Declan. (1979). 'J.M. Synge and the Songs of the Folk,' *Hermathena*, (126): 7–37.
Kiberd, Declan. (1995). *Inventing Ireland: The Literature of the Modern Nation*. London: Jonathan Cape.
Kiberd, Declan. (2000). *Irish Classics*. London: Granta Books.
O'Donnell, Ian. (2005). 'Lethal Violence in Ireland, 1841 to 2003: Famine, Celibacy and Parental Pacification,' *British Journal of Criminology*, 45(1): 671–95.
O'Donnell, Ian. (2010). 'Killing in Ireland at the Turn of the Centuries: Contexts, Consequences and Civilizing Processes,' *Irish Economic and Social History*, 37: 53–74.
Ó Súilleabhain, Sean. (1972). 'Synge's Use of Irish Folklore.' In: Maurice Harmon (ed.), *J.M. Synge: Centenary Papers 1971*. Dublin: Dolmen Press, 18–34.
Pat. (1907). 'That Dreadful Play,' *The Irish Times*, January 30, p. 9.
Synge, J.M. (1907). (1995). '*The Playboy of the Western World*.' In: *The Playboy of the Western World and Other Plays*. Edited and Introduced by Ann Saddlemyer. Oxford: Oxford University Press, 95–146.
Synge, J.M. (1907a). 'Letter to the Editor,' *The Irish Times*, January 31, p. 5.
Synge, J.M. (1907b). (1983). 'To Stephen MacKenna, April 17,' *Collected Letters*, 1 vol, 1871–1907, Oxford: Clarendon, 332–3.
Synge, J.M. (1907c). (1979). *The Aran Islands*. Oxford: Oxford University Press.
Synge, J.M. (1907d). (1983). 'To Stephen MacKenna, April 9,' *Collected Letters*, 1 vol, 1871–1907, Oxford: Clarendon, 329–30.
Trotter, Mary. (1998). 'Which Fiddler Calls the Tune? The *Playboy* Riots and the Politics of Nationalist Theatre Spectatorship,' *Theatre Survey*, 39(2): 39–52.
Yeats, W.B. (1907). (2005). 'To John Quinn, February 18, 1907,' *Collected Letters*, 4 vols, 1905–1907. Oxford University Press (eds. John Kelly and Ronald Schuchard), 630.

7

Is Theriocide Murder?

The death of an animal sometimes elicits strong human emotions. When an animal companion dies we experience heartbreak and grief. So, too, mediated images of animals who die as a result of environmental or other types of disaster on occasion produce spontaneous eruptions of anger and sorrow. Who can forget the grisly images of countless oil-encrusted birds and fish who died in 2010 when BP's Deepwater Horizon rig spilled roughly 4 million barrels of oil into the Gulf of Mexico? Moreover, in the aftermath of Hurricane Katrina, in 2005, when gruesome TV news images displayed the floating bodies of dead dogs, cats and cattle, about $40 million was donated by concerned viewers for the rescue and relocation of surviving animals.

Emotions of anger and outrage are sometimes also displayed when the public learns that animals have been killed during a terrorist attack. When the Irish Republican Army bombed the Changing of the Guard ceremony in Hyde Park next to the Queen's London palace in 1982, eleven soldiers and seven horses were killed. Other than their families, few of us can recall the names of the dead soldiers. But an injured horse—called Sefton—lives on in the national psyche and is memorialized in a life-sized statue unveiled at the Royal Veterinary College. Most of us will recall the global furore that followed the killing of Cecil the lion outside

Zimbabwe's Hwange National Park in July 2015. Fear and anger are sometimes the dominant emotions that accompany what was assumed to be the activities of a psychopathic cult bent on serial theriocide, as happened after the maiming of numerous horses and cows in England and Wales during the 1990s and into the new millennium.

However, to most people, most of the time, the overwhelming majority of theriocides are seen neither as wrong nor as illegal. They are invisible, not even worthy of comment. Yet, I believe that one day, sooner rather than later, some theriocides presently considered socially, morally and legally acceptable will be regarded as heinous enough to be criminalized (and not as property crimes but as crimes of violence). Were vivisection to be criminalized, for example, then a distinct possibility is that those who kill animals during scientific experimentation will be prosecuted for murder. This chapter therefore takes up again the question that was first explicitly posed at the end of Chap. 2: Is theriocide murder? The way forward is led by Jacques Derrida, who wryly asks, 'Do we agree to presume that every murder, every transgression of the commandment "Thou shalt not kill" concerns only man … and that in sum there are only crimes "against humanity"?'[1]

The Criminalization of Theriocide

In the past four decades numerous works of moral philosophy and critical animal studies have insisted that the killing of animals should not be tolerated. Except for the occasional passing comment, however, none has directly or in any concerted way addressed whether in certain circumstances the killing of an animal other than a human might be murder.[2] Tom Regan, for example, even while demanding the criminalization of vivisection ('the blackest of all black crimes'),[3] has always stopped short of denouncing it as murder.

For some of the same reasons that the progressive wings of sociology and criminology have been slow to embrace the study of animal abuse so, too, they have not yet examined whether the killing of animals—theriocide—should be named murder and, if so, with what consequences and for whom.

However, a fundamental shift in opinion might now be in the offing. This possibility has arisen as an effect of a new willingness to view certain harmful human attitudes, words and actions towards animals as self-interested and wrongful and therefore deserving of the pejorative epithet 'speciesist'. The narrow legalistic term 'crimes against animals', for example, has been replaced by the broader concepts of 'animal abuse', 'harms to animals' and 'violations of animals' rights'. The several categories of 'bestiality', and the obsolete 'among Christians a crime not to be named', are nowadays theorized as wrongful actions better termed and thought about as animal sexual assault.[4]

Other types of animal abuse are also in the process of being theorized anew. For example, Raghnild Sollund, who has been at the forefront of theorizing about the legal and illegal trade in wildlife, seems committed to the idea that it is more honest to rename the trafficking in animals and animal body parts abduction and kidnapping.[5] Moreover, also consider the argument by Carmen Cusack that because cows are subject to non-consensual insemination, the act of inseminating and milking a cow is tantamount to rape.[6] If we follow the same logic, then the electronic stimulation of bulls, pigs and other male animals—in order to collect and use their semen—is a similarly non-consensual practice and must also be thought of as rape.

The same spirit of theoretical reappraisal lies behind a recent proposal on ecocide to the Law Commission of the United Nations (UN). (This returns us, in a way full circle, to the UN's denial of universal rights for animals that is challenged in Chap. 1.) The activist barrister Polly Higgins argues that 'ecocide is in essence the very antithesis of life', as a result of which she proposes that, for purposes of international law, ecocide may be defined as:

> the extensive destruction, damage to or loss of ecosystem(s) of a given territory, whether by human agency or by other causes, to such an extent that peaceful enjoyment by *the inhabitants* of that territory has been severely diminished.[7]

This is indeed a useful working definition of ecocide. But it fails to specify what 'destruction' and 'damage' might be in any given case. Destruction of what and damage to what, precisely? Destruction of plants? Of animals? Damage to streams? To mountains? To mountain lions? To cats and dogs?

Higgins herself has addressed some of these problems by importing a revised wording of the 1998 Rome Statute's definition of environmental damage as a result of war crimes. Article 8(2)(b)(iv) of the statute specifically criminalizes '[w]idespread long-term and severe damage to the natural environment which would be clearly excessive in relation to the concrete and overall military advantage'.[8] Higgins' desired revision to Article 8(2)(b)(iv) is to substitute 'community' for 'military'. But does this solve the problem? Probably it doesn't, because a difficulty with her original formulation of ecocide lies in the vague construction of 'inhabitants'. Who and what are to be included as inhabitants and by what criteria? Who and what will therefore be excluded?

Presumably in recognition of these very questions, Higgins soon thereafter modified her original proposal to embrace harm to animals. Now, in proposing to the UN that ecocide be defined as the fifth crime against peace—that is, after genocide, crimes against humanity, war crimes and crimes of aggression—she explains that ecocide is a crime against peace because it can lead to: (1) loss of life, injury to life and severe diminution of enjoyment of life for humans and nonhuman beings; (2) the heightened risk of conflict arising from impact upon human and nonhuman life which has occurred as a result of the above; and (3) adverse impact upon future generations and their ability to survive.[9]

The attempt to identify both human and nonhuman beings as among the potential victims of ecocide—rather than the all-encompassing but ultimately vague 'inhabitants'—is a very positive advance in the direction of species inclusiveness. Note also how adroitly Higgins refers to nonhuman *beings*! (Also note that to speak of 'nonhuman beings' is perhaps not the escape from a Wittgensteinian vicious circle that it appears. To speak of *nonhuman* beings is ironically to privilege humans because it errs in exactly the same way as does the designation of human females as non-male humans.) Regrettably, however, the proposal that the UN should define ecocide as the fifth crime against peace seems to have stalled. Its resurrection would be most welcome. Perhaps the impetus for renewal will come from the struggles over environmental justice by activist indigenous groups in several regions of South America. Indeed, just such a push from below happened in October 2015, at the international summit on climate change, when the president of Ecuador, Rafael Correa called for a 'Universal Declaration of the Rights of Nature' and the creation of an International Court of Environmental Justice.

At about the same time as Higgins and her colleagues Damien Short and Nigel South were attempting to invigorate the concept of ecocide, I was starting to think about whether an act of theriocide might on occasion rise to the level of murder. Thus, in the relative backwater of an academic journal's Abstract, I posed the following scenario[10]:

> I wish I had a penny or a peso for each of the many times in the past few years that I have listened in on a conversation or read something about human rights and animal rights and then been forced to think through to the variety of its possible conclusions what for three shipwrecked and hungry survivors in a lifeboat on the high seas is the proper thing to do about their thirst and imminent starvation. Suppose that the three survivors of this shipwreck are an adult human, the ship's cabin boy and a dog. Suppose also that they are several days away from rescue and without hope of acquiring food or potable water from their salt-water environment. For purposes of survival in this dire situation, may one of the two humans kill and eat one of the other two survivors? If so, which one? To these two questions almost certainly the response by two of the shipwrecked survivors themselves, by would-be in-contact radio rescuers, by medical consultants, by theological experts and by the general public would be: 'it's alright to eat the dog.'

My staging of the above scenario was intended to encourage greater honesty in how we talk about the killing of our fellow creatures. Clearly, the abrupt ending of this rights talk—'it's alright to eat the dog'—left the real business of life and death unfinished. To wit, I had intentionally chosen to leave for another occasion the exploration of one of the possible outcomes of the fictional lifeboat situation: if the dog were to be eaten by the human survivors, would or should this theriocide qualify as a murder? (Without wishing to complicate matters further—or not too much—suppose that, instead of a dog, the third surviving member of the lifeboat was an orangutan, an endangered member of the family of Great Apes.)

On this and similar questions I'm willing to travel some of the way with Tom Regan. He has suggested that, with certain principled provisos and absent special considerations, it is acceptable for humans to eat a member of another animal species if they are in a survivor-mode action of self-defence.[11] Regan goes on to argue, somewhat controversially, that this is justified because the *prima facie* loss of life for most of us is greater than it is for most animals. Self-preservation is not akin to speciesism, granted, but from *their* viewpoint most animals would strongly resist Regan's conclusion—they would disagree with it, in other words, however it is framed. Perhaps the proper solution to who lives and who dies in the lifeboat would be either to toss a coin or else to let the beings in competition with each other for survival have at it and fight to the death.[12] To be fair to Regan, however, he has also written, in the context of the moral wrongness of vivisection, that there are 'disanalogies' between lifeboats and research laboratories. None of the survivors on the lifeboat is there because his or her rights were violated, yet:

> [a]s soon as we enter a laboratory in which animals are experimented upon … the moral scene changes dramatically. When one solitary animal is brought into a laboratory, there to be used in pursuit of human benefits, that animal's right to be treated with respect has been violated.[13]

There are some, perhaps most, who will respond with wincing, their faces aghast, to the suggestion that theriocide might be murder. On reflection these naysayers could point out that it is quite acceptable to eat animal flesh either because this is what we have all always done or because it is better to kill livestock humanely with a stun gun in a slaughterhouse than for them to have no life at all. Confronted with the reply that however it is that animals have come into being, we are morally obliged never to kill them, they could then change tack and additionally argue that to define some theriocides as murder would be to dilute the severity of the social censure of the wrongful killing of a human. This would be an error, they could suggest, because an even greater number of wrongful killings will ensue if the murder of humans is censured more weakly than it once was. (Thirty years ago, of course, just such a short-sighted response awaited the feminist proposal to expand the concept of rape from an action based solely on physical force to one which was preceded or accompanied by psychological, emotional or economic coercion.)

The claim that theriocide is or might be murder surely hinges on the well-reasoned construction of another claim, namely, that the animals whose killings are so described are persons or beings with irrevocable moral and legal rights.[14] These rights are enshrined in the concept of legal personhood. At a minimum, they entitle their bearers to life, to bodily liberty, to respect and to dignity. *If and only if animals acquire legal personhood does the question of whether they are capable of being murdered make any sense.*

Legal Personhood for Animals

Three of the most pressing issues about legal personhood for animals are (1) the criteria of legal personhood; (2) the species that merit legal personhood; and (3) the sort of justice that those convicted of killing animals with legal personhood will be served.

In respect of the first issue, the most prominent arguments have been made by Peter Singer in his best-selling book *Animal Liberation*. Singer's act-utilitarianism, which flows more or less directly from the Benthamite principle of utility, claims that all sentient animals should be given equal consideration in their avoidance of suffering. Between species who are capable of suffering and those who are not, Singer seems to place a dividing line somewhere between a shrimp and a mollusc. In his own words[15]:

> The grounds we have for believing that other mammals and birds suffer are, then, closely analogous to the grounds we have for believing that other humans suffer. It remains to consider how far down the evolutionary scale this analogy holds. Obviously it becomes poorer when we get further away from man. To be more precise would require a detailed examination of all that we know about other forms of life. With fish, reptiles, and other vertebrates the analogy still seems strong, with molluscs like oysters it is much weaker. Insects are more difficult, and it may be that in our present state of knowledge we must be agnostic about whether they are capable of suffering.

For permitting the sacrifice of some animals at the altar of scientific experimentation if it maximizes the total happiness of the many, Singer's act utilitarianism regularly receives short shrift from sections of the animal rights community—particularly from members of critical animal studies such as Joan Dunayer and Gary Francione. Because Singer has always disavowed the notion of animal rights, it must additionally be said that it is well-nigh impossible to see how animals will ever be able to emerge from their lethal legal wilderness if they are *not* the bearers of rights that are both moral and legal.

Precisely this problem seems to be the point of departure for Tom Regan's deontological approach to animal rights. In his book *The Case for Animal Rights*, Regan argues that inviolable moral rights inhere in those animals who satisfy the criterion of being what he terms 'a subject-of-a-life'[16]:

> [This] involves more than merely being alive and more than merely being conscious … [I]ndividuals [who] are subjects-of-a-life … have beliefs and desires; perception, memory, and a sense of the future, including their own future; an emotional life together with feelings of pleasure and pain; preference- and welfare-interests; the ability to initiate action in pursuit of their desires and goals; a psychophysical identity over time; and an individual welfare in the sense that their experiential life fares well or ill for them, logically independently of their utility for others and logically independently of their being the object of anyone else's interests.

For Regan, animals who satisfy the subject-of-a-life criterion have inherent value. They should therefore never be treated as a means to an end. They are ends in themselves. Ipso facto, animals with inherent value have the same basic rights as human moral patients, including the right to respectful treatment and the right not to be harmed, either by inflictions or by deprivations. As such, we must not eat animals, nor use them as receptacles of value, whether in hunting and trapping or in science and education. But these rightful human–animal practices are not to be seen as kind or compassionate. Rather, they are dictated by respect and dignity and justice.

Which animals merit legal personhood? It is at this point that things get decidedly sticky. Perhaps there is consensus on the inclusion of all mammals. But what of invertebrates? Or birds such as corvids and parrots? Or insects? Or bivalves? Moreover, should a similarly respectful line of questioning be granted to plants? Should trees have standing? Regan himself recognizes that different species vary in the strength of their respective claims to legal personhood. In his view all mammals have a strong claim. Most animals other than mammals have a weak claim. Ultimately, then, Regan's list lends itself to the accusation of speciesism: the animals with a strong claim to legal personhood are the ones most like us.

The crucial importance of establishing legal personhood for animals is addressed in Steven Wise's *Rattling the Cage: Towards Legal Rights for Animals*. Wise's chief complaint in this book is that without legal standing neither animals nor their representatives will be able to seek redress for the many ways in which their fundamental interests are routinely ignored and violated. He argues that because the US Congress has granted legal personhood to non-sentient entities such as corporations, municipalities and ships, animals' relative powerlessness in civil law can surely be overcome. Wise's chosen route for this task is to penetrate existing legal barriers not through congressional legislation but at what he regards as these barriers' weakest and most flexible site, namely, judge-made law. In the not-too-distant future, Wise believes, some fair-minded judge, following the principles of liberty and equality, will be persuaded to conclude that the same basic rules about the entitlement to and acquisition of legal rights for humans should also apply to certain other animals.

Wise himself suggests that not all species are entitled to legal rights. This is so, he contends, because only if it can be shown that a given animal's autonomy is in essential respects very similar to that of humans—at least to that of human infants, young children and severely retarded adults—will it be both possible and desirable to convince judges that the animal is entitled to legal rights. By 'essential respects' Wise refers to an animal's brain structure, genes, cognitive abilities and levels of consciousness, each of which he instantiates with considerable scientific evidence. As such, he concludes, legal rights should be extended to the roughly 10,000 surviving bonobos and 200,000 chimpanzees.

On 4 December 2014, in the New York Appellate Division case of *Nonhuman Rights Project vs. Patrick C. Lavery*, Wise and the Nonhuman Rights Project sued for a writ of habeas corpus that would free Tommy, a

26-year-old chimpanzee, who was kept in a cage by his owner in Gloversville, New York. Wise argued—following the principles of animal rights established in his book *Rattling the Cage*—that the chimpanzee deserved the human right of bodily liberty. But the court, explicitly relying on the work of academic lawyer Richard Cupp, an opponent of animal rights, denied the suit. The court used contracturalist reasoning to deliver its verdict:

> [U]nlike human beings, chimpanzees cannot bear any legal duties, submit to societal responsibilities or be held legally accountable for their actions. In our view, it is this incapability to bear any legal responsibilities and societal duties that renders it inappropriate to confer upon chimpanzees the legal rights—such as the fundamental right to liberty protected by the writ of habeas corpus—that have been afforded to human beings.[17]

Had Tommy the chimpanzee succeeded in acquiring legal rights then this ruling could have been hailed as a key stepping stone towards the amelioration of the lives of other animals as well. (But it is hard to see how meaningful legal rights could ever be granted to any species that lack the privileged characteristics of chimpanzees and bonobos in Wise's calculus.)

Despite the failure of this particular suit, there is a real possibility that a court will one day be persuaded by oral argument that one or more nonhuman species are entitled to legal personhood. Besides the suit by the Nonhuman Rights Project for Tommy's bodily liberty, other advances include a positive vote in the Balearic parliament in Spain, which in 2007 granted effective legal personhood and basic rights to all Great Apes, as has also happened in New Zealand. In Argentina, in late December 2014, a court decided that Sandra, a 28-year-old orangutan sequestered in a zoo in Buenos Areas, was philosophically and legally a nonhuman person with basic rights to freedom and that she should therefore be released to a chimpanzee sanctuary; by mid-2017 this had still not happened. Similar legal proceedings are currently underway in Colombia and Brazil.[18] When the day of legal personhood finally arrives for some species other than humans, it will perhaps also ensure some humans who commit theriocide will be prosecuted and convicted of murder.

Towards the Abolition of Speciesism

What is the next chapter in our relationship with our fellow creatures? Volumes of rights talk and acres of Earth Jurisprudence have as yet been unable to undo the fact that legal personhood has never been a status of animals other than humans. Not in past millennia and not now.

If and when animals are granted legal personhood—animals of whatever species, hue or stripe, that is—one has to wonder how effective their apparent victory will be. Emptying their cages and cutting their chains would just be the beginning. Difficulties will abound. Consider pet keeping. Except for working animals—dogs recruited as guards or guides or as herders of cattle, for example, or cats used only as mousers—we interact with non-farm domesticated animals in a spirit of companionship rather than that of a master–slave relationship. So much is this so that we regard our animal companions as family members. We give them names and recognize their distinct personalities. We love them and, when they die, we mourn them. At the same time, the truth is that our companion animals are actually animals whom *we appoint* as our companions.

With this caution in mind, now suppose that a court grants the right to life to our animal companions. Because they cannot really be said to have had much of a say in their recruitment and appointment, does it therefore follow that their right to life—to bodily liberty, to put this right another way—means that our animal companions can only be emancipated if we release them from their appointed confinement with us? In the short term, what if these animals don't want to leave their companion humans? Perhaps our cats and dogs prefer a life of indentured companionship rather than one with erratic food supply, little emotional support and the risk of predators. I know that if my companion animals were left outside, given no food or water and altogether ignored, they would be utterly traumatized and die (I would be traumatized as well, although I could no doubt stumble through). In the long term, does their right to life—to *their* life, not ours—mean the end of us keeping them as animal companions? The animal rights community seems quite divided on this issue.

Also consider 'livestock' (deadstock). Billions of cattle, sheep and pigs are killed each year on factory farms. The situation of livestock differs from that of companion animals, however, in at least one crucial way: we cherish our animal companions but we kill our livestock. We raise our livestock with the specific intent of killing them and eating their flesh.

Now suppose that a court grants legal personhood to livestock. Their right to life and bodily liberty would presumably mean liberation for those animals who are currently in the process of being raised and who are awaiting slaughter. Some of the ensuing elements of this very scenario have been pondered by John Coetzee[19]:

> The paramount right is the right to life. In the case of domesticated animals, there is a twist to their right to life that is not always recognized. For the breeding of such animals, particularly livestock, is tightly controlled by the people who own them (own them body and soul). In practice this means that animals are called into being as dictated by the market (the market for their flesh). If tomorrow we approved and enforced a right to life for livestock, the immediate effect would be a moratorium on births as livestock owners cut back on no longer profitable herds. To put the case in an extreme form: a right to life for pigs would mean that in a few years the only pigs left on earth will be in zoos and sanctuaries.

Suppose, finally, that the right to life is extended to animals in zoos. Presumably this will mean that pigs will fast become an endangered species. The only pigs left will be in sanctuaries.

The social distance between rights on paper and rights on the ground is very lengthy indeed. Its terrain is strewn with huge obstacles. There is therefore good reason to think that the abolition of speciesism will, in the long run, be just as uncertain as it has been for slavery, racism, sexism, ableism and other forms of tyranny. This is so not least because a host of countervailing economic and cultural powers will be hard at work resisting and undermining animals' newfound legal status. Private property and carnivorism are tough nuts to crack. As long as we use animals for our own speciesist ends—whether as private or public property—their owners will be able to dispose of them almost exactly as they wish and with little or no consequence. Legal personhood for animals, in other words, might turn out to be more symbolic than real.

In the meantime, how can theriocide be deterred? Probably not at all, if the attempt to oppose it is chiefly through the incarceration of offenders. Almost from its invention, more than two hundred years ago, the modern prison has been shown to be a gigantic, harmful and costly failure. Violence only begets more violence. Can offenders be reprogrammed through psychological counselling? This might work for those with warped masculinities or for those who kill animals for pleasure. But it is most unlikely to change the mind-set of those who kill the vast majority of animals: those who own slaughterhouses, run product-testing laboratories, toil in state apparatuses and command armies.

There are no quick or ready-made answers to how speciesism can be eliminated. But I know just enough to know of two strategies that might help. One is the introduction of universal humane education. Compassion for our fellow creatures should be encouraged in all children. Humane education should be a required part of all curricula from kindergarten onwards. The other strategy, which might with the greatest sensitivity and care be used as an extension of the first, is the use of spectacle, the awesome power of which we are only now beginning to understand. Many of us love to look at violence and its numerous representations. We devour it. Suppose, then, that a process of 'glassification' were to be applied to the brick-and-mortar and steel walls of factory farms, product-testing laboratories and the like. To reverse the processes of invisibilization, we could render their zones of concealment and confinement transparent. Let these horrific institutions be glassified![20] Urge those who eat animal flesh to visit slaughterhouses and see for themselves the grisly facts of wholesale animal slaughter. Urge consumers to visit laboratories which test their desired products on animals: let them see first-hand the awful suffering of caged chimpanzees, dogs and cats, and those of mice, rats and rabbits who are routinely injected with lethal doses of cancerous cells or who are administered blinding drops of shampoo concentrate.

These strategies may take two or more generations to work. Some will say that patience is not a virtue. But for animals and us, what is the alternative?

Notes

1. Derrida (2002: 415–16).
2. Authors of these passing comments include the anthrozoologist James Serpell, describing as murder the slaughter by the ancient Romans, who, for centuries, loved to watch the torture and killings of thousands of exotic animals (1996: 176; see also Toynbee, 1973: 21–23); the feminist scholar of science and technology Donna Haraway, outraged that humans are allowed to kill animals in laboratories without being charged with murder—'Every living being except Man can be killed but not murdered' (2008: 78); the ethologist Marc Bekoff, complaining that '[w]ords such as euthanize, dispatch, harvest, and cull are frequently used to refer to instances in which people with different motivations and intentions kill healthy animals. It's about time these polite words are changed to the harsher word, murder' (2017); and the feminist animal advocate Joan Dunayer: '[l]awmakers have characterized lethal trapping of nonhumans as lawful killing. They could just as easily characterize it as murder' (2004: 17ff).
3. Regan (2007: 134–36).
4. On the moral wrongfulness of animal sexual assault see, for example, Beirne (1997) and Beirne et al. (2017).
5. See Sollund (2011: 438, n.3, 2015) and Goyes and Sollund (2016: 88).
6. Cusack (2013).
7. Higgins (2010: 62–63, emphasis added).
8. Cited in Higgins (2010: 65–66).
9. Higgins (2012: 157, emphasis added). For an excellent historical discussion of the several proposals to the UN for laws against genocide and ecocide see Higgins, Short and South (2013).
10. Beirne (2011: 349). Without the presence of animals other than humans, this sort of scenario was some time ago wrestled with by the legal philosopher Lon Fuller (1949) in his fictitious 'Case of the Speluncean Explorers'. Similar life-and-death scenarios regularly populate the philosophical forum of 'trolley problems'.
11. Regan (1983: 324). Regan formulates three principles that could justify the overriding of rights: (1) the 'miniride principle', whereby one should choose to harm the innocent few to save the rights of the innocent many (1983: 305–07); (2) the 'worse-off principle', whereby one should choose to harm the many if not doing so entails that another course of action would leave some of the few worse off than any of the many

Is Theriocide Murder? 211

(1983: 307–12); and (3) the 'liberty principle', whereby the innocent have the right to self-defence even if this overrides the rights of others (1983: 331–34).

12. Tossing the coin is the solution devised by Francione (2008: 13–14).
13. Regan, 'Preface' to the 2004 edition of *The Case for Animal Rights* (p. xxxi).
14. On the many difficulties involved in determining whether a particular member (such as an infant) of a particular species (such as an infant chimpanzee or an infant porpoise, dolphin or whale) qualifies as a "person", see DeGrazia (2006).
15. Singer (1973). Jeremy Bentham (1789: 283) had famously stated that:

    > the day may come, when the rest of the animal creation may acquire those rights which never could have been withholden from them but by the hand of tyranny … It may come one day to be recognized, that the number of legs, the villosity of the skin, or the termination of the os sacrum, are reasons equally insufficient for abandoning a sensitive being to the same fate. What else is it that should trace the insuperable line? Is it the faculty of reason, or perhaps, the faculty for discourse? … the question is not, Can they reason? nor, Can they talk? but, Can they suffer? Why should the law refuse its protection to any sensitive being? … The time will come when humanity will extend its mantle over everything which breathes …

    The utilitarian lineage actually goes backwards from Singer to Bentham to Cesare Beccaria. Bentham referred to Beccaria as 'Oh! my master, first evangelist of Reason … you who have made so many useful excursions into the path of utility, what is there left for us to do?—Never to turn aside from that path', while Beccaria himself had urged 'Be just with all the beings that surround you. Remember that even the smallest creatures, crushed by cruel and arrogant Man, are endowed with a little ray of life' (cited in Beirne 1999: 130).
16. Regan (2004: 243).
17. *People ex rel. Nonhuman Rights Project, Inc. v. Lavery*, 124 A.D.3d 148, 152 (3d Dept. 2014). See also Cupp (2015).
18. For an update on animal protection legislation in Australia, South Africa, Israel, Brazil, the US and China, see Cao and White (2016: Chaps. 6–12).
19. Coetzee (2009: 120).

20. The idea of glassification has been applied to slaughterhouses by Pollan (2002) and then taken up and its difficulties in voracious capitalist societies brilliantly expounded by Pachirat (2011), who worked undercover for five months in an industrial slaughterhouse in rural Kansas, where 2500 cattle were killed each day. One every 12 seconds!

Bibliography

Animal Studies Group. (2016). *Killing Animals*. Urbana, IL: University of Illinois Press.

Beirne, Piers. (1997). 'Rethinking Bestiality: Towards a Concept of Interspecies Sexual Assault,' *Theoretical Criminology*, 1(3): 317–40.

Beirne, Piers. (1999). 'For a Nonspeciesist Criminology: Animal Abuse as an Object of Study,' *Criminology*, 37(1): 117–48.

Beirne, Piers. (2011). 'On the Facticity of Animal Trials in Early Modern Britain, Or A Note onthe Curious Prosecution of Farmer Carter's Dog for Murder,' *Crime Law and Social Change*, 55(5): 359–74.

Beirne, Piers, Jennifer Maher and Harriet Pierpoint. (2017). 'Animal Sexual Assault.' In Jennifer Maher, Harriet Pierpoint and Piers Beirne (eds.), *The Palgrave International Handbook of Animal Abuse Studies*. Basingstoke: Palgrave Macmillan, 59–85.

Bekoff, Marc. (2017). 'Why Can Only Humans be Murdered? What About Nonhuman Animals?' *Psychology Today*, February 16. Available www.alternet.org.

Bentham, Jeremy. (1789). *An Introduction to the Principles of Morals and Legislation*. Edited by J.H. Burns and H.L.A. Hart. London: Athlone Press.

Cao, Deborah and Steven White. (eds.). (2016). *Animal Law and Welfare – International Perspectives*. Berlin: Springer.

Coetzee, John M. (2009). 'On Appetite, the Right to Life, and Rational Ethics.' In: Paola Cavalieri (ed.), *The Death of the Animal. A Dialogue*. New York: Columbia University Press, 119–21.

Cupp, Richard L. (2015). 'Human Responsibility, Not Legal Personhood, for Animals,' *Engage*, 16(2). Available www.fed-soc.org/publications/detail/human-responsibility-not-legal-personhood-for-nonhuman-animals.

Cusack, Carmen M. (2013). 'Feminism and Husbandry: Drawing the Fine Line between Mine and Bovine,' *Journal for Critical Animal Studies*, 11(1): 24–45.

DeGrazia, David. (2006). 'On the Question of Personhood Beyond Homo Sapiens.' In: Peter Singer (ed.), *In Defense of Animals: The Second Wave*. Oxford: Blackwell, 40–53.

Derrida, Jacques. (2002). 'The Animal That Therefore I Am (More to Follow),' *Critical Inquiry*, 28(2): 369–418. Translated by David Wills.
Derrida, Jacques. (2009). *The Beast & the Sovereign*. 1 vol. Edited by Michael Lisse, Marie-Louise Mallet and Ginette Michaud. Translated by Geoffrey Bennington. Chicago: Chicago University Press.
Dunayer, Joan. (2004). *Speciesism*. Derwood, MD: Ryce Publishing.
Francione, Gary L. (2008). *Animals as Persons: Essays on the Abolition of Animal Exploitation*. New York: Columbia University Press.
Fuller, Lon L. (1949). 'The Case of the Speluncean Explorers,' *Harvard Law Review*, 62(4): 616–45.
Goyes, David Rodríguez and Ragnhild Sollund. (2016). 'Contesting and Contextualising CITES: Wildlife Trafficking in Colombia and Brazil,' *International Journal for Crime, Justice and Social Democracy*, 5(4): 87–102.
Haraway, Donna J. (2008). *When Species Meet*. Minneapolis: University of Minnesota Press.
Higgins, Polly. (2010). *Eradicating Ecocide: Exposing the Corporate and Political Practices Destroying the Planet and Proposing the Laws Needed to Eradicate Ecocide*. New York: Shepheard-Walwyn.
Higgins, Polly. (2012). *Earth Is Our Business: Changing the Rules of the Game*. London: Shepheard-Walwyn.
Higgins, Polly, Damien Short and Nigel South. (2013). 'Protecting the Planet: A Proposal for a Law of Ecocide,' *Crime, Law and Social Change*, 59(3): 251–66.
Pachirat, Timothy. (2011). *Every Twelve Seconds: Industrialized Slaughter and the Politics of Sight*. New Haven, CT: Yale University Press.
Pollan, Michael. (2002). 'An Animal's Place,' *New York Times*, November 10. Available www.nytimes.com.
Regan, Tom. (1983). (2004). *The Case for Animal Rights*. Berkeley, CA: University of California Press.
Regan, Tom. (2007). 'Vivisection: The Case for Abolition.' In: Piers Beirne and Nigel South (eds.), *Issues in Green Criminology: Confronting Harms Against Environments, Humanity and Other Animals*. Cullompton: Willan, 114–39.
Serpell, James. (1996). *In the Company of Animals*. Oxford: Basil Blackwell.
Singer, Peter. (1973). 'Animal Liberation: A Review of Stanley Godlovitch, Roslind Godlovitch and John Harris (eds.), *Animals, Men and Morals*,' *The New York Review*, April 5.
Sollund, Ragnhild. (2011). 'Expressions of Speciesism: The Effects of Keeping Companion Animals on Animal Abuse, Animal Trafficking and Species Decline,' *Crime, Law & Social Change*, 55(5): 437–51.

Sollund, Ragnhild. (2013). 'Animal Trafficking and Trade: Abuse and Species Injustice.' In: Reece Walters, Diane Westerhuis and Tanya Wyatt (eds.), *Emerging Issues in Green Criminology: Exploring Power, Justice and Harm.* Basingstoke: Palgrave Macmillan, 72–92.

Sollund, Ragnhild. (2015). 'With or Without a License to Kill: Human Predator Conflicts and Theriocide in Norway.' In: Avi Brisman, Nigel South and Rob White (eds.), *Environmental Crime and Social Conflict: Contemporary and Emerging Issues.* Burlington, VT: Ashgate, 95–121.

Sollund, Ragnhild. (2017). 'Routine Theriocide of Animals Seized in Traffic.' In: Jennifer Maher, Harriet Pierpoint and Piers Beirne (eds.), *The Palgrave International Handbook of Animal Abuse Studies.* Basingstoke: Palgrave Macmillan, 453–74.

Taylor, Nik and Heather Fraser. (2017). 'Condoned Animal Abuse in the Slaughterhouse: The Language of Life, the Discourse of Death.' In: Jennifer Maher, Harriet Pierpoint and Piers Beirne (eds.), *The Palgrave International Handbook of Animal Abuse Studies.* Basingstoke: Palgrave Macmillan, 179–99.

Thomas, Keith. (1983). *Man and the Natural World: Changing Attitudes in England 1500–1800.* Oxford: Oxford University Press.

Toynbee, Jocelyn. (1973). *Animals in Roman Life and Art.* London: Thames & Hudson.

Wyatt, Tanya. (2013). *Wildlife Trafficking: A Deconstruction of the Crime, the Victims and the Offenders.* Basingstoke: Palgrave Macmillan.

Index[1]

A

Act Concerning Wrecks of the Sea (1275), 127n106
Act of Plowing by the Tayle (1635), 26
Adams, C., 34, 41n38
Addison, J., 143, 158n6
Aelian, 53
Agnew, R., 41n42
Animal abuse
   animal spectacles and as entertainment
      menageries, 14–16, 49, 93
      zoos, 25, 31, 206, 208
   kidnapping (*see* Wildlife trade)
   Old Testament
      Exodus, 74, 83, 85
      Genesis, 24, 25, 83, 84
      Leviticus, 24, 25, 85
      Samuel, 84
   and religion
      Calvinism, 63, 64
      Judaeo-Christianity, 54
      Protestantism, 63, 64, 99, 107, 147, 171
      Roman Catholicism, 83, 107, 154
   See also Animal cruelty; Animal neglect; Carnism; Theriocide
Animal cruelty
   animal baiting, 29, 53, 141, 142
   hunting and bloodsports, 5, 24, 29, 30
   See also Theriocide
Animal deaths, 14, 23, 117n24
   See also Theriocide
Animal justiciability, 6, 75, 79, 82, 91, 118n26

---

[1] Note: Page numbers followed by 'n' refer to notes.

216 Index

Animal killing sites, *see* Theriocide, sites of
Animal neglect, 5, 24, 26, 27
Animal rights, viii, xvii, 4, 8, 40n29, 41n50, 85, 201, 204, 206, 208
  See also Legal personhood, for animals
Animals
  in Britain, vi, 7, 64, 71–114
  as companions (appointed as such), 18, 26, 136, 197, 207, 208
  criminal prosecution of, 75, 98, 108 (*see also* Animal trials)
  domesticated, 1, 18, 24, 30, 65n7, 74, 88, 99, 117n24, 207, 208
  as edibles
    cows and other cattle, 18, 35, 137, 143, 208
    fishes, 20, 21, 147
    lambs, 28, 147
    pigs, 1, 2, 18, 20, 208
    See also Flesh
  hybrids, 25, 65n4, 136
  justiciable, 6 (*see also* Animal trials, justiciability)
  killing humans, 62
  killing of
    euphemisms for, 5, 14, 20–22, 37
    See also Theriocide
  as property of humans, viii, 4, 14, 23, 77, 92
  as signs of satire, 55–57, 136
  species of, 119n38
    bears, 29, 33, 53, 54, 116n18
    bulls, 53, 56, 57, 88, 137, 142, 199
    chimpanzees, 205, 206, 209
    cows, 18, 35, 50, 84, 88, 198, 199
    deer, 51, 53, 57
    dogs, 7, 8, 19, 27, 31, 33, 37, 51, 53–55, 57, 60, 66n16, 73, 79, 82, 84, 88, 92, 98–112, 116n18, 119n41, 122n75, 122n76, 124n85, 125n97, 125n98, 126n100, 136–142, 159n8, 159n9, 197, 207
    elephants, 33, 35, 38n3, 54, 111, 113
    equines, 88, 92
    foxes, 21, 27, 29, 54, 60, 79, 88, 116n18
    insects, 35, 74, 88, 203
    leopards, 33, 53, 117n24
    lions, 53, 54, 57, 60, 116n18, 197
    mammals, 35, 203–205
    molluscs, 35, 203
    monkeys, 33, 50, 53, 111, 113, 126n106
    oxen, 25, 50, 88, 137
    pigs, 1, 2, 19, 20, 33, 57, 79, 86, 88, 89, 92, 96, 120n50, 159n9, 199, 208
    rodents, 29, 30, 88, 90, 119n38 (*see also* Vermin)
    shrimps, 35, 203
    snakes, 27, 84, 88
    wolves, 16, 27, 54, 79, 84, 88, 99, 116n18, 122n72
    wild, 30, 31, 74, 88 (*see also* Wildlife, animal trials)
Animal sexual assault, 23, 36, 199, 210n4
Animal trials
  animal justiciability in, 6, 75, 79, 82, 91, 117n26

biblical support for, 83
courts
  coroners, 7, 97, 101
  ecclesiastical, 74, 82, 87, 88, 117n28
  secular, 6, 74, 88, 108
courts, crimes of animals
  prosecuted in bestiality, 84, 85, 87, 88, 110, 113, 118n30, 199
  heresy, 84, 118n29
  homicide, 4–6, 13–38, 74, 75, 82, 89, 110, 114n5, 115n11
  pauperies, 79, 80, 116n19
  witchcraft, 84
criminal intent, 22, 75
deodands, 7, 93–97, 108, 121–122n65
geographical location
  Brazil, 66n13, 89, 119n42, 206, 211n18
  Denmark, 89, 120n52
  England, 7, 8, 17, 26, 52, 63, 73, 92, 94, 96, 97, 99, 106, 108, 111, 137, 139, 198
  France, 4, 62
  Ireland, 26, 96, 97, 109, 159n11, 159n13, 167, 171, 187, 190, 194n42
  Italy, 88, 89, 99
  New Haven colony, 125n96
  New Zealand, 33, 111, 206
  Scotland, 7, 73, 96, 98–100, 109
  Switzerland, 89
geohistory, 71–114
  periodicity, 73, 88
punishment, vii, 51, 54, 75, 76, 82, 83, 111, 118n33, 175

records of, 6, 7, 85, 87, 89, 92, 93, 101–103, 115n11, 120n48, 179
Animal Welfare Act (2006), 34
Animism, 110
Aquinas, T., 83, 84, 117n28, 118n30
Arne, T., 155
Art, 5, 49, 50, 57, 58, 76, 137, 139, 162n32, 181, 191
  anti-Catholic/anti-popery, 8, 107, 143, 152
  auditory component of, 153
  British, 7, 158n1 (*see also* Hogarth, W.)
  Dutch, 61, 76, 191
  Flemish, 50, 57, 76
  francophobia in (*see* Hogarth, W.)
  Golden Age, 49, 50, 58, 137, 139
  and nationalism, 156, 158n1
  Paulus Potter, 5 (*see also Life of a Hunter*)
  as satire, 50, 55–57, 60, 61, 65n4, 105
  triumphalism in, 181, 191
  World Upside Down tradition (*see Life of a Hunter*)
Aulette, J., 40n22

B

Barrett, K., 41n41
Beccaria, C., 211n15
Beef, 209
  bovine ideology, 21
  butchers, 66n15
  carnism, 143
  English nationalism and, 155
  as symbol, 143
  See also Carnism

Index

Beirne, P., vii, viii, 39n10, 39n15, 39n19, 65n4, 67n33, 127n118, 161n28, 210n4, 210n10, 211n15
Bekoff, M., 210n2
Bentham, J., 16, 38n4, 41n50, 118n33, 211n15
Bentley, J., 31
Bisschop, L., 41n21
Blackstone, W., 20, 22, 39n10, 39n11, 120n55, 121n65
Bloom, L., 183
Boekhout van Solinge, T., 40n33
Bourgeois, M., 181, 191n1, 193n26
BP's Deepwater Horizon, 32, 197
Bracton, H., 94, 96, 121n56
Bretherton, G., 171, 192n5, 192n11
Breugel, P., the Elder, 50
Brewster, M., 39n18
Brisman, A., 41n41
Bristow, E., 41n48
Britain
  England, 7, 8, 17, 26, 39n15, 52, 63, 114n5, 137–139, 144, 147, 157
  Scotland, 7, 96–98, 109
  See also Animal trials; Hogarth, W.; Nationalism
Broos, B., 65n6
Brueghel, J., the Younger, 50
Buijsen, E., 65n6, 65n9, 65n10
Burns, R., 40n21, 41n43
Butchers, 2, 17, 148, 156
  See also Hogarth, W.; Slaughterhouses

C

Cahill, A., 41n42, 41n45
Calais, *see* Hogarth, W.
Cao, D., 211n18

Carney, J., 179, 193n22, 193n31
Carney, P., 193n22
Carnism, 41n38, 136, 143
Carrabine, E., 159n10
Chassenée, B., 86, 87, 119n35
Coetzee, J., 208, 211n19
Cohen, E., 38n2, 91, 115n8, 115n11, 117n26, 120n49
Cole, L., 125n98
Conley, C., 185, 193n32
Courts, *see* Animal trials, courts
Crimes
  animal sexual assault, 23, 36, 199, 210n4
  bestiality (*see* Animal sexual assault)
  ecocide, 199–201, 210n9
  genocide, 22, 40n26, 200, 210n9
  homicide, 4–6, 13–38, 74, 77, 82, 83, 89, 110, 115n9, 183
  parricide, 9
  theriocide, as murder, 5, 13–38, 197–209
Cruelty, *see* Animal cruelty
Cupp, 211n17
Cusack, C., 199, 210n6

D

Damhoudere, J., 6, 76–78, 80–82, 84, 116n13, 116n14, 116n15, 116n16, 116n17, 116n18, 116n19, 116n20, 117n23, 117n25, 118n30
Darnton, R., 124n94, 127n107
Darwin, C., 112, 127n110
Deodands, 7, 93–97, 108, 121n57, 121n62, 121–122n65

Derrida, J., 35, 38n3, 40n26, 41n49, 198, 210n1
Dodd, G., 38n8
Dooren, T., 41n53
Dunayer, J., 204, 210n2

E

Eeckhout, A., 66n13
Einberg, E., 158n4, 158n6, 162n30
Embourgeoisement, 147
England, 8, 17, 26, 39n15, 52, 63, 73, 92, 94, 96, 97, 99, 106, 108, 111, 137–139, 144, 147, 154, 155, 179, 198
  See also Animal trials; Britain
Erwin, T., 111
Euphemisms, 5, 14, 20–22, 24, 32, 37
Evans, E., 7, 66n15, 96–98, 100, 102, 107, 108, 110, 111, 115n5, 115n6, 115n9, 116n12, 117n23, 118–133n31, 119–138n34, 119n40, 120–143n41, 122–166n65, 122–169n68, 122n71, 123n80, 125n96
  as animal rights activist, 118n34
  The Criminal Prosecution and Capital Punishment of Animals, 6, 57, 73, 85–93

F

Factory farming
  and pollution, 24
  theriocide in, 34, 36 (*see also* slaughterhouses)
Ferron, J., 87
Fichtelberg, A., 41n37

Fielding, H., 105, 149, 161n26, 161n27
Finkelstein, J., 90, 91, 110, 114n5, 115n8, 115n11, 117n28, 119n46, 120n48, 126n102
Fitzgerald, A., 40n28, 41n48, 114n4, 115n8
Flesh, edible, of animals, 142, 143, 202, 209
  See also Carnism; Factory farming; Hogarth, W., Potter, P.; Veganism
Food, *see* Animals, as edibles
Forrest, E., 155, 156, 162n31
Forrest, T., 155
Foucault, M., 16, 38n4, 166
Foxe, J., 71, 72, 107, 114n2
France, 8, 62, 82, 83, 88, 89, 96, 108, 111, 115n8, 123n79, 135, 136, 142, 147, 152, 154, 155, 157, 159n11
  See also Animal trials; Hogarth, W.
Francione, G., 114n4, 204, 211n12
Francis, F., 187
Fraser, H., 40n26, 40n28
Frazer, J., 115n8, 118n34, 119n42
Friedland, P., 75, 82, 114n6, 115n8, 115n9, 115n10, 117n25, 117n27, 125n97
Fudge, E., 67n28, 73, 114n5
Fukushima, 31, 32, 210n10

G

Galle, T., 57
Garrick, D., 148, 154, 161n23
Gay, J., 149
Glassification, 209, 212n20
Goethe, J., 51, 65n6
Goyes, D., 40n33, 210n5

Grandin, T., 28, 40n25
Gray, A., 41n48
Great chain of being, 64, 83,
    108, 109

H

Hallie, P., 67n28
Haraway, D., 210n2
Harm to animals, *see* Animal abuse;
    Animal cruelty; Animal
    deaths; Theriocide
Hasson, P., 186
Hay, D., 107, 124n85, 125n95
Hediger, R., 31, 41n37
Hicks, M., 110
Higgins, P., 199–201, 210n7,
    210n8, 210n9
Hinch, R., 41n48
Hogarth, W., 135–158, 161n29
    beef consumption, 143,
        155, 156
    Calais, 8, 135, 150,
        152–155, 161n28
    francophobia, 8, 143
    music in Hogarth's art, 136, 147
        Rule Brittania, 155
        *Song in Praise of Old English
        Roast Beef, A*, 149, 150
    patriotic animals
        cattle, 135–158
        dogs, 135–158
    patriotism, 8, 135–137, 140,
        141, 156
    Sublime Society of Beefsteaks, 155
    works
        Beer Street, 1751, 135, 136,
            147, 148, 157
        Beggar's Opera, The, 1728,
            149, 157

*Election Entertainment, An
    (Humours of an Election* 1),
    1754, 148, 157
England (Invasion Series 2),
    135, 157
Enraged Musician, The, 1741,
    157, 161n29
France (Invasion Series 1),
    1756, 135, 157
*Gate of Calais, Or, O The Roast
    Beef of Old England*,
    1748, 8, 135, 150,
    152–155, 157
Gin Lane, 1751, 135, 136,
    147, 157, 159n9
*Hogarth: The Painter and his
    Pug* (1747), 140,
    141, 157
*Hudibras Encounters the
    Skimmington (Hudibras* 7),
    1726, 161n29
*Hudibras' First Adventure
    (Hudibras* 3), 1727, 148, 157
*Idle'Prentice Executed at Tyburn,
    The (Industry and Idleness* 6),
    157, 161n29
*Industrious 'Prentice Married to
    his Master's Daughter
    (Industry and Idleness* 6),
    1747, 148, 157
The Lady's Death, 1745, 2, 159n9
March to Finchley,
    1749, 135, 157
Miss Mary Edwards,
    1742, 137, 138
*O The Roast Beef of Old
    England (Gate of Calais)*,
    1749, 8, 135, 155
Southwark Fair,
    1731, 158, 161n29

Taste in High Life, or Taste à la Mode, 1742, 144, 147, 158
Transubstantiation Satirized, n.d., 151, 154, 158, 162n30
Holden, A., 122n72
Holland, *see* Netherlands, the
Homicide, 4–6, 13–38, 74, 77, 82, 83, 184, 186
Hone, W., 103, 104, 122n76, 123n82, 124n84, 124n85, 124n86, 124n87
Humphrey, N., 93, 120n51
Hunting discourses, 21
Husbandry manuals, 29, 93, 108
Hyde, D., 189
Hyde, W., 90

I

Institutes of the Christian Religion, 63
Invisibilisation, process of, 209
  See also Euphemisms; Speciesism
Ireland
  homicide in *Fin-de-Siècle* Ireland, 166, 182–187
  in *Outrage Reports*, 176, 183, 187
  See also Animal trials; Synge, J.M.; *Playboy of the Western World*

J

Jackson, B., 116n19, 122n73, 122n75, 125n97
Johnson, B., 97
Jones, W., 102

Justiciable animals, 6, 71–114
  See also Animal trials; Legal personhood, for animals

K

Kelty-Huber, C., 41n39
Kemp, M., 51, 58, 64, 65n6, 65n8, 66n17, 66n18, 67n36
Keys, J., 66n16
Kiberd, D., 174, 176, 192n9, 192n12, 192n16
Kramer, R., 40n21
Kunzle, D., 61, 66n23, 67n25, 67n36

L

Lee, P., 38n5
Legal personhood, for animals, 203–207
  in Argentina, Brazil, Colombia, New Zealand, Spain, U.S., 206
  See also Animal justiciability
Le Quéré, C., 41n44
Le Vau, L., 15
Leveridge, R., 149, 150, 161n27
Life of a Hunter, 52
  Diana and Actaeon myth and, 144
  Dutch Golden Age and, 58
  Hermitage Museum and, 5, 59
  Legend of St. Eustace and, 52
  as satire of animal trials, 55–57
  as world upside down, 60
  works by Paulus Potter
    Bear Hunt (1649), 55
    Cattle and Sheep in a Stormy Landscape (1647), 55

Life of a Hunter (cont.)
   Cows Reflected in the Water
     (1648), 55
   Figures with Horses by a Stable
     (1647), 55
   Life of a Hunter
     (c.1647–1650), 49–67
   Wild Boar Hunting in a Forest
     (1641), 55, 62
   The Young Bull (1647), 55, 56
Lombrosianism, 114, 118n34
Long, M., 41n41
Louandre, C., 98, 99, 122n70
Lynch, M., 40n21, 41n41, 41n43

M

MacDonnell, A., 179–182, 184
Machyn, H., 71
MacKenna, S., 194n41
MacLachlan, I., 38n8
Maher, J., 39n18, 40n33
Malleus Maleficarum, 74, 84, 118n29
Markham, G., 126n99
Martin, J., 87
Mascall, L., 108
Maurits, J., 58, 59, 65n5, 66n13
Menageries, *see* Animal abuse
Michalowski, R.,
   40n21, 40n22, 41n43
Middleton, J., 143
Milgrom, J., 39n17
Militarism
   and factory farming, 5, 24
   and pollution, 24
   and vivisection, 24
   See also Hogarth, W.; Theriocide, sites of
Milton, J., 141
Montaigne, M., 6, 62–64

N

Nationalism, 41n38, 142,
   154–156, 158n1
Netherlands, the, 57, 60, 63, 64
   See also Hogarth, W.; Potter, P.
Newell, W., 96
Nichols, J., 114n1, 162n32
Nihan, C., 24, 25, 39n15,
   39n16, 39n17
Nocella, A., 31, 41n37
Nonhuman Rights Project
   ("NhRP"), 205, 206
Nurse, A., 39n18, 40n31

O

O'Donnell, I., 193n27
Ordinance for Prohibiting Cock-
   Matches (1654), 26
Orwell, G., 105
Ó Súilleabhain, S., 192n14
Ovid, 51, 52

P

Pachirat, T., 39n13, 40n28, 212n20
Paine, T., 105, 106, 124n92,
   124n93
Panopticism, 16
   See also Bentham, Jeremy;
   Foucault, Michel
Parkinson, J., 101
Patriarchy, 172
Patriotism
   and francophobia, 8
   and Ireland (*see Playboy of the Western World*)
   and national identity, construction of English, 156, 172
   in the Netherland, 50

Paulson, R., 158n3, 158n4, 159n8, 161n23
Pauperies, 79
  See also Animal trials
Pérelle, A., 15
Peterson, A., 40n34
Pierpoint, H., 39n18
Playboy of the Western World, 165–167, 171, 172, 181–183, 186, 190, 192n3, 194n42
  anti-Catholicism in, 152
  and J.M. Synge, 8, 9, 165–191
  Aran islands and, 181
  cast of
    Michael James Flaherty, 166–167
    Shawn Keogh, 167
    Christy Mahon, 166, 171, 181, 182
    Old Mahon, 172, 190
    Pegeen Mike, 167
    Widow Quin, 167, 192n3
    Father Reilly, 167
  homicidal precedents for
    James Lynchehaun, 186
    William Maley, 186
  Irish peasantry, portrayal of in, 185, 188
  nationalism in, 171
  parricide in, 8, 9, 165–191
  riots at performances of
    Abbey Theatre, Dublin, 165, 166, 183, 194n42
    Beijing, 194n42
    Britain, 194n42
    Galway, 194n42
    New York City, 166

Philadelphia, 166
Royal Irish Constabulary, 186
An Toraíocht Dhiarmada agus Gráinne, 190
Pollan, M., 211n20
Porter, R., 148, 161n25
Potter, P., *see Life of a Hunter*

R

Raber, K., 125n98
Regan, T., 13, 30, 38n1, 41n35, 198, 202, 204, 205, 210n3, 210n11, 211n13
Reyes, C., 39n18
Reynaert, 60
Richardson, J., 156
Rich, J., 148
Rickman, C., 105, 124n88
Ritvo, H., 73, 114n5, 159n15
Rogers, B., 147, 159n8, 160n18, 160n19
Rubens, P., 50
Ruskin, J., 67n28

S

Salter, C., 31
Salt, H., 8, 118n33
Schwartz, B., 39n15
Scotland, 73, 96
  See also Animal trials; Britain
Sentience, 3, 35
Serpell, J., 210n2
Shakespeare, W., 97, 99, 122n71, 122n72, 126n99, 139–141, 143, 161n23, 162n32
Shannon, L., 73, 114n5, 125n98

Short, D., 201
Slaughterhouses, see Animal killing sites
Sloet, L., 101, 122n78
Smith, A., 67n31, 156
Sollund, R., 39n21, 40n33, 120n52, 199, 210n5
Sorenson, J., 41n36, 41n47
South, N., 41n41, 201
Speciesism
  abolition of, 207–209
  anthropocentrism, vii
  speciesist language, 10, 14
Sportization, 29
Squires, P., 40n31
Stallybrass, P., 66n23
Stokvis, B., 66n14
Stretesky, P., 40n21, 41n41, 41n43
Sublime Society of Beef Steaks, 8, 148
Swift, J., 141
Synge, J.M., 9, 165–191
  See also Ireland; *Playboy of the Western World*

T

Tarde, G., 113
Taylor, C., 41n53
Taylor, N., 40n26, 40n28
Teniers, D., 50
Tester, K., 73, 114n5, 115n8
Theriocide, 17, 24, 27, 30, 33
  criminalisation of, as murder, 198–203
  definition of, 24
  etymology, 23–25
  sites of
    climate change, 24
    cruelty and neglect, 24, 27
    factory farming, 24
    hunting and bloodsports, 24
    militarism, 24, 33
    pollution, 24, 33
    slaughterhouses, 17, 24
    state, 24
    state-corporate, 33
    trafficking (animal kidnapping), 30
    vivisection, 24
    wildlife trade, 24
  See also Animal abuse
Thomas, K., 20, 39n12, 39n14, 114n2, 114n5, 126n103, 158n3
Thompson, E., 31, 124n85
Thornhill, Sir J., 148, 160n20
Timbs, J., 160n20, 160n21, 160n22
Topsell, E., 125n99
Toynbee, J., 210n2
Transubstantiation, 154
Trusler, J., 156, 162n32
Tuckett, M., 101
Tusser, T., 125n99

U

Uglow, J., 143, 158n4, 160n16
Ulpian, 77, 117n24
Universal humane education, 209
Urban, M., 41n46

V

van Balckeneynde, A., 59
van der Meer, J. J., 60
  See also Reynaert
van der Straet, J., 57
van Heemskerck, E., the elder, 65n4

Index

van Ostade, A., 50
van Poelenburgh, C., 54, 65n8
van Solms, Princess Amelia, 59
van Veen, P., 63
Vermin, 28, 74, 83, 88, 125n98
Vespucci, A., 57
Vialles, N., 38n5
von Amira, K., 102, 123n80

W

Walsh, A., 65n6, 65n8, 66n12, 66n13, 66n16, 66n21, 67n25, 67n36
Walters, R., 41n40, 41n41
Weber, M., 108, 125n97
White, R., 41n40, 41n42, 211n18
Wielant, P., 116n14
Wildlife trade, *see* Theriocide, sites of
Wise, S., 115n8, 205, 206
Witchcraft, 84, 88, 110
Wolloch, N., 65n1, 65n7
World Upside Down, 60
Wouwerman, P., 49
Wyatt, T., 40n33

X

Xenophobia, *see* Patriotism

Y

Yeats, W., 166, 175, 183, 193n28
Yeomans, L., 120n54

Z

Zoos, *see* Animal abuse

CPSIA information can be obtained
at www.ICGtesting.com
Printed in the USA
LVHW07*1922230318
570971LV00017B/295/P